MW01703525

Warehouse Management
and
Inventory Control

Warehouse Management and Inventory Control

Dr. J P Saxena

Consulting Engineer
Saudi Cement Company
Saudi Arabia
&
Former Director
National Council for Cement and Building Materials
New Delhi, India

VIKAS PUBLISHING HOUSE PVT LTD

VIKAS PUBLISHING HOUSE PVT LTD

576, Masjid Road, Jangpura, **New Delhi** - 110 014
Phones: 24315313, 24314605 • Fax: 91-11-24310879
E-mail: *helpline@vikaspublishing.com*

First Floor, N.S. Bhawan, 4th Cross, 4th Main,
Gandhi Nagar, **Bangalore** - 560 009 • Phone: 2281254

F-20, Nand Dham Industrial Estate, Marol,
Andheri (East), **Mumbai** - 400 059 • Phone: 28502333, 28502324
E-mail: *ajayvikas@vsnl.net* • Mobile: 98208 39959

35, Palm Avenue, **Kolkata** - 700 019 • Phone: 22872575

C-8, Ist Floor, Nelson Chambers, 115 Nelson Manickam Road,
Aminjikarai, **Chennai** - 600 029 • Phone: 23744547, 23746090

Mahender Lok Apartments, Ist Floor, H No. 104,
Kankar Bagh, **Patna** - 800 020 • Phone: 2347410

Distributors:

UBS PUBLISHERS' DISTRIBUTORS PVT LTD

5, Ansari Road, **New Delhi** - 110 002
Phones: 23273601, 23266646 • Fax: 23276593, 23274261
E-mail: *ubspd@ubspd.com* • Internet: *www.gobookshopping.com*

- 10, First Main Road, Gandhi Nagar, **Bangalore** - 560 009 • Phone: 2253903
- 60, Nelson Manickam Road, Aminjikarai, **Chennai** - 600 029 • Phone: 3746222
- 8/1-B, Chowringhee Lane, **Kolkata** - 700 016 • Phones: 22521821, 22522910
- 5-A, Rajendra Nagar, **Patna** - 800 016 • Phone: 2672856, 2673973
- 80, Noronha Road, Cantonment, **Kanpur** - 208 004 • Phones: 2305793, 2305799
- 143, M P Nagar, Zone -1, **Bhopal** - 462 011 • Phones: 5203183, 5203193
- 40/7940, Convent Road, **Ernakulam** - 682 035 • Phones: 2353901, 2363905

Distributors for Western India:

PREFACE BOOKS

223, Cama Industrial Estate, 2nd Floor,
Sun Mill Compound, Lower Parel (W), **Mumbai** - 400 013 • Phone: 24988054

ISBN: 81-259-1210-X

Copyright © 2003, **Vikas Publishing House Pvt Ltd**

All rights reserved. No part of this publication may be reproduced in any form without the prior written permission of the publishers.

This book was developed, edited and produced at:

Consultant Publisher: P K Madhavan

Project Coordinator: Pradeep P

Editorial Team: Chitra M S, Kameswar Rao
Shankari R, Sanjeev V

Vijay Nicole Imprints
C-7, 1st Floor, Nelson Chambers,
115, Nelson Manickam Road,
Aminjikarai, Chennai - 600 029
Phones : 23743062, 23745826
E-mail : iipvni@vsnl.net

website : **www.vijaynicole.com**

Information contained in this book has been obtained by the Publishers from sources believed to be reliable. The publisher and its authors make no representation or warranties with respect to accuracy or completeness of the contents of this book, and shall in no event be liable for any errors, omissions or damages arising out of use of this information, and specifically disclaim any implied warranties or merchantability or fitness for any particular purpose.

Laser Typesetting & Cover Design: **Vijay Nicole Imprints**, Chennai

Printed at Sanjay Printers, Delhi - 110032

Preface

Study of methods and development of systems relating to 'Warehousing and Inventory Control' are important for efficient operation of warehouses. In recent years, computerization has improved the efficiency of the warehouse operations to a great extent. At the same time, computerization has not replaced the need for conceptual understanding of warehouse and inventory control. Warehouse operations are not limited merely to accounting of materials, but they have commercial and legal implications especially when the material received is found deficient in quantity or is not of acceptable quality or is damaged during transit. There is a need for procedures, systems and controls in these activities.

The need for professional approach in the activities of warehouse and inventory control has also been realized due to large size operations, especially in large industrial units or companies having a number of units spread all over the world. The activities of warehouse and inventory control are no longer considered routine. Realizing the demand for warehouse and inventory control professionals, various universities and institutions have started offering courses in the areas of storekeeping, inventory control and spare parts management.

Even though a number of books were published on the subject, this book aims to update with the recent practices, procedures and systems for effective management of warehouse and control of inventory. Attempt has been made to provide procedures compatible to computer applications.

As many organizations go for ISO certification, the book also addresses the requirements for conformance to ISO Standards. The book has been organized in twenty chapters to deal with aspects of planning, organizing, execution and control of activities of warehousing and inventory control.

Chapter 1 discusses organizational structure of stores division, activities of warehousing and inventory control and day-to-day operations. Functions and responsibilities of the key personnel in the stores division are also discussed.

Chapters 2,3 and 4 deal with requisitioning, replenishment of inventory, receipt, inspection and issue of materials. Chapter 5 discusses various aspects of stocktaking. Types of discrepancies noticed and the methodology of their resolution are discussed in chapter 6.

Chapter 7 focuses on control of tools, surplus materials and scrap materials. Tools are very important for operation, maintenance and repairs of plant and machinery.

Chapter 8 deals with storage and handling practices for representative items which require special care. The items covered in the chapter are not exhaustive.

Chapter 9 discusses advantages of computerization in warehouse operations, and interaction between stores division and other departments like production, maintenance, finance and marketing. The chapter focuses on the selection of computer system for establishing the database, information retrieval and management reporting. This chapter also deals with the features of a popular software for inventory control and storekeeping.

Performance evaluation in warehouse and inventory control is essential. Chapter 10 identifies various performance parameters and performance indicators as used by different levels of management for evaluation of the performance of stores division.

Chapter 11 addresses the issues related to Quality Assurance and ISO Standards. These which include formulation of specifications, inspection of materials, handling, storage, packing and delivery of materials and quality records.

Chapter 12 deals with planning and organizing for store division. Chapter 13 deals with security, safety and maintenance of stores.

Chapters 14–20 are dedicated to inventory control. Chapter 14 deals with classification of inventory and strategic considerations. Chapter 15 deals with codification. Standardization and standardization program is dealt in chapter 16.

Inventory control concepts, model and techniques have been dealt in chapters 17 and 18 with emphasis on dynamic nature of inventory. Management of spare parts which is one of the key issues in efficient repair and maintenance of the plant and machinery, is dealt in chapter 19. Chapter 20 deals with valuation of inventory.

This book is suitable to students of Master of Business Administration (MBA), Bachelor of Business Administration (BBA), Postgraduate Diploma in Business Administration (PGDBA), postgraduate Diploma in Industrial Management (PGDIM), Postgraduate Diploma in Materials Management (PGDMM), Certificate Course in Storekeeping and Inventory Control, and production Management.

The book will also be useful to Inventory Engineers, Production Engineers, Inventory Controllers, Warehouse Officers, Inspection Controllers, Materials Planners, Materials Inspectors, Materials Managers, Stores Managers and Consultants.

The author is grateful to various experts who have contributed through discussions at various stages which have made it possible to bring the book out. The author is also grateful to his wife for her cooperation and support in bringing out this book.

Dr. J P Saxena

Contents

List of Figures

List of Tables

List of Appendices

List of Abbreviations

AC	Acquisition Cost
DR	Discrepancy Report
DRN	Dispatch and Receipt Note
DVC	Direct Issue Voucher
EOQ	Economic Order Quantity
EOT Crane	Electric Overhead Traveling Crane
FIFO	First In First Out
FOC	Free on Charge
FSN	Fast, Slow and Non-Moving
G/L	General Ledger
GM	General Manager
GOLF	Government, Ordinary, Local, Foreign Sources
HIFO	Highest In First Out
HML	High, Medium and Low
IAF	Inventory Adjustment Form
IC	Inspection Controller
ICC	Inventory Carrying Cost
ID	Identification
ISO	International Standards Organization
L/C	Letter of Credit
LIFO	Last In First Out
MDRR	Material Receipt and Inspection Note
MI	Material Inspector
MIN	Materials Inspection Notice
MIR	Materials Inspection and Receipt
MR	Material Requisition
MRIN	Material Receipt & Inspection Note
MRP	Materials Requisition for Purchase
MRPU	Materials Requisition for Purchase Update
NIFO	Next In First Out
NRUM	New, Re-built, Used and Manufactured

OEM	Original Equipment Manufacturer
OW	Officer Warehouse
PI	Performance Indicator
PO	Purchase Order
PP	Performance Parameter
PUOM	Purchasing Unit of Measure
RN	Return Note
ROQ	Reorder Quantity
SASO	Saudi Arabia Standard Organization
SC	Stock Code
SD	Stores Division
SDE	Scare, Difficult, Easy to Obtain
SOS	Seasonal, Off-seasonal
SRC	Stock Record Controller
SRIN	Store Requisition & Issue Note
SUOM	Stocking Unit of Measure
TQC	Total Quality Control
TQM	Total Quality Management
US$	US Dollar
UV	Ultra Violet
VED	Vital, Essential and Desirable
WH	Warehouse
WQ	Working Quantity
YTD	Year TO Date

Part I

Warehouse Management

Chapter 1

Warehouse Organization

INTRODUCTION

Warehouse is an essential limb of an industrial unit. It is the depository of all materials required by the industrial unit and supplies materials as and when required. Different types of materials are required for different operations in a production unit. Some examples are given in the Table 1.1.

Table 1.1 Materials Required for Various Purposes

S. No.	Materials	Purpose
1	Raw materials	Production of the product.
2	Spares & Consumables	Repair and maintenance works
3	Packing materials	Packaging
4	Chemicals	Quality control testing
5	Electrical items	Installation and maintenance of electric installations
6	Electronic items	Repair and maintenance of electronic systems
7	Kitchen items	For requirements of canteen
8	Stationery items	Office work
9	Tyres and tubes	Transport vehicles
10	Lubricants and oils	Lubrication works
11	Tools and tackles	Repair and maintenance works

The variety of items stored is so large that a planned system is necessary to keep them safely and in order. The stored items should be identified and issued with minimum efforts and in minimum time. This calls for the followings:

- an organization structure suitable to carry on various activities efficiently and productively
- defining the functions and duties of each focal official

- developing operational systems for standardization in operations and uniformity in actions in various situations
- to develop systems and ensure safety of men and materials
- to decide on authority for decision making on various issues
- to develop and maintain records for proper accounting, management information and analysis for improving the procedures and policies.

POSITION OF WAREHOUSE/STORES DIVISION IN THE ORGANIZATION

The position of the Stores Division in an organization depends mainly on the size of the organization. Various arrangements are in use to manage the activities of the warehouse. In medium and small sized organizations, the Stores Division is normally under the control of the Works Manager. Stores Manager works at par with other functional managers like Purchase Manager, Manager Administration, Finance Managers, Sales Manager, etc. (Fig. 1.1). In larger organizations, the Stores Manager reports to the Materials Manager, who directly reports to the General Manager. Materials Management is normally a corporate activity in a large organization and is independent of the works management. Purchase Division and Stores Division, both are under the control of the Materials Manager (Fig. 1.2).

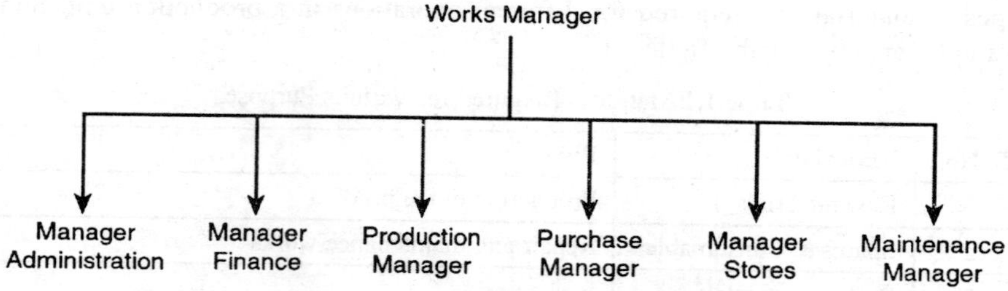

***Fig. 1.1** Organization Structure of a Small / Medium Sized Organization*

In big multi-unit or multi-location organizations, the operations are large and a lot of coordination is required to optimize the benefits of the large size of the organization. For example, very costly items could be stored in one store or at one location to meet the requirements of all the units. This helps in reducing the inventory cost as well as in obtaining the best prices due to large volume of the purchases.

Under the control of works Manager, the Stores Division works in closer coordination with the Production and Maintenance departments. Stores Division has to work according to the needs of these departments irrespective of the systems requirements. Inefficiencies of the Production and the Maintenance departments are normally overlooked and Stores Division has to always adjust and accommodate to the requirements of these departments. In this situation, though a better coordination is achieved between the Stores Division, Production Department and Maintenance Department, the benefits of working on professional systems, are sacrificed at times, Excessive indenting, delay in indenting or not indenting the required items, frequent issues, frequent return of unused materials, wrong ordering, wrong specifications, wrong inspection or delay in inspections are common features and shortcomings of this arrangement. Non-moving or slow moving items increase in the inventory due to poor control by the operation side. This happens due to little or no control of the Stores Division on the actions of Production and Maintenance departments.

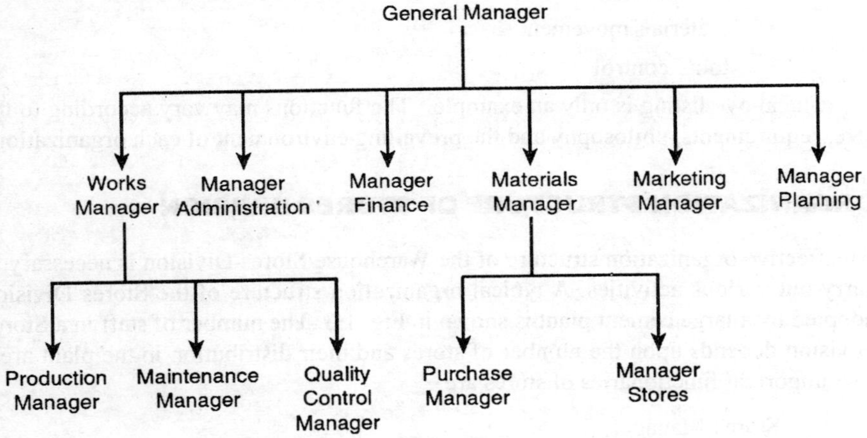

Fig. 1.2 Organization Structure of a Large Organization

Stores Division works relatively on professional lines under the control of the Materials Management Department, which is a corporate department. It is in a position to formulate policies and procedures independent of other departments. These policies and procedures are formulated, keeping in view the requirement of the organization as a whole. The wrong actions of other departments are not covered up easily. Normally such an independent working of Stores Division helps in bringing professionalism, efficiency and productivity.

ACTIVITIES IN A WAREHOUSE/STORE

The various activities in a warehouse/store can be classified as below:

(i) Requisitioning of materials

- replenishment of stock items
- requisitioning of new/out of stock items
- processing and approval of purchase requisitions
- amendments/cancellation of purchase requisitions
- updating status, follow-up and control of purchase requisitions

(ii) Materials inspection

- handling of control samples
- recording of additional/ new specifications
- receipt and inspection of materials
- reporting and handling of discrepancies

(iii) Warehousing operations

- issue of materials i.e. stock items/direct issues
- issues on loan basis
- stock taking
- materials movement
- tools control

The above listing is only an example. The functions may vary according to the size, requirements, philosophy and the prevailing environment of each organization.

ORGANIZATION STRUCTURE OF STORES DIVISION

An effective organization structure of the Warehouse/Stores Division is necessary to carry out various activities. A typical organization structure of the Stores Division adopted by a large cement plant is shown in Fig. 1.3. The number of staff in a Stores Division depends upon the number of stores and their distribution in the plant area. The important functionaries of stores are:

- Stores Manager
- Engineer, Inventory Control
- Warehouse Officer
- Inspection Controller
- Inventory Controller
- Store Keeper(s)
- Supervisor, Stock Records Section

The designations of various functionaries may differ from organization to organization. The basic functions and duties of these functionaries are presented in Appendices 1.1 - 1.7, which are representative only and should be tailored to the needs of each organization.

ORGANIZATIONAL MATTERS FOR EFFICIENT WORKING OF STORES DIVISION

The efficiency and productivity of the Stores Division depend upon the management of various organizational matters. These organizational matters have a direct impact on the day to the day operations of the Stores Division and include the followings:

- delegation of authority
- record keeping
- printing of stationary

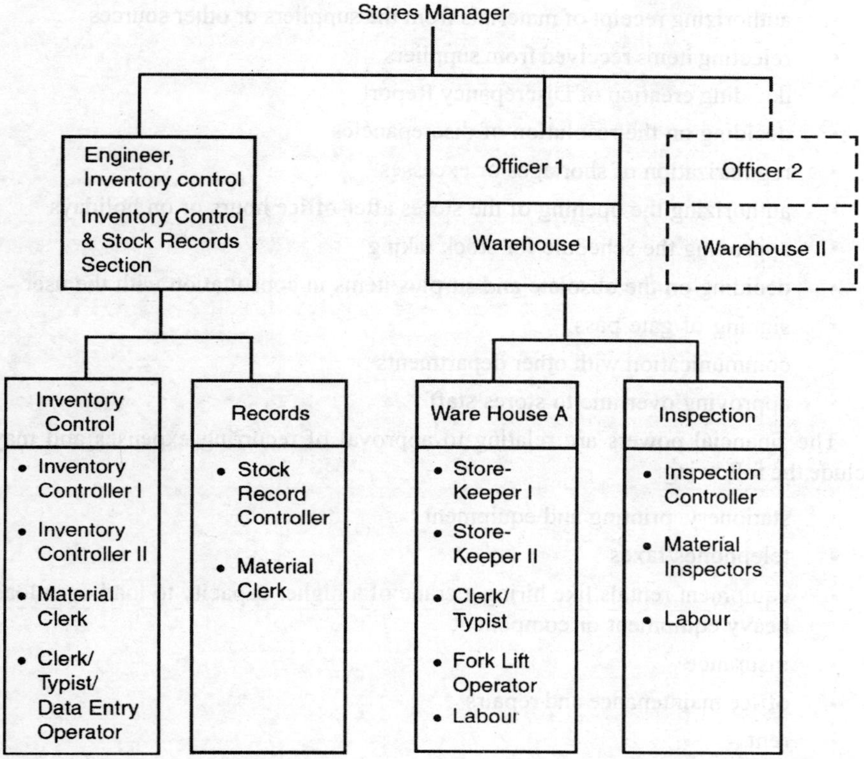

Fig. 1.3 *Organization Structure of a Stores Division*

Delegation of Authority

Delegation of authority is necessary to enable each functionary to take decisions or get decisions from the authorized persons in the most effective manner and in shortest possible time. Delegation of authority is normally divided in two broad areas, which are:

- Administrative powers
- Financial powers

The stores functions are basically operational and decision-making is basically in the area of administrative matters. Some recurring expenses are also incurred, which are sanctioned by the Stores Manager. Powers are delegated to enable decision-making nearest to the place of activity. For example, Warehouse Officer may be authorized to receive all incoming and outgoing materials. Stores Manager may be authorized to approve creation of a new stock item or delete stock item from the system.

The delegation of administrative power in respect of activities of stores may include the followings:

- fixing the store issue timings
- authorizing the issue of materials

- authorizing receipt of materials from the suppliers or other sources
- rejecting items received from suppliers
- deciding creation of Discrepancy Report
- deciding on the resolution of discrepancies
- regularization of shortages or excesses
- authorizing the opening of the stores after office hours or on holidays
- approving the schedule for stock taking
- deciding on the obsolete and surplus items in consultation with the user
- signing of gate pass
- communication with other departments
- approving overtime to stores staff

The financial powers are relating to approval of recurring expenses and may include the following:

- stationery, printing and equipment
- telephones/faxes
- equipment rentals like hiring a crane of a higher capacity to load or unload heavy equipment or component
- insurance
- office maintenance and repairs
- rent

Store Records

Maintenance of store records Stores Division should always keep the records up-to-date. It is absolutely essential for the safety of materials and their quick verification. Stock balance of an item may be nil, even if the item has been received but not entered in records. The balance will continue to show nil stock till it is updated. The user may be waiting for the item and repair and maintenance work may be delayed due to wrong information. Similarly, an item issued physically but issue entry not made in the record will still show the item in the stock. This will delay replenishment of the item. In another case, Insurance Claim of an item will be delayed if the Inspection Note and the Discrepancy Report for the item are not finalized and their details not entered in the records. Various records maintained in the stores are:

- Material Requisitions (MR)
- Material Requisition for Purchase (MRP)
- raw materials file (separate file for each raw material)
- material delivery status record
- invoice file
- insurance claims
- critical items review file

- discrepancies noticed and their status
- management reports
- correspondence with various departments
- standardization correspondence
- codification File
- management decisions
- trade literature
- supplier's visit record
- list of drawings and manuals
- contracts files
- personal files of employees

Weeding out of records Stores Division generates lot of paper work in the process of receipt, issue, inspection and stock taking of items. As per procedures, every action of the stores department should be documented. This results in large amount of paper work. Like wise, a number of records are created due to intensive interaction with a large number of departments and persons. Thus, proper racks, a file room and a system for maintaining the files year-wise, subject-wise and according to the criticality of the subject matter are required. However, as time passes, a large number of records lose their importance and therefore should be weeded out at regular intervals. Retaining unwanted records creates difficulty in accessing information.

The management should make a policy on weeding out of the records laying down the criteria of weeding out of each record. This involves indicating the period of retention of the file, frequency of weeding out exercise, identifying the responsible position, who should be authorized for screening the file and destroying the unwanted papers.

The weeding out of records should be properly documented. The period of retention for each record is decided keeping in view the type of industry, technological changes, frequency of changes and importance of the record for administrative, financial or legal requirements.

Printing of Stationery

Stores Division uses various standard formats for recording the transactions of receipt, issue, stocking items, inspection of items and physical verification of stock items. It is one area, where standardization has been achieved to a very high level. Since the activities of the Stores Division are of continuous and repetitive nature, printing of format is essential and economical. Printing of formats facilitates recording of data in an organized manner for quick and accurate analysis. Printed formats improve the efficiency to a very great extent. Stores Division should lay down a policy on printing of stationery/formats, which will cover the following issues:

- What to print
- When to print
- Frequency of printing
- How much to print

- Review of printing material before sending for printing
- Authorized person to decide on printing
- Obtaining inputs of other departments on issues relating to them
- Authority to approve printing contract

Wastage of stationery resulting from obsolete formats with minor changes brought out from time to time can be avoided by policy guidelines on printing. Also, the printed formats already in use should be thoroughly checked and a decision on what to be added or deleted should be taken.

The Stores Manager should review the requirements of printing of various formats and of any other documents. Normally printing should be done once/twice a year. However, in unforeseen circumstances, Stores Manager can decide to print the formats more frequently as may be required. In cases where inputs of other departments are necessary, the Stores Manager should ensure that all required inputs are obtained from other departments before clearing the documents for printing. The replenishment of the printed stationery should be as per schedule and the responsibility of printing should be assigned to an official, who should ensure that all the requirements are met within time.

APPENDIX 1.1

FUNCTIONS AND DUTIES OF STORES MANAGER

Basic Functions

Manages the activities of the Stores Division regarding efficient receipt, storage, maintenance and issue of all materials, equipment, spare parts, etc. stored in the warehouse and associated areas. Ensures the maintenance of up-to-date stock levels of materials, equipment and consumables that are regularly used and participates in the forecasting of future requirements.

Duties

(i) Manages and supervises the activities of personnel assigned to Stores Division.

(ii) Plans and coordinates the safe and efficient receipt, storage and issue of all materials and equipments. Duties also include allocating storage and issue of all materials and ensuring the efficient, safe and accurate handling of materials to minimize losses and/or damage, and to optimize space and facilitate easy access.

(iii) Plans and develops warehousing procedures for management's approval, ensuring sufficient control to minimize losses and maintain high safety standards. Duties also include preparing detailed procedures for issuing and receiving stock, loading, unloading and storing materials.

(iv) Plans, coordinates and oversees the processing of physical inventories documentation, ensuring that any discrepancies are satisfactorily explained.

(v) Coordinates the materials documentation and stock data, ensuring that materials and their movements are accurately entered into file, replenishment and stock data is maintained and updated, and all stock data reports necessary for various analyses are regularly issued and processed.

(vi) Maintains strict material control, including reviewing orders and determining validity of request according to job requirements prior to releasing material and ensuring that all surplus materials are returned to the warehouse.

(vii) Recommends quantities and types of surplus materials and equipment to be sold and processes the relevant documentation. Coordinates with other division heads, their immediate needs of the surplus stock, and documents specifications, age, condition, book prices, etc. of approved stock to be sold. Supervises the disposal or sale of dangerous items such as gases, chemicals, petroleum products or explosives.

(viii) Coordinates the reports and recommendations to the management regarding materials control systems and procedures, stock-levels, and forecasts of a need as a result of historical data comparisons and coordination with other Division Heads.

(ix) Performs other duties such as training subordinates, ensuring good housekeeping and observance of safety rules, following up on queries and preparing special reports.

APPENDIX 1.2

FUNCTIONS AND DUTIES OF ENGINEER, INVENTORY CONTROL

Basic Functions

Supervises the planning, coordinating and controlling of the replenishment of materials efficiently and in an effective manner based on optimum inventory levels. Implements and reviews systems and procedures. Recommends improved and efficient methods for reduction of costs.

Duties

(i) Requisitioning and replenishment of stores items

- Supervises and participates in planning and preparation of accurate Purchase Requisitions/ Repair Requisitions for stock replenishment and user requested items. Reviews with users various parameters such as specifications, substitutes, reconditioning of items etc. Arranges for drawings to facilitate sourcing.
- Reviews the requisitions received from the users and ensures proper approval, item codes, working quantity, etc.
- Schedules review of all commodities or material groups and develops material catalogs.

(ii) Monitoring and Follow-up

- Monitors and reviews to ensure conformity with schedule.
- Prepares, updates and closely monitors stocks of all vital items.

- Coordinates closely with Purchasing as well as Delivery & Shipping Section for timely delivery of urgent and vital items.
- Supervises accurate postings of all transactions/ computer data entry and updating.
- Scrutinizes discrepancy reports.
- Follows up discrepancies with Purchasing for resolution.
- Processes the reconciliation of discrepancy.

(iii) Planning and Controlling

- Coordinates with Planning in setting levels, codification, standardization, ABC analysis, identification of non-moving and obsolete materials.
- Coordinates with Officer, Warehouse in physical stock taking, assists in preparation of explanation in case of discrepancies and reports/ recommends procedures to minimize recurrence.
- Maintains and updates the lists of items, which require government approval/licenses.

(iv) Systems Improvement

- Constantly reviews existing systems and methods for improvements.

APPENDIX 1.3

FUNCTIONS AND DUTIES OF INVENTORY CONTROLLER

Basic Functions

- to arrange for timely replenishment of items for the groups and subgroups
- to monitor movement of vital items
- to maintain manuals and catalogs
- to coordinate with similar level personnel
- to ensure complete specifications in all requisitions
- to supervise Inventory personnel

Duties

Replenishment of Items

- Accurate and timely replenishment of stores items.
- Analysis of requisitions based on commodities or groups/subgroups. Processing user's requisitions.
- Analysis of forecasted requirements based on review and feedback from users.
- Arranges updating descriptions, specifications, working quantities etc., based on the feedback from inspection or users.
- Constant review of similar items for merging
- Reviews non-moving and nil stock items for initiating corrective action.

Specifications

- Describes and forms specifications, develops synonyms for various items used.

Catalogs and manuals

- Maintains and updates lists of equipment, catalogs and manuals for assigned area of work.

Coordination

- Coordinates with personnel in warehousing, purchasing, customs and traffic and plant operations for providing clarifications.

APPENDIX 1.4

FUNCTIONS AND DUTIES OF WAREHOUSE OFFICER

Basic Functions

Supervises the activities of the warehousing and inspection section, including improvements, planning, executing and controlling the safe and efficient handling, storage, maintenance and issue of all materials, equipment and spare parts stored in the warehouse and associated areas and ensuring their security and protection. Also responsible for inspection of all incoming and outgoing materials.

Duties

Receiving, storing and issuing

- Supervises the activities of personnel assigned to warehouse and inspection section.
- Coordinates the safe and efficient movement, storage and issue of all materials and equipments required by the company. Includes planning and allocation of storage space for optimum utilization and facilitating easy access. Ensures suitable storage conditions/environment for each class of materials as per accepted practices and recommendations of manufacturers. Monitoring and ensuring safety, security and good housekeeping of all storage locations and materials.
- Examines the items received through return notes and repair requisitions for further actions
- Arranges identification of all non-moving/obsolete/expired/damaged items and recommends for suitable action after scrutiny.

Inspection

- Plans, supervises and coordinates the off-loading and storage of major deliveries. Coordinates closely with inspection personnel as well as division head for additional manpower, equipment, etc., and for inspection of the consignment.

- Materials Inspection Notice is sent to users as per procedure. Coordinates with Engineer, inventory control for inspection of complex incoming materials.
- Supervises inspection personnel for materials inspection of incoming materials and also from users for repair of the items.
- Supervises routine inventory activities as an administrative function. Arranges reviews of all inventories accurately and efficiently and coordinates with Engineer, Inventory Control for centralized processing of items.

Reviewing and recommending procedures

- Reviews and recommends procedures for loading, unloading, storing, issuing and control of materials to improve efficiency, minimize losses from deterioration or damage and to maintain a high standard of safety and security.

APPENDIX 1.5

FUNCTIONS AND DUTIES OF INSPECTION CONTROLLER

Basic Function

- To supervise the activities of materials inspectors.
- To process discrepancy reports as and when needed.
- To receive, inspect and ensure proper packing and dispatch of items/equipment for outside repairs.
- To process scrap declaration forms in line with approved policy.
- To inspect critical and/or high value materials in coordination with requisitioning User.

Duties

(i) Supervises the activities of materials inspectors. Ensures the safe unloading of all incoming materials, inspects in coordination with the users to ensure that specifications are in line with purchase requisitions/purchase orders, and determines discrepancies regarding quantities, damages, and specifications. Accepted materials are handed over to respective storekeepers/ users after completion of inspection reports. Discrepancy reports are prepared for unaccepted materials and raised for resolution by purchase division.

(ii) Coordinates with Unit Foremen/Section Engineers for additional information where substitutes are received or when stock items or acceptable drawing is not available for comparison. Follows up closely with respective users to get the necessary inspection reports for further processing for materials such as electronic cards which require testing.

(iii) Receives, inspects and ensures the appropriate packing and dispatch of items received for outside repairs.

(iv) Prepares discrepancy reports for excess/shortage of supplies, incorrect materials received or damages. In case of wrong supply, coordinates with user for obtaining polaroid photographs of existing items in use with relevant drawing/s. Prepares a detailed report, as an attachment, showing the differences between the required and supplied items, particularly for overseas suppliers. Reviews the possibilities of alternative use of received materials.

(v) Coordinates with Inventory Control personnel for updating of specifications, part numbers, etc.

(vi) Ensures that inspection and sampling procedures for bulk material deliveries are implemented accordingly. Ensures that proper samples are collected before handing over them to Quality & Process Control.

(vii) Arranges for the required computer entries for status reports. Recommends improvements in existing procedures for achieving improved efficiency.

(viii) Receives and reviews Scrap Declarations with related materials. Checks for appropriate approvals and justifications. Arranges the processing of documents relevant to the disposal of the materials as per established policy.

APPENDIX 1.6

FUNCTIONS AND DUTIES OF STOCK RECORDS CONTROLLER

Basic Functions

Responsible for executing and overseeing the efficient, accurate and timely posting of all transactions - receipts, issues, returns, amendments, etc. Processing, maintaining and retrieving all related documents and records. Generation of various Computer reports. Coordination with Finance for resolution of discrepancies.

Duties

Documentation and data processing

- Processes all documents and transactions for receipts, issues, returns, loans, adjustments, etc. upon authorized and approved documents.
- Supervises postings and updating of all data and generation of reports.
- Preparation and maintenance of statements of raw materials and production materials for receipts, issues and adjustments.
- Closing of monthly and yearly activities.

Control of important issues

- To control restrictive issues like uniforms, safety items to employees and update their records for the same.
- Maintains records of loans and borrowings and follows up with supervisors for settlement.
- Resolves discrepancies and coordinates with similar level positions within the division.
- Liaison with Warehouse Officer for adjustments and updating of stock balances at the time of stock checking and updates computer records as per approved procedure.

Monitoring sub-stores

- Monitors stock position in user-controlled sub-stores and reports status to the section heads.

APPENDIX 1.7

FUNCTIONS AND DUTIES OF STOREKEEPER

Basic Functions

Supervises and participates in the receiving, checking, tagging, binning, storage, physical movement, safety and security of materials, and good house keeping. Identification of non-moving and obsolete stores materials. Proper operations and maintenance of materials handling equipment. Implementation of procedures and control. Independent charge of main stores and coordinates with other sections of the division.

Duties

Receiving, checking and storing

- Supervises and participates in the receiving, checking, tagging, binning, physical movement and good housekeeping of assigned storage locations, implementation of procedures and control.
- Ensures proper operation and maintenance of all assigned materials handling equipment.
- Reviews, plans and recommends efficient allocation of storage space.
- Ensures timely movement of materials from inspection area to bins and bins to delivery point as per procedures.

Safety, security and housekeeping

- Ensures regular availability of charged fire extinguishers in their proper location and arranges for the subordinates to be fully aware and trained to combat fire or any other hazards.
- Responsible for safety and security of assigned stores and all materials. Ensures that all storage areas are properly secured and access is allowed to authorized persons only.
- Responsible for good housekeeping and protecting materials and facilities from dust, rust, moisture, heat and other elements which may cause deterioration.
- For optimum utilization of space and standardization, assigns and reassigns bin locations as and when necessary and keeps related sections informed.
- Segregating expired items and recommends for their disposal.

Inventory audit

- Supervises the Stores Assistants/Assistant Storekeepers assigned for his area.
- Coordinates and assists in Inventory Audit.

CHAPTER 2

Requisitions and Replenishment of Materials

INTRODUCTION

A very large number of items are kept in stock in a large industrial unit. Stock items have a regular usage and are replenished when the stock level reaches the reorder stage. Review and monitoring of the reorder level of each stock item is done at regular intervals. The review is done by Inventory Control Section and then by the user to estimate the quantity of the item to be procured when necessary. A review on the quantity to be procured is made after taking into consideration the requirements of production and regular repair and maintenance. The requirement is based on the trend of past consumption of the item, say five years. In case there is a plan for special repair of the plant and machinery or a plan for overhauling the plant, the spares are planned for the specific requirements of the special repairs or overhauling and added to the regular requirements.

The variety of stock items being very large, it is not feasible to review all the items at one time. A review plan is made for review of items of different groups. A schedule is prepared to review similar items at a time in a group. Thus all the items are reviewed according to the schedule spread over the whole year.

Besides the stock items, there are other spare parts that are required for repair and maintenance of plant and machinery, but their consumption is not regular. The decision on the quantity to be purchased is made by the user keeping in view the condition of the machine and the plan for repair.

Materials Requisition (Appendix 2.1) once approved by the competent authority of the user department is again reviewed by the Inventory Control Section, which recommends the quantity to be purchased based on the stock level of the item at that time. The Stores Division prepares a Materials Requisition for Purchase (MRP) (Appendix 2.2), which is then approved by the manager of the Stores Division and is forwarded to the Purchase Division for procurement. Procurement of stock items as well as items not consumed regularly is done on the basis of a Materials Requisition for Purchase (MRP), which is approved by a competent authority, before any action is initiated on it.

NEED FOR REQUISITIONING THE MATERIAL

Requisitioning of material is one of the most important activities of the warehouse. The process of requisitioning forces the stores to examine the stock level of the items and their requirements for the future. Review by the user is an important input in deciding the quantity to be purchased, which is based on the requirements of the plant on a realistic basis keeping in view the plans of production, repairs and maintenance. The extensive review helps the Stores Division to avoid any stock-out situation. It also helps in avoiding procurement of those items, that are not required, and also controls over-stocking of various items. Surplus stock may result in obsolete items and even spoilage of items during their long storage.

The review of quantity for replenishment or for new purchases of materials also helps in appropriate attention to various materials. Stock level and past consumption review informs the Stores Division about the urgency of purchasing some items over the others, and also about the need to delay purchases of the items that are not moving. The non-moving or slow-moving items, if not controlled, will result in excessive inventory and blockage of money.

REPLENISHMENT OF STOCK ITEMS

Replenishment of stock items takes into consideration various factors, such as:

- lead time for procurement
- minimum, maximum and reorder levels of the stock items
- review of critical items
- review by user department
- scrutiny by Inventory Section
- determining the reorder quantity

Ascertain Leadtime

Average lead time is computed for stock items that are repeatedly purchased. Further, checking is done based on the groups/subgroups of items as per requirements.

For new items to be stocked and also for stock items sporadically used, the lead time is established from the established lead time list of similar materials.

Ascertain Minimum, Maximum and Reorder Levels

Minimum, maximum and reorder levels of items of a group/ subgroup in the inventory are generated by the computer in quantitative terms on the basis of the available historical data of past consumption.

In cases where relevant historical data for an item is not available or where further information is needed to correctly establish the levels (especially for new stock items), advice of the user department is taken regarding minimum, maximum and reorder levels to be considered. Special care is required for items of sporadic nature or where equipment is likely to be scrapped in the near future.

For items where changes in consumption patterns and/or leadtime are observed, old replenishment levels should be updated based on the latest data at the time of replenishment of the items.

Stock Replenishment Report

Items for replenishment should be consolidated groupwise using the main group/ subgroup code. A Materials Replenishment Report (Appendix 2.3) is generated for items based on the replenishment control levels, stock balance and quantity on order (if any)/outstanding MRP.

The Stock Replenishment Report (MRR) (Appendix 2.3) indicates the following details:

- item code #
- bin location
- item description
- unit code
- stock balance
- last five years' consumption,
- YTD consumption for current year
- working quantity
- reference of previous MRP/PO
- reorder quantity proposed

The report details out all the items/groups/subgroups of items. The report is then evaluated and if required, necessary changes are made. The report is allocated a Material Requisition (MR) (Appendix 2.1) number. A schedule for review of items in various groups and subgroups is prepared, which is spread over the whole year.

Selection of Items Based on Groups/Subgroups on a Monthly Basis or As and When Required

On a monthly basis or as and when required, a report is to be generated for items when the stock balance reaches the reorder level or is lesser than the reorder level and will be selected groupwise.

Selection of Critical Items

A list of vital stock items that are essential for plant operation, not usually available locally and have a long leadtime, should be prepared on the basis of past data. During the course of normal issue and replenishment, the list of critical stock items is updated.

Items on this list should be reviewed at least every 30 days and if there is any unusual consumption or change in leadtime or delay in ordering/shipping of any item, the same should be selected for further review with the concerned user.

Preparation of Materials Requisition Report

The item range is selected for replenishment of items. A Material Requisition (MR) report for the selected items with ROQ is generated by the computer and reviewed. Necessary changes are made in the report. Items not required are deleted from the list. For other items, the quantity to be purchased is either increased/reduced or not changed. A printout of the report is then taken out.

Dispatch of Requisition to User Department

The Computer allocates a sequential Material Requisition (MR) number to the printout. Necessary remarks or additional details for any item are given in the report that assists the user in reviewing the printout. After approval of the report by the manager of the Stores Division, the same is logged & dispatched to the user department.

The MR description/specification of each item is reviewed by the user department and where errors are noted or additional details are required about the description of items to facilitate correct procurement, corrections/additions are made to the MR. The user takes into account various factors, for example preventive maintenance schedule, approved modification (if any), existing condition of equipment, working quantities etc., and makes estimates on future consumption quantity. These estimates are entered itemwise in the specified column by the user and each entry is initialed.

Scrutiny of Revised Replenishments, Requisitions, and Consolidation

The report received from the user department is scrutinized to ensure that quantities or remarks have been entered against each item and initialed. Incomplete reports or requisitions where questions raised by Inventory Section have not been answered, should be referred back to the user department for rectification. Reports reviewed by the user should be kept for consolidation with other material requisitions or reports of similar category items for a predetermined period, say one week, after which they should be processed individually.

Review Order Quantity

The Inventory Section reviews each item on the consolidated Requisition/Report in light of the estimated annual consumption quantity given by the user, and in conjunction with details of stock balance, leadtime/re-order level, maximum and minimum levels, and any outstanding MRP. The order quantity for each item is then established and indicated on the consolidated Requisition or Report against each item.

Appropriate remarks against each item regarding samples, and other relevant information from the user is highlighted on the Replenishment Requisition or Report for transfer to the MRP when prepared.

REQUISITION FOR NEW AND OUT OF STOCK ITEMS

Procurement of stock items can be divided into two categories:

- New stock items
- Out of stock items

The user/originating department prepares a Material Requisition for spares, consumables, and equipment required by it. The MR is approved by the competent authority. According to delegation of powers, different levels of management are given authority to approve the MR up to different amounts. Routine requirements are approved by the concerned manager of the user/originating department, but high-value requirements are approved by the concerned person in a level above that of a manager. The MR approved by the appropriate level is forwarded to the manager of the Stores Division.

Scrutiny of MR

MR upon receipt in the Stores Division, is scrutinized for the following:

i. MR is initiated by the person in accordance with the list of authorized persons as informed by the user departments.

ii. MR is approved by the authority according to the delegation of authority.

iii. The 'date required' is indicated on the MR.

iv. Check whether the date required is in accordance with the standard leadtime applicable for the requested material. In case a short leadtime is indicated, justification for the same should be obtained from user/originating department

v. Full justification should be given for urgent requirements. Urgent requirements, whether for local or overseas procurement must be approved as per policy from time to time.

vi. The desired mode of shipment, in case of procurement from overseas, i.e. Air Parcel Post, Courier, Airfreight or Sea Freight is to be indicated by the requisitioner. In case any special instruction is required to be given, the same should be recorded on the MR.

vii. If a new item has to be stocked, reason/justification recommending the new item in the stock should be written clearly. Factors to be considered for creation of new stock item are:

   - The item should have a continuity of usage.
   - High probability of failure qualifies an item as a stock item. If the item is not likely to fail for years it should not be classified as stock item. Some stores follow the principle that if the item is issued/used at least once a year, the usage is considered as regular usage. Such an item is categorized as stock item.
   - Criticality of item for the machine and criticality of the machine are important considerations for creation of stock item. Even if the item is not likely to fail for 2 or 3 years, but its failure may affect the production, it is necessary to keep the item in stock.

- Imported items and item of critical nature with long lead time should be stocked.

viii. For a stock item where the stock balance is nil or insufficient, and the item is required in more quantity than currently available in stock, the MR must clearly indicate the following:

- Item code and BIN Location of each item to avoid duplication of code.
- The latest stock balance.
- Appropriate remark/justification for the quantity required in excess of the stock balance.
- Approval of the Departmental Head.

ix. The description and technical specifications on the MR are reviewed to ensure the following:

- Description or technical specifications of the required item must be complete and Working Quantity (WQ), nature of item (vital, essential, general) should be written.
- Details including those on name plate of main equipment (Mother Unit) or facility for which the item is required should be indicated on the MR.
- Wherever applicable, drawings, sketches, photographs or samples must be enclosed to facilitate procurement of correct items.
- Other details such as asset code of main equipment, cost code, unit of measure, and previous MRP reference, must be mentioned.
- In case where a sample is given with the MR, the same should be correctly reflected on the MR description. Each sample must be properly tagged by the user with necessary details, that is, MR item number, brief description, etc., and indicating its status such as defective, new, returnable, etc.

PREPARATION OF MATERIALS REQUISITION FOR PURCHASE

After scrutiny of MR, the Stores Division prepares a Materials Requisition for Purchase (MRP) (Appendix 2.2) A MRP has the following information:

- MR number.
- In case of new items for direct issue, it has the file number corresponding to the equipment/facility for which the item is requested.
- MRP number. A sequential number is generated by the computer.
- Item code. In case of a new item, an item code is given for the item.
- Bin location of the item.
- The previous purchase order and purchase requisition number reference.

Distribution of MRP

The approved MRP together with a copy of the relevant MR is distributed as indicated below:

- Original - Purchasing Division.
- Two copies - Stores Division for inspection & expediting respectively.
- Another copy of MRP together with MR copy to User/ Originator Department/ Division.

MRP amendments based on data entry errors, merging, splitting of MRP, or their cancellation should be authorized by the manager of the Stores Division after concurrence of the Purchasing Division and the concerned user/originating department.

Amendment of Materials Requisition for Purchase

The MRP is then forwarded to the Purchasing Division for procurement action. During the scrutiny of the MRP by the buyer, sometimes deficiencies are noticed in specifications. This is brought to the notice of the Stores Division for clarifications. If the clarifications need involvement of the user/originating department, the issues are referred to the user/originating department for clarifications. The MRP is modified on the basis of clarifications received by the user/originating department through the stores Division.

During the evaluation of offers received from the suppliers, sometimes a new version of the item, change of part number or new features are found in the specifications. In some cases, the cost of purchase is found to be very high. In such cases, a reference is made to the user department to review specifications and/ the quantity to purchase. The views of the User are incorporated in the MRP, regarding specifications and the quantity. The MRP is then revised by the Inventory Section on the recommendation of the buyer. It is necessary that user consents to the proposed changes in the MRP.

Materials Requisition for Purchase Update

The revised Materials Requisition for Purchase is termed as Materials Requisition for Purchase Update (MRPU) (Appendix 2.4). MRP's amendments to the quantity, unit code, item description, merging of two or more MRP's, transfer of items between one or more MRP's or cancellation of an item in the MRP's are to be made on MRPU. The original MR is attached as a supporting document to the MRPU and filed in sequential order in the MRPU file.

Expediting Copy

On receipt of the expediting copy, the same is filed in numerical sequence in the expediting MRP file. Copies of any clarification/memos or additional documents received from Purchasing Division and/or user/ originator of MR are attached to the expediting copy of MRP.

Inspection copy of MRP is filed in the Outstanding Inspection Copy of the MRP file. Copies of catalogs, drawings, Polaroid photos, pieces/slices of samples of material, facilitate identification/inspection of material, and which are either originally received with the MR or obtained during processing of MRP in the Purchasing Division, are attached to the Inspection copy of MRP. After arrival of the material, the Materials Inspector of Materials Inspection and Receipt (MIR) Section checks the Materials Dispatch and Receipt Report (MDRR) . After inspection and acceptance of materials, the relevant MDRR number, item number, quantity received and other references are entered item wise on the Material Inspection Status File.

The Inspection copies of the MRP together with the MDRR and other receipt documents are passed to the Warehousing Officer. The Warehousing Officer, after allocation of Bin Location and physical binning of items/direct issues, forwards the inspection copies of MRP together with MDRR and other receipt documents for preparation of Materials Receipt & Inspection Note (MRIN).

Updating Receipt Status of MRP

On receipt of the materials, the details of Materials Dispatch & Receipt Report (MDRR) and other receipt documents should be entered on the MRP Status Report against the relevant MRP number indicating arrival of material. This provides an interim update of information to user departments and Purchasing Division regarding receipt of materials. A Final update is done after the materials have been inspected and accepted by the concerned users and on receipt of the copy of Material Receipt & Inspection Note (MRIN).

APPENDIX 2.1 MATERIAL REQUISITION (MR)

Plant Location:.................

SECTION	DEPT.	INITIATED BY:	RECOMMENDED BY	APPROVED BY	DATE OF MR	DATE REQD.	REF. #	COST CODE:

MAIN EQUIP./SUB ASSY. FOR WHICH PARTS ARE REQUIRED	SI. #	ITEM #/ WAREHOUSE/ LOCATION	DESCRIPTION & PART #	U/M	QTY. REQD.	WQ	MATERIAL/ ITEM		PREVIOUS MRP/ P.O REF.
							TYPE	NATURE	
DESCRIPTION									
Year:									
Manufacturer:									
Model:									
Type:									
Serial #									
Power Supply/Rating									
KW									
Voltage									
Phase									
Frequency									
Ampere									
RPM									
Asset Code #									

JUSTIFICATION FOR REQUIREMENT AND/OR KEEPING IN STOCK (Attach separate sheet if necessary)	
REMARKS BY STORES DIVISION FOR CLARIFICATION/ JUSTIFICATION	

NOTE:
1. All items introduced for the first time to inventory shall be treated as "W" (when Required) until consumption pattern is established at least for 3 years.
2. For replacement of existing Equipment/Machine, related spares in Inventory must be considered. This is to be advised on the MR.

STORES DIVISION USE ONLY	REQUISITION		MR #	MRP #	FILE #	DATE:
	RECEIVED BY:	DATE:				

Distribution: White & Pink: Stores Division (Pink to be returned to Originator). Blue: Originator.

APPENDIX 2.2 MATERIAL REQUISITION FOR PURCHASE (MRP)

NO.: DATE:

PLANT	REQUIRED BY	MARKET	DESCRIPTION MACHINE	INITIATED BY	PREPARED BY	REVIEWED BY	STORES MANAGER	PURCHASE MANAGER	BUYER	
Req.Seq.	Description			Part ID MRP NO.	Loc. NURM	Qty. to order UOM	Last Pur. Price/Av. Price	Prv. P.O.V. No. & Date	Pending Quantity	
									MRP	PO

NOTES:

DISTRIBUTION: Original-Purchasing, Green-Warehouse, Yellow-Store Division (Inventory), Pink-User Department

APPENDIX 2.3 MATERIAL REPLENISHMENT REPORT (MRR)

Date:

Report Selection Criteria

Item Range From ……… To ……..

Material Item Type Range From ……… To ……..

Material Item Type Range From ……… To ……..

Sl #	Item #	Type, Nature	Description	WQ	Stock	ROL	O/S QTY	ROQ	MRP Qty value	AUP(US$)	Quantity	
	ABC Class				UM	MAX	PO				Year	Quantity
	Default				Stock Value	MIN	MRP					
	Warehouse Location											
1	R110-030-0000	AA	Tiles, Vinyl	0	76	5.73		58	58	3.95	94	20
	C				PC	13.76					95	35
	AA126302				300 Apprx.	1.14					96	6
											97	17
											98	15

APPENDIX 2.4 MATERIALS REQUISITION FOR PURCHASE UPDATE (MRPU)

Page .... of ....

TO:	PLANT :	MRP #		BUYER CODE	MRPU #	
		REVISION.#			DATE	

Line #	REV U/C/A	PART ID	Ware House	Bin Location	Part Description	U/M	Quantity

REMARKS :

PREPARED BY	RECOMMENDED BY	APPROVED BY	ENTERED BY
	STORES MANAGER		

Distribution : **Original** - Inventory Control, **Pink**- Warehouse (Inspection), **Blue** - User Department, **Yellow** - Purchasing.

U = Updated
C = Cancelled
A = Added

CHAPTER 3

Receipt and Inspection of Materials

INTRODUCTION

An industrial unit uses different types of materials such as raw materials, spares, consumables, machine components, and assemblies. It is very necessary that all incoming materials are properly received, checked, counted or measured and inspected to ensure that:

- Correct material is received as required.
- The quantity of the material received is as indicated in the receiving documents.
- Quality of the material received is as specified in the purchase order.

RECEIPT OF MATERIALS

Materials are received at warehouse from the following:

- Customs &Traffic Section of the company, which may be located at a different place such as another city
- Buyers
- Transporters
- Suppliers

In order to ensure proper receipt of incoming materials, all receipt documents are to be thoroughly verified prior to unloading. Materials are received either against a Materials Requisition (MR) Appendix 2.1 or a Materials Dispatch & Receipt Report (MDRR) (Appendix 3.1). MR are used for items of small value purchased against cash, whereas MDRR is used for all other materials.

Receipt of Materials from Customs and Traffic Section of the Company

Customs and Traffic Section of the Company receives the materials from the suppliers, both foreign and local, and even arranges materials from the local markets to meet the urgent requirements. Materials received from Customs and Traffic Section are handled as below:

- All materials both from local and overseas sources excluding those transported by local buyers or direct delivery from suppliers/transporters are forwarded by Customs & Traffic Section against Materials Dispatch and Receipt Report (MDRR) comprising originals & 3 copies in blue, green & pink.
- Separate MDRRs are prepared by Customs & Traffic Section for each group of items, that is, Cash Purchase, Bulk Purchase Requisition, Air Parcel Post/ Courier, Air-Freight, Sea freight, etc.
- Full details of items dispatched together with total number of boxes/packages are indicated on the MDRR.
- On arrival of materials, the supervisor, of the Materials Inspection & Receipt Section (MIR) collects the MDRR from the driver, and verifies that the supporting documents, that is, packing list/delivery advice/copies of invoices, wherever applicable, are available with the MDRR.
- Once the supervisor of the, MIR Section is satisfied that the necessary documents are available and are in order, the material is unloaded from the vehicle.

Receipt of Materials Directly from Buyers

Materials procured by buyers are received directly from them against either a Material Requisition (MR) or a Materials Dispatch & Receiving Report (MDRR).

Receipt of Materials Against MR

Only cash purchase items of small value, which are not destined for stock or are not fixed assets, are received against MR. Materials received from buyers against MR are handled as below:

- Materials are delivered by the buyer to the Materials Clerk, Inventory Control Section together with the original MR and Invoice.
- The Materials Clerk after verifying that the material conforms to the MR, informs the user/originator to inspect and collect the material.
- Acknowledgment of acceptance and receipt is obtained on the invoice from the representative of user/originator department inspecting the goods, and his name should be written on the invoice clearly.
- Materials together with the pink copy of the MR is handed over to the representative of the user/originator department.
- The original MR and acknowledged invoice is returned to the concerned buyer for settlement with finance.

Receipt of Materials Against MDRR

All materials from the buyers, other than those received against a MR, are received on MDRR and are handled as below:

- After receipt of the MDRR, the supervisor, of the Materials Inspection & Receipt Section will verify that the details on the MDRR are complete, and that the necessary backup documents that is copy of invoice, delivery advice, etc., (wherever applicable) are available.
- Along with the materials, the documents are handed over by the driver to the Materials Receipt & Inspection Clerk for checking and unloading. If everything is in order, the clerk hands over an acknowledgment slip.
- After confirming that the material is in order, with respect to quantity only, the yellow copy of MDRR with acknowledgment is returned to the concerned buyer while the original together with the blue, green and pink copies is retained by the Stores Division for further processing.

Receipt of Materials Directly from Suppliers/Transporters/Company Vehicles

Direct delivery of materials from suppliers, transporters, and company vehicles is arranged for spares or consumables which are received at the Main Warehouse, Open Storage Yard or Sub-Stores by trucks/trailers or containers. Raw Materials are received at the relevant Stores or Open Storage Yards by Trucks. In both cases, receipt documents are verified and processed further.

(i) Direct receipt of spares and consumables

Direct receipt of spares and consumables is handled in the following manner:

- All spares and consumables delivered by suppliers, transporters, and company vehicles should be accompanied by necessary delivery documents, that is Delivery Advice, Dispatch Notes, etc.
- The Supervisor, Materials Inspection & Receipt Section checks the documents to ensure that all details including P.O. Box number, supplier's name, quantity delivered, etc., are available for identification of the materials. After the necessary check is completed and it is established that the material is as specified in the documents, it is unloaded in the relevant storage area.

(ii) Direct receipt of raw materials

The Stores Division prior to the receipt of any raw materials informs all the concerned personnel including the transporter's drivers and weighbridge operators, the location of the designated unloading area. The receipt procedure and required documentation for all items in this category are as detailed below:

- Dump trucks transporting raw materials must possess Dispatch and Receipt Note (DRN) (Appendix 3.2)

- The driver hands over the DRN to the weighbridge operator, who records the gross weight (weight of truck plus cargo). The DRN is retained at the weighbridge.
- The driver is then directed by the weighbridge operator to proceed to the designated unloading area to discharge the cargo.
- The transporter's truck after unloading the material, proceeds once again to the weighbridge where the empty weight (tare weight) is ascertained and the net weight calculated. Both the weights are recorded on the retained DRN, the original of which is handed over to the transporter's driver. The blue and pink copies are retained by weighbridge, operator.
- At the end of each day, the weighbridge operator groups together materialwise both copies of DRN and sends them to the Stores Division for further processing.

Receipt of Loan Items

It is a usual practice to give some items on loan to other organizations on request. Once the lent items are returned and received at the warehouse, the following procedure is followed:

- Items obtained on loan from other companies are received against Delivery Advice/Issue Note of the company concerned.
- The Supervisor, MIR Section confirms that the items are as per receipt documents. The material is then unloaded.
- After unloading & confirming the receipt of number of items/packages as per the Delivery Advice/ Issue Note, the Supervisor of MIR Section signs on the receipt document as an acknowledgment and returns one copy to the driver.
- Further checking and inspection is carried out as detailed in earlier sections.

UNLOADING OF MATERIALS

Materials arriving by pickup/flat bed trailers or in containers is unloaded by the Stores Division, whereas in case of raw materials the unloading is done by the transporter, in accordance with the unloading procedures.

Unloading by the Stores Division

The Supervisor, of MIR Section arranges timely unloading of cargo in the correct location. He is responsible for ensuring that all unloading is performed in a safe manner and safety requirements are followed. They are:

- To clear the unloading area of previously received materials, equipment, or other obstructions.
- Use of safety helmets, gloves, shoes plus any other safety gear deemed necessary after taking into account the nature of material.
- Unloading and handling of equipment to be done by authorized and trained personnel only.

Unloading by Transporters

Materials are to be unloaded by the transporters by following the directions as stated below:

- Unloading is to be in the designated area of the assigned yard.
- Materials should be unloaded in a systematic manner to allow efficient unloading of subsequent cargoes.
- Transporters must ensure that all safety, traffic and environmental requirements are followed and unloading is performed in a safe manner.

INSPECTION

Inspection can be divided into two stages They are:

- Pre-dispatch inspection
- Post-receipt inspection

The type of inspection of materials depends upon various factors, such as:

- size of the item: small, medium or large
- nature of items, that is machine parts, chemicals, explosives, or materials sensitive to environmental conditions
- cost of items
- materials requiring special testing facilities
- bulk materials, where any rejection of material has serious repercussions.

Pre-Dispatch Inspection

In case of an order for plant and machinery, where the performance of the machine greatly depends upon quality control during manufacturing and assembly, it is essential that the inspection is carried out at various stages of the manufacturing/fabrication. Once assembled or fabricated, there is no possibility of checking the parts, that are inside the machine. Since both dismantling and assembly of any equipment or machine involves both cost and effort, further checking of the internal parts is discouraged once the fabrication/assembly of the machine is complete. It is the objective of the supplier as well the buyer that the plant and machinery, once installed, performs without any problem. Stage inspection ensures that the quality control during manufacturing is as per relevant standards and would help in maintaining the quality of the product.

Pre-dispatch inspection is normally done in the supplier's works by his own staff. In case of reputed suppliers, the buyer relies on the quality control system of the supplier. However, in some cases the buyer asks the supplier to submit the copies of the inspection reports for his information and record. This is a very common practice for materials used in pressure vessels, where lot of welding is involved. The quality of welding is very important for the life as well as performance of the pressure vessel. Similarly, the chemical composition of the material is very crucial in case of castings.

Stage inspection in this case is very essential to ensure the correct composition of the product and also to ensure the proper heat treatment required to achieve the desired quality.

Depending upon the criticality of the item due to its importance or high cost, the buyer may even depute his own inspectors to the works of the supplier, for stage inspections or may even hire the services of specialists from other reputed expert organizations for the purpose. The buyer may also ask test reports of certain tests from reputed testing laboratories to ensure that all necessary tests are carried out at the appropriate stages to maintain the ultimate quality of the final product.

Pre-dispatch inspection is essential in cases of import of raw materials, where bulk quantity is involved. Any rejection of the material at the destination, or the need for its return from the destination to the supplier, results in many problems, such as loss of valuable time and money. The buyer is very careful in such cases and definitely does not want to take any risk on the quality of the material. He therefore appoints reputed Inspection Agencies to inspect the material before dispatch both for the quantity being shipped as well as for its quality. The Expert Agency conducts all necessary tests, including physical and chemical testing as required to ensure that the material being dispatched conforms to specifications as mentioned in the agreement. In case the material ready for dispatch does not conform to the specifications, the consignment is rejected to avoid any problem later on at its destination.

The payment term in case of imports is normally through a letter of credit (L/C). Payments are made to the supplier by the bank on presentation of the documents by the supplier. The buyer takes special care to ascertain the quantity and quality of the material loaded on the ship, before release of payment by the bank. The buyer or supplier, as agreed upon, appoints a surveyor to conduct a draft survey of the material on the ship to establish the quantity of material actually loaded on the ship. The surveyor takes into consideration all the required parameters for establishing the quantity of the material such as bulk density of the material, level of the ship in the water before loading and after loading, weight of the ship and fuel, or any other weight relevant to the calculations. In addition, physical and chemical testing of the material is also carried out to ensure that the quality of material loaded is in conformance with the quality agreed upon. Pre-dispatch inspection, although involving a lot of money, is important and essential to safeguard the interest of the buyer.

Post-receipt Inspection

Post-receipt inspection is normally done at the warehouse/works of the buyer. It can be divided into two stages. The first stage is termed as preliminary inspection and is carried out by the Material Inspector of the warehouse. The second stage is known as the final inspection and is carried out by the representative of the user department/ originating department.

Inspection by Material Inspector in the Warehouse

Various activities in the first stage of inspection done by the Material Inspector of the warehouse are:

- segregation and counting of packages
- unpacking, identification and visual checking
- information to user/originating department

(i) Segregation and counting of packages

The following steps are taken for segregation and counting of packages:

- After unloading, the supervisor of the Materials Receipt and Inspection Section, arranges for the segregation of packages in accordance with the receipt document.
- Packages received from overseas should be arranged separately from those received from the local market.
- Each package from the overseas vendors should be identified by means of the shipping marks related to the documents.
- Any package found missing, or any excess compared to the number/marks on the documents should be immediately brought to the notice of the Officer, Customs & Traffic Section by the supervisor for initiating appropriate action.

(ii) Unpacking, identifying and visual checking

The supervisor, Materials Receipt and Inspection Section, allocates the items to the Materials Receipt & Inspection Clerks. Required labor is made available to assist in unpacking. The following steps are taken for unpacking, identifying and checking of the materials:

- Each package, wooden box, and carton is carefully opened and arranged item by item on the floor or inspection tables. Delicate items are laid on cardboard or plastic sheets.
- Each item is identified from the Materials Dispatch and Receipt Report (MDRR), Packing list, Delivery Advice, or Copy of Invoice of Purchase Orders.
- The physical condition of each item is visually checked for any possible damage.
- Once the inspection is completed, necessary remarks regarding shortages, damages or unidentified items are made on the receipt documents.
- If satisfied that the material conforms in all respects to the Purchase Order and the control sample, the Clerk, Materials Receipt and Inspection Section accepts the same by noting 'Inspected and Accepted' on the relevant receipt documents and signs the same.
- If case of any difference, a Discrepancy Report (DR) is prepared which is dealt with separately in Chapter 6.

Information to User/Originating Departments

(i) Material arrival

On arrival of the material, the following procedures are under taken:

- Immediately on arrival of materials, a copy of MDRR and/or photocopies of receipt documents are handed to the Inventory Control Section by the Materials Receipt and Inspection Section.
- The Materials Clerk of Inventory Control Section compares the receipt documents with the Materials Requisition for Purchase to identify the user/originator and advises the concerned department of the material arrival.
- After the preliminary inspection is completed by the Supervisor, Materials Receipt and Inspection Section, the user/originating department is informed for conducting inspection.

(ii) Issue of Materials Inspection Notice

The Materials Receipt and Inspection Clerk prepares the Material Inspection Notice (s) (MIN) (Appendix 3.3) and forwards the same to the user/originator department requesting inspection in the following cases:

- for all new items, whether intended for stock or direct issue
- for all items received on loan
- for all project items
- for all free of charge (FOC) supplies received without a Materials Requisition for Purchase (MRP)/Purchase Order (PO)
- for stock items where no previous stock quantity/control sample is available
- for all items, if the item received is different from the item requested in the Purchase Order (PO)
- wherever doubt exists as to the acceptability of material which includes, but is not limited to, poor appearance/finish/quality and/or minor damage or is old/used/reconditioned

(iii) Follow-up

The Supervisor, MIR Section ensures that the inspection is initiated at the earliest by the user/ originating department but not later than three working days from the time of issue of notice. Where department(s) fail to respond within the time limit, the matter is brought to the attention of Stores Manager, who coordinates with the concerned Department Manager to carry out the inspection.

Inspection by User/Originating Department

(i) Inspection of materials in main warehouse/relevant store

The user/originating department(s) after receipt of Materials Inspection Notice(s) (MIN), deputes an Engineer or Foreman for inspection. The deputed Engineer Foreman together with the Supervisor, MIR Section proceeds to the relevant storage area where the material is laid out. He inspects the material and either accepts or rejects the same. If the material is acceptable, he signs the MIN. However, if the material is rejected, reasons for rejection are noted in full on the MIN and then signed by the Engineer or the Foreman.

In cases where the Engineer or Foreman is unable to make an on-the-spot decision, or the item is such that testing is required prior to acceptance, the item is taken to the appropriate workshop. Normally not more than three working days should be allowed from the inspection date to accept or reject the material. Any item not accepted/rejected within three working days is brought to the notice of the Manager, Stores Department, who should contact the concerned Department Head for appropriate action.

(ii) Inspection of materials taken by user/originating department to their workshop

For all the items taken to the user/originating department's workshop for testing, acknowledgment of receipt is to be noted on the MIN. All items should be accepted or rejected within seven working days of the receipt of material by the testing workshop.

However, certain items require more than 7 days, before a decision to accept or reject is taken. For example, a minimum of seven days inspection and a maximum period of 21 days is given for the inspection of electronic cards. In any case, there should be a time limit for completing the inspection by the user/originating department workshop, either to accept or to reject the material under inspection.

CONTROL SAMPLES

A Control Sample is a complete unit of a new item which has been selected or approved by the user. It is either obtained from the supplier by the Purchasing Division or a sample piece is taken from any previous purchase and is kept separately in stock for the purpose of comparison or checking similar items for quality assurance.

Used defective items approved by the user, which are complete and representative, may also be kept in stock locations as Control Samples. The Control Samples obtained from the supplier for approved material, are utilized in inspection of supplies, to confirm that approved specifications and quality of purchased material are maintained.

Handling of Control Samples

The handling and utilization of Control Samples for carrying out inspection is an important issue. The Control Samples should be properly marked for identification and should be kept in bin location by clearly marking it as a Control Sample. The Control Sample should be handled carefully to avoid any confusion at a later date.

Approved Control Samples for ordered materials are forwarded by Purchasing Division to Warehouse for safe-keeping until arrival of the ordered material. The Inventory Control Section arranges for the marking/tagging and keeps the Control Samples in safe storage. The tag should have a brief description of the item, related MRP number, MRP item number, or any other reference as may be necessary. Against the relevant item number on the inspection copy of MRP, details of receipt of Control Samples are written. The details of the Control Samples are also entered in the Control Samples Register.

Safe-keeping of Control Samples

Control samples received from the Purchasing Division, whether for stock items or for direct issues are taken on charge as Free of Charge (FOC) supply on Return Note. The samples are then stored in the relevant bin locations with tags marked 'This is a Control Sample', to be issued only in case of emergency after approval by the Manager, Stores Division. The Control Sample is stored in a steel closet with locking arrangement and the key is kept safely. General consumables, safety items, any other material, and one unit of each item marked as Control Sample should be kept in stock in the relevant bin location. In case an old Control Sample is already available, the same will be de-tagged and kept with rest of the stock for future issue. In its place, the new Control Sample will be stored with proper tagging. Control Samples for direct issue items, after inspection & acceptance, and after recording the transfer in the Control Sample Register, are kept in the warehouse. Low value Control Samples of common-use items, are usually issued to the concerned user department together with the newly received material. At the time of replenishment of stock items, details of the control samples are indicated on the Inspection copy of MRP for facilitating the inspection of material on its receipt.

Inspection with the Help of Control Samples

Control Sample is a very strong tool for inspection. Some of the details of the materials procured cannot be specified by dimensional details, or are difficult to describe in words. Control Samples clearly explain all the details about the item purchased.

On arrival of the materials from the supplier or any other source, the details of the item to be inspected are noted from the inspection copy of the MRP. In addition, the relevant Control Sample is taken from the steel closet or from the concerned bin location for completing the inspection. After completing the inspection, the Control Sample is replaced in its respective location.

The Control Sample is a very reliable reference material for checking the item received. The presence of the Control Sample at the time of inspection removes any doubt about the item and the inspector becomes very confident about accepting or rejecting the item. Any employee with a little experience can handle the inspection with the help of the Control Sample. It is a strong tool for training new Material Inspectors.

DOCUMENTATION FOR ACCEPTED MATERIALS

Stock Items

The details of MDRR for all stock items, which have been accepted by the user/ originator, are recorded in the MDRR Register. The MDRR is forwarded to the Warehousing Section together with the relevant documents (MRP, MDRR, Packing List, etc.) for records.

In case of items received on loan, the details of Delivery Note/Issue Note of the lending company are recorded in the MDRR Register. After making all entries in MDRR Register, all documents are forwarded to Warehousing Section for records.

Direct Issue Items

Direct issue items, which are of an extremely urgent nature, after acceptance, are handed over to the user from the inspection area itself against receipt of the Direct Issue Stores Voucher (DISV) (Appendix 3.4). Receipt of the Direct Issue Stores Voucher (DISV) is recorded in the MDRR Register and is forwarded to the Warehousing Section for processing of MRIN (Appendix 3.5).

All other direct issue items, which are not urgently required, after inspection and acceptance by the user/originating department, are forwarded to the Stock Record Controller together with all relevant documents for further processing.

MATERIALS UNDER DISCREPANCY

Whenever any difference between the material ordered & the material received is noted, either by the MIR Section or by the user/originating department, the observation is recorded in a Discrepancy Report, giving full details of the discrepancies noted. The DR number is noted on the MDRR and is forwarded to the Stores Keeper. Material under DR is handled separately in Chapter 6.

APPENDIX 3.1 MATERIAL DISPATCH AND RECEIPT REPORT (MDRR)

Plant:

Sl. # ....
Date: ....

Sl. #	Purchase order (PO)		Material Requisition for Purchase (MRP)		Part ID	U/M	PART DESCRIPTION	PO Quantity	Dispatched Quantity	Received Quantity	Rejected Quantity	Discrepancy Report No. & Date	MRIN No. & Date
	PO #	Line #	MRP #	Line #	Bin -1 Bin - 2	LOC							

Remarks:

	No. of Packages		Attachments: copies of	Dispatched	Received
	Dispatched	Received	Purchase Order		
Wooden Boxes			Invoice		
Cartons			Packing List		
Others			Delivery Advice		

Packages Receipt Condition	Damaged	Opened
No. of Wooden Boxes:		
No. of Cartons:		
No. of Others:		

Prepared By	Date	Dispatched By	Date	Driver's Name	Vehicle #	Received at Plant By	Date	Inspected & Counted By	Date	Authorized Signature	Date	Entered By	Date

Distribution: Original & yellow - Purchase Division, Green - Warehouse, Pink - Inventory Control

APPENDIX 3.2 DESPATCH AND RECEIPT NOTE (DRN)

Transport Contractor:	……		Date ……..	
Truck/Trailer No.	……		Driver's name & signature	……….
			Sig. Of Company Representative	……….
Weight (tons):				
	Gross: ……..		Time in at the plant	……….
	Tare : ……..		Time out from the plant	……….
	Net : ……..			
Weigh Bridge No.:	…….	Name & Signature	………….	
			(Weighbridge Operator)	

Distribution: Original - Transport Contractor, Blue - Customs & Traffic Section, Pink - Stores Division, Yellow - Supplier/Source

APPENDIX 3.3 MATERIALS INSPECTION NOTE (MIN)

No. : ....

Date : ....

Plant :

Store Division

To :			**Inspection is requested to be completed within 3 days.**			
Department		Division		**Information**		**Inspection**
MRP #		PO #	MDRR #			
MRP / PO Header						
MRP Item #/(s)						
Remarks (if any) :						
Materials Inspector / Name / Signature		**Inspection Controller**		**Officer, Warehouse**		**Date**

User Department / Division

1. All items are acceptable / Not acceptable.
2. Item #s. .... only acceptable, balance not acceptable

(For Item/s which is / are not acceptable, please give details / technical reasons.)

Line #	**MRP Item #**	**Reason (s) for non acceptance**

If the above space is not enough, please attach a separate sheet.

	Job Title	**Name**	**Emp. No.**	**Signature**	**Date**
Inspected / Accepted by					

For Direct Issue Items	**Job Title**	**Name**	**Emp. No.**	**Signature**	**Date**
1. Received by:					
2. Issued by:		Signature:	Date:	Officer, Warehouse:	

Distribution : **Original & Blue** : Warehouse. **Pink** : User Dept./Div. **Yellow**: Finance

APPENDIX 3.4 DIRECT ISSUE STORES VOUCHER (DISV)

No: ....

Date : ....

PLANT		MRP#		PO#		MDRR# / Date		User Dept./Div.	

Sl.#	MRP Ln.#	PO Ln.#	Part ID	Part Description	U / M	Qty Received	Remarks

Expense G/L Code	Issued By	Initial	Signature	Date	Received By	Emp.#	Name	Initial	Date	For Finance use
			Warehouse Officer							

Distribution : Original & Blue - Finance, Pink- Store Division, Green - User Dept./Div.

APPENDIX 3.5 MATERIALS RECEIPT AND INSPECTION NOTE (MRIN)

Page #..................

MRIN #	Date:

PLANT	Prepared By:	P.O.# :	P.O. Head :	VENDOR ID	INVOICE #
		Date :			DATE

Seq. No.	Part ID / Part Description	LOC BIN 1 BIN 2 NURM SC	Asset G/L# / Expense G/L #	QUANTITIES: ORDERED	QUANTITIES: RECEIVED	QUANTITIES: BACK -ORDERED	QUANTITIES: ADJUSTED	REMARKS

Stores Division							FINANCE		
	ENTERED BY		CHECKED BY		RECEIVED BY			VERIFIED BY	
	SIGNATURE	DATE	SIGNATURE	DATE	SIGNATURE	DATE		SIGNATURE	DATE

DISTRIBUTION : Original & Green - Finance, Yellow : Stores Division (Stock Recorc NURM: Normal, Urgent,Regular and Manufactured

CHAPTER 4

Issue of Materials

INTRODUCTION

Issue of materials is one of the routine activities of the warehouse. Yet, it is very important and has a bearing on the productivity of other departments of the organization, especially of the production and maintenance departments. The User departments often demand immediate issue of the materials for attending to urgent repairs of plant and machinery. Sometimes issues are requested without proper authorization. The warehouse staff find it difficult to meet such demands due to limited manpower resources.

In a large industrial unit, there may be number of warehouses scattered over a large area at different locations. The warehouse staff are often under tremendous pressure to meet frequent and unscheduled requests for issue of materials, more so when the material requisitions are made at the same time from different warehouses. Issue of materials, therefore, is to be regulated during predetermined hours and with a proper fool proof system for safety of the materials and their accounting.

Some of the stores are under the control of user departments for operational convenience. For example, raw material stores are normally under the control of Production Department. Systems are developed to maintain efficiency on one hand and proper record-keeping on the other hand, to maintain proper accounting and cost control.

In many cases the materials are issued on loan basis and may be received back after some time or may be settled permanently by sale deal. Materials on loan basis could be issued to the buyer within the organization to identify an item by its sample for its purchase. Mostly, the issue of material in such cases is on a temporary basis and the sample is returned to the stores once the procurement of the item is completed. In other cases, where the purchasing activity is located in a city at a different location, the buyer sends the sample collected from the suppliers to the stores for obtaining the approval of the user for the sample. After obtaining the decision of the user in accepting or rejecting the sample of the supplier, the sample is again issued and returned to the buyer.

Materials are also issued on a temporary basis on loan, or permanently on a sale basis to outside agencies such as contractors or other organizations having similar business. Proper documentation is necessary to link the item easily on its return to the store. The recording system should be designed properly to close the transaction of issue and receipt both from the point of view of quantity and cost.

Some of the items are required on urgent basis, for use, immediately on their arrival from the supplier. In some other cases, the materials are procured for a specific project or a major shutdown. These materials are issued directly to the user after inspection without being taken in the inventory first. A separate procedure is followed in such cases for proper accounting and booking of the expenditure to the concerned head of account.

In case of sudden breakdown of a machine after normal office hours or on holidays, materials are issued on emergency basis without following normal procedures because of the absence of the store staff. A different procedure is followed to take care of such contingencies.

Considerations in Issue of Materials

Important considerations regarding issue of materials are:

- Materials should be issued under proper authorization.
- Material should be issued to authorized persons only.
- Items to be issued as per the requirements of the user should be identified correctly.
- Quantity issued should be correct as per issue note. It should neither be less nor more.
- Documentation relating to the issue of materials should be complete and indicate the following:
    - Who has indented the material?
    - Who has authorized the issue?
    - Whether the person authorizing the issue has the delegation of power from the management?
    - How many items are required?
    - How many items are in stock?
    - How many items are issued?
    - What quantity of each item is required?
    - What quantity of each item is in stock?
    - What quantity of each item has been issued?
    - If the item under issue is linked to the appropriate financial head of account for booking of expenditure to the concerned cost center?
    - If the stock balance of the material after the issue, tallies with physical stock balance of the items in the store bins?

Issue procedures and documentation should be so designed as to enable the user to get the materials without any delay and with minimum effort. The records and documents should enable proper cost computation, cost control, and management reporting. Store records should be able to provide up-to-date stock level of all items at all times, and the stock level in the record should tally with the physical stock balance of the items. This will provide the desired safety for the items and help in avoiding any pilferage and theft.

PROCEDURE FOR ISSUE OF STOCK ITEMS

- The User Department prepares the Store Requisition and Issue Note (SRIN) (Appendix 4.1) with appropriate authorization in line with the company policy, based on which, the Store Division issues the requisitioned item.
- The Issue Clerk before issuing the materials matches the signature of the approval authority with the specimen signature already available with him. Further, he checks other relevant information on the Issue Notes such as price, class, description, location, unit of measures, etc. The Store Division is responsible for conformation of authority limits before any issue is made.
- Incomplete/ unacceptable Issue Notes are returned to the concerned department, after mentioning the reasons for rejection. On receipt of the corrected Issue Notes from the user, the same is then processed.
- The Issue Clerk checks the stock balance. After confirmation of stock availability, an Issue Note number is allocated, which is signed by the Issue Clerk and then forwarded to the Officer, Warehouse or the Stores Manager for approval.
- Once the Issue Note is approved, the same is given to the user who hands over the Issue Note to the Stores Keeper at the counter for collecting the item. The person who receives the item(s) signs on the Issue Note.
- Distribution of the Issue Notes is as follows:

- Pink copy	-	User
- Green copy	-	Finance Department
- Original (white)	-	Stores Division

- Details on the Issue Note such as the Issue Note number, date, item #, location, U/M, Quantity Issued, and Cost Code are entered in the computer file. After entry, the Issue Clerk signs the Issue Note. Printouts of the Issue Note entered during the day are arranged for cross-checking with the hard copy of the Issue Note. The green copy is sent to Finance. The original is retained in Stores Division for filing.
- Due to operational reasons, emergency issues from inspection area are made without the required authorization provided the authorization is received on the next working day. In such cases the user prepares the SRIN and hands over the same to the person who issued the item. The Issue Note is later on attached to the MDRR so as to indicate that the quantity has already been issued.

- There are certain categories of items in stock, for example, steel plates, pipes, and electrical items etc., which are reserved for issuing to a particular departments. If any other department requires these items, they have to take approval from the concerned department.
- Care is taken that item is issued on FIFO (First in First out) basis, except for certain categories of items (re-condition items), where the issue is done on LIFO (Last in First out) basis. In this case the item received last is issued first.

PROCEDURE FOR EMERGENCY ISSUES

- For emergency requirements, the Stores Keeper issues the material from stock after normal working hours and on holidays for emergency breakdown of critical equipment.
- The Stores division prepares a list of employees every month indicating the duration (date range), their name, telephone number, building number and room number. These employees are assigned an 'on-emergency-call status' for issue of materials. A copy of the list is forwarded to all departmental heads for information.
- In case of emergency issues, the user contacts the Stores Keeper, who is on call status.
- The Stores Keeper issues the item from the concerned store to the user, and necessary details such as location, item description, quantity, reasons for issue, the user's name, and his signature are entered in the register.
- The user prepares the Issue Note on the next working day with proper approval and hands it over to the Stores Division for processing.

PROCEDURE FOR DIRECT ISSUE

- Items of an extremely urgent nature can be issued directly by the Officer, Warehousing Section to the user/originating department from the inspection area.
- After acceptance of the item(s), the same are handed over to user against receipt of the Direct Issue Stores Voucher (DISV) (Appendix 3.4).
- Receipt of Direct Issue Stores Voucher (DISV) is to be recorded in the MDRR Register and forwarded to Warehousing Section for processing of MRIN.
- All other issue items, together with all the relevant documents, are forwarded by the Officer, Warehousing Section to the Stock Record Controller for further processing after inspection and acceptance by the user/originating department.

PROCEDURE FOR ISSUE FROM USER-CONTROLLED STORES

- This procedure applies to the issue of bulk materials such as raw materials. Because of the nature of these items, with regard to their daily usage and special handling, the Production Department directly controls the issue of the bulk materials from stores/yards.

- On a daily basis, the concerned user advises the Officer, Warehousing (OW) about the raw materials issued for production.
- The Officer, Warehousing calculates the total quantity of material issued during the month, and tallies that with the total figure of the monthly consumption report received from the user. If any discrepancy with regard to occurs, the same is checked and corrected by obtaining all the relevant documents issued during that period. The frequency of such checking may differ from organization to organization.
- When shortage of material kept in the yard occurs (for e.g., due to gusts of wind, raw material that gets blown away cannot be reclaimed either from the surface or from other factors), the Manager, Production Department advises the Manager, Stores Division about the shortages and other relevant details through a written document.
- Based on the user's information, the Stores Division prepares a write-off approval request and forwards it to the General Manager for his approval. Once approval is obtained, the copies are distributed to the Production Department, the Finance Department and the Stores Division. The Stores Division then adjusts the stock accordingly through Inventory Adjustment Form (IAF) (Appendix 4.1).
- The concerned user department prepares Stores Requisitions & Issue Note (SRIN) for all issues made during the month with the approval of the Production Manager and forwards it to the Stores Division for processing.
- The Stores Division is responsible for regularizing the issue documents.
- The Issue Clerk allocates an Issue Note Number; and details such as Issue Note Number, date, item number, location, unit of measure, quantity issued, and cost code are entered in the computer file.
- Distribution of the Issue Notes are as follows:

- Pink copy	User
- Green copy	Finance Department
- Original (white)	Stores Division

PROCEDURE FOR MATERIALS ISSUED ON LOAN BASIS

Procedure for Issue of Stock Items as Samples

- Whenever a sample is required to facilitate correct purchase, the concerned buyer prepares a Store Requisition and Issue Note (SRIN) for issue from stock on a loan basis.
- The Buyer obtains approval of the Head of Purchasing on the SRIN and sends the to same the Stores Division for processing.
- After authorization by the manager of Stores, the Officer, Warehouse arranges to issue the material to the concerned buyer and obtains his signature. The buyer is responsible for timely return of the loan.

- Entry of SRIN, including the name, initial and employee number of the borrower and estimated date of return of loan, is made in the store records.
- For non-returnable samples for purchasing purpose, the concerned buyer prepares Store Requisition and Issue Note (SRIN) and obtains approval of the Head of Purchasing.

Procedure for Issue of Stock Items to Outside Agencies

- The Manager, Stores Division reviews any request from an outside agency for issue of material on loan basis.
- After reviewing the stock balance, anticipated consumption during the loan period, and obtaining concurrence of user department where applicable, Manager, Stores forwards his recommendation to GM, who gives orders for issue on loan basis or on sale basis.
- The Stock Records Controller prepares SRIN and obtains approval of the Manager, Stores Department.
- The issue and processing of SRIN is done in the same way as detailed earlier; except that the concerned outside agency's representative's signature and details are obtained on the SRIN.
- The issue and processing of SRIN to any outside agency should be based on a complete set of correspondence documents such as agency request, loan approval, agency confirmation of acceptance of item, estimated time for return of loan, and means of transport. All documents should be attached to the approved SRIN. Further, a copy of confirmation of the receipt of the item by the outside agency is kept with other related documents.

Return of Stock Items Issued as Samples

- On completion of the Purchase process, the buyer returns the borrowed material to the Stores Division.
- The Officer, Warehousing Section receives the returned material and after ensuring that it is in the same condition as when it was issued, advises the Stocks Record Controller to prepare a Return Note (RN) (Appendix 4.3)
- The Stock Record Controller prepares the Return Note (Appendix 4.3) and after authorization by the manager of the Stores Division issues the copy of the RN to the concerned buyer as acknowledgement for the items received.

Settlement of Loan

- Follow-up on outstanding loans

  The Manager, Stores Division arranges a computer report on outstanding loans, sends the same to concerned buyer, and advises him to either return the loan or to deposit the cost of the material.
- Offsetting of settled loans

After obtaining the receipt of lent materials and noting the SRIN number against which the item was issued on loan, the Stock Record Controller makes necessary entries for settlement of the loan and offsets the loan in the computer file.

- Settlement of outstanding loans against payment
  - Where the borrower cannot and/or elects to settle the loan by payment, the Manager, Stores Division obtains the GM's approval for settling the loan on cost.
  - The Stores Division initiates a Return Note (Appendix 4.3) to correct the record. After entry of the RN in the computer, the Stock Records Controller prepares an SRIN for the same outstanding item on sales basis for approval by the Stores Manager.
  - The approved SRIN, after authorization by the Stores Manager is forwarded to the Finance Department for invoicing.

APPENDIX 4.1 STORES REQUISITION AND ISSUE NOTE (SRIN)

Page No. ....…

Date: ....

PLANT/USER	INITIATED BY	RECOMMENDED BY	APPROVED BY	
MACHINE		REQUIRED FOR		
RECEIVED BY		REVIEWED BY	ISSUED BY	ENTERED BY
EMPLOYEE	SIGNATURE			

SEQ.	LOCATION	PART ID DESCRIPTION	NURM BIN	EXP. GL NO.	AUP US$ CONTROL ID	QUANTITY UOM	EXTENDED VALUE US$

Distribution: Original - Store Division, Green - Finance, Pink - Originator.

SRIN TOTAL VALUE US$

APPENDIX 4.2 INVENTORY ADJUSTMENT FORM (IAF)

Delete Not Applicable (See Foot Note)

SURPLUS	SHORT	

PLANT :

IAF #	To :		Department					Stock Counted by : Stock Verified by :		Date :
	Sl.#	Item #	W/H	Bin Location	U/M	G/L Code Asset	Expense	Quantity	Revised Original Variance	Value (US$) Revised Original Variance
	1									
		Description								
		Remarks								
	2									
		Description								
		Remarks								
	3									
		Description								
		Remarks								
	4									
		Description								
		Remarks								
	5									
		Description								
		Remarks								

Recommended by :	Concurred by : (Internal Auditor, if applicable)	Approved by :	Valued by :	Entered by : Date
Date	Date	Date	Date	Verified by : Date

Distribution : **Original** - Finance, **Blue** - Stores Division

Note : Each Form is to be utilized for either Surplus or Short , and not for both.

APPENDIX 4.3 RETURN NOTE (RN)

PLANT :

RETURNING DEPARTMENT	DIVISION	SECTION	AUTHORIZED BY: NAME : SIGNATURE : DATE :	RN # DATE

ORIGINATING DEPARTMENT | **FINANCE DEPARTMENT**

ITEM NO	PART ID	BIN LOCATION	DESCRIPTION & NAME PLATE DETAILS	UNIT CODE	QUANTITY RETURNED	ASSET CODE	COST CODE	REF. : SRIN # MRIN #	DEBIT ACCOUNT	CREDIT ACCOUNT	VALUE

REASON (S) / JUSTIFICATION FOR RETURN :	CERTIFICATION FOR WORKING CONDITION / SUITABILITY FOR FUTURE USE. : AREA / EQUIPMENT / POINT OF FUTURE USE :	NOTES & COMMENTS : (STORES DIVISION)

	STORES DIVISION			FINANCE
RETURNED BY : SIGNATURE : EMPLOYEE # : DATE :	INSPECTED BY: SIGNATURE : DATE :	RECEIVED BY : SIGNATURE : DATE :	INPUT BY : SIGNATURE : DATE :	VERIFIED BY : SIGNATURE : DATE :

Distribution : **Original** - Finance, **Green** - Stores Division, **Pink** - Originating Dept./Div.

CHAPTER 5

Stocktaking

INTRODUCTION

Stocktaking means manual counting of store items and tallying the physical balance with the quantity as recorded in the books. Stocktaking is a routine and continuous exercise in a warehouse and is a strong management tool to ensure that materials procured are accounted for correctly and that the critical items are physically available as shown in the records. Mostly, the number of items in stock tallies with the number of items on record. Occasionally, some discrepancies are noticed where the physical balance of the items is found to be less or even more than the balance in the records. Both these situations are not acceptable. Once any discrepancy is noticed, it is essential to establish the cause of the discrepancy. Was the discrepancy due to wrong posting or wrong placement of the item in the store or was it due to any other reason?

The report of the stock taking team is a very valuable input to the management to get an indepth knowledge about the operations of the warehouse. It can detect any wrong practice, and also find out if the procedures laid down for stock accounting are being followed properly, and if not, the reason for the same. The report also provides an opportunity to the management to examine its systems and identify areas of improvements. Stocktaking also brings to light the existence of items, which have been purchased during an emergency at a very high price but have not been used even after a long gap of time.

Trained surveyors are engaged for carrying out the stocktaking of raw materials, which are normally stocked in open yards in heaps of different sizes and heights. In case of shortage of material, the report of the surveyor may help identify any wrong practice being followed, either in the Stores Division or by the transporter bringing the material, or even in the Production Department while booking the material for production activities.

In case of certain critical items, both shortage or excess is serious from the point of view of security and safety. For example, in case of explosives, any excess in the quantity of the explosive raises questions about its source. At the same time, a shortage in the quantity of the explosive is alarming for possible misuse of the same. Stock taking for such items should be very detailed and strict. Any difference in the quantity in the records and the physical quantity should immediately be investigated, and the matter should be reported to the higher authorities. This is important as the safety of human beings is involved.

Need for Stocktaking

Stocktaking is essential for the following reasons.

- To detect shortage/excess of materials in the stores.
- To detect if the shortage excess is due to negligence, mistake, or a willful wrong act on the part of any employee.
- To make sure that important/critical items are physically available in the store in good condition for use when needed.
- To assess the real value of inventory in the stores, especially in case of in-process inventory.
- To take immediate action in utilization of the items with limited remaining shelf-life. For example, castable refractory, vulcanizing materials, cable-jointing materials and medicines have limited shelf-life. If it is noticed during stocktaking that the remaining shelf-life of any item is short, immediate action could be taken in using the item before the expiry date or to issue it to another user.
- To develop an appropriate market strategy for a finished product not sold for long. In case of a huge build up of stock of the finished product and no hope of sale in the near future, it may be prudent to sell the item at a lower price, or, efforts should be made to find new markets or customers.

REASONS FOR HIGHER PHYSICAL BALANCE IN THE INVENTORY

At times, it is noticed that the number of items are either higher or lower than the book balance. The following reasons can be attributed for higher physical balance of store items:

- The Storekeeper had made an issue entry in the book, but did not really issue the item.
- The user, upon issue of the item, did not take the item away from the store.
- Materials returned by the user were received but an not entered in the records.
- Materials issued on loan are received back but appropriate entry was not made in the records .
- Mistake in identifying the items in the Inventory due to wrong description/ lack of details. An item could be wrongly identified as another item and placed in another location.
- Additional quantity found in another location, which was not linked in records.

- Materials received from the supplier in excess of the ordered quantity was not entered in the records.

REASONS FOR LOWER PHYSICAL BALANCE IN THE INVENTORY

Various reasons for lower physical balances may be:

- Mistake in issue entry. If an item A is wrongly issued in place of another item B, the stock balance of item A will be less than the quantity in stock, whereas the book balance of the item B actually not issued will be less than its physical balance.
- Higher quantity issued than the quantity ordered for.
- Mistake during inspection when the material is received from the supplier. Short delivery of material not detected at the time of inspection, and an entry for full order quantity is made in the books.
- Pilferage by the storekeeper.
- Pilferage by the user representative, while getting the material issued.
- Pilferage by the security staff itself.
- Materials issued on loan temporarily without proper issue entry. Later on, the stores keeper forgets about the temporary issue.
- Theft of the material.
- Materials lost in storage and handling. This happens, especially in case of materials in powder form which are blown away by the wind, or leak out from the trucks during transportation or during loading/unloading of the material. Some chemicals evaporate during storage and will show less quantity than the book balance.

Factors Having Influence on Stocktaking

The stock taking approach depends upon various factors, some of them are:

- Number of items in stores/warehouses.
- Number of stores/warehouses.
- Type of warehouse/store, that is, whether it is in an open yard or in a closed area.
- Environmental conditions during stocktaking. The process of stocktaking may be difficult in a very hot or very cold climate. It is difficult to count items stocked in the open during the rainy season.
- Some periods are not suitable for stock taking. for example, the period when most of the staff go on leave during the annual vacation of their children. Similarly, periods during festival-time such as Christmas in Europe and USA and Id in the Middle East should be avoided, as the staff strength in this period will be stringent.

- Nature of items for example, small items or heavy items, chemicals and explosives etc. Each item has to be handled differently and therefore time taken in physical verification differs from one category to another.
- Professionals required to check the items for example, electronic /electrical engineers are required to check electronic/electrical items.
- Availability of required manpower.
- Type of store records, whether manual or computerized.
- Availability of proper tools and tackles for handling of materials; availability of correct measuring tapes, weighing scales, and other tools required for unpacking and packing affects the time taken for stocktaking.

Who should do Stocktaking

Normally stockchecking should be done by Store Keeper himself from time to time taking into account the importance of the items. However, in view of the large volume of work, teams of inspectors are formed, who follow a schedule approved by the Stores Manager. These teams can comprise of employees of the Stores Division itself. In case of shortage of staff, team members can be drawn from other departments also; they are temporarily withdrawn from their normal duties and are asked to complete the stock taking work within a given schedule. In certain cases, specialist staff may be required to correctly identify the items in the stores. For example, electrical items should be checked by persons with electrical engineering background. Electronics engineers should be called upon for checking electronics items and so on. External auditors or surveyors could also be appointed for stock taking of in-process materials.

Approach in Stocktaking

Depending upon the availability of the resources, different approaches are adopted for stocktaking. The various approaches adopted are discussed here:

- Wherever possible, just before issuing the item, the available stocks are counted by the concerned Store Keeper.
- Based on value slabs, criticality, and usage, some of the items are counted once in a year.
- Non-moving items are checked once in a year.
- Stocktaking by External Auditor is done on a yearly basis in co-ordination with the Internal Auditor.
- Upon resignation or transfer of a person from the store, all items related to that store are counted and verified.
- Stocktaking is done of new stock items created during the month/in a quarter.
- Yearly stocktaking is done in the beginning of the year. In some stores, to facilitate quick stocktaking, the normal store operations are suspended for few days or are done during limited hours of the day so that stocktaking work is carried out without any hindrance.

- In a warehouse having large number of inventory items, stocktaking is a regular activity and organized in such a way that normal work is not disturbed. A schedule is prepared to check items of certain categories by one or more teams. All the items in the stores should be preferably checked once a year. More attention should be given to high value items, critical items, and items of attractive nature. The help of professionals from other departments may be taken for stocktaking of specialized items.
- Surveyors are appointed from expert organizations for checking of raw materials and in-process materials, especially for materials in powder shape or rock or stored in special shaped containers, which cannot be easily measured on a direct scale.

Stocktaking Planning and Processing

As discussed in earlier sections, stocktaking is a very exhaustive exercise, which involves lot of physical work in handling of materials, counting them or measuring the quantity and making proper records. A detailed planning of the total work is very essential. The planned actions should be commensurate to the availability of appropriate manpower and other facilities required for completing the work. Different teams should be formed for taking stock of different materials simultaneously. Once a program is prepared, it should be executed as per plan with minimum deviations. Any unforeseen disturbances in the program should be quickly looked into and adjustments should be made immediately. The work plan should be organized in such a way that it should not affect the normal working of the warehouse. One of the most important aspect of successful stocktaking is that stock balance of all items are posted properly before commencing stocktaking.

The Stores Manager should ensure that all necessary help, such as adequate number of team members, labor, background papers, measuring tools and tackles are provided to the stocktaking teams to carry on their work without hindrance. The team should carry with them standard formats to record their findings indicating items code, item location, quantity physically available, cross reference of item in various stores etc. A computer report of items/group of items selected is generated. Checking of each item is carried out manually as scheduled and checked against the book balance.

The team must ensure that a given category of items are checked completely at one stretch. If items are available at another location, the total quantity of stock items should be checked at the same time to avoid any possibility of covering the shortage in one place by the quantity available at other place.

REPORTING OF SHORTAGE/EXCESS

Any shortage/excess as found should be signed by the stocktaking team member as well as the concerned Store Keeper. One copy of this should immediately be sent to Stores Manager for information. The report should give details of the item found in shortage/excess, the quantity for the shortage/excess and its cost. Reasons of shortage, if established should be brought out in the report.

Rectification of Shortage/Excess

In case of any difference in the stock level and the physical balance of the item in the store, transactions pending posting are checked for. It should be examined and established if the discrepancy, shortage, or excess is due to delay in posting normal transactions on time (receipts and issues). All adjustments affecting quantity and value are investigated and the reasons behind that are established.

If any such transactions (whether relating to receipts or issues) exist, the counted balance is adjusted accordingly. If the balance does not match before or after the above mentioned adjustment an Inventory Adjustment Form (IAF) (Appendix 4.2) is prepared after proper investigation and forwarded to the Internal Audit, for further investigation. The matter is referred to the Finance Department recommending internal adjustment. The adjustment is processed and recorded after the authorization is received from the Finance Department.

SRINIVASAN B

CHAPTER 6

Discrepancies and Their Resolution

INTRODUCTION

Material, upon receipt in the warehouse, is inspected to ensure that the same is in conformance with the ordered specifications, quality and quantity. A large number of items from very low value to very high value are received every day in the warehouse. Normally, suppliers take great care to see that the quantity and quality of materials dispatched/delivered are exactly the same as agreed upon in the purchase order. However, it is every day experience that there are deviations either in the quantity or the quality of the material received from that specified in the purchase order. In case of minor deviations in specifications, the materials are accepted if they can perform the function for which they were acquired. However, materials that cannot be used are rejected. The cost of the items received with minor deviations in specifications or quality and acceptable to the user is negotiated and mutually agreed up on. If the deviation is only in the quantity, the matter is taken up with the supplier and settled amicably.

Wrong materials received from the local market can be easily replaced by the correct material, but in case of supplies received from foreign sources lot of formalities are involved in exporting the rejected material and re-importing the replacement material. Exporting the rejected material involves not only lot of efforts in packing, handling, transportation, and insurance but also involves additional cost. Keeping in view these factors, suppliers may request the buyer to keep the material with him either at cost price or even at lower cost. In case the material is of low value, the supplier may even suggest that the buyer keep the item free of cost. If the buyer is not keen to keep the item and the cost of the material supplied and rejected is low, the supplier may even advise the buyer to throw away the material or destroy the same. If the rejected material is costly, the supplier may bear the transportation cost of the rejected material and may ask the buyer to return the same to his works or to any other place. The decision in the matter depends upon the nature of the item, its cost, quantity, cost of packing, forwarding, transportation, insurance, and export formalities. Any deviation in the quantity and quality of the material received is termed as a discrepancy. A discrepancy is reported through a discrepancy report (DR). A discrepancy report (Appendix 6.1) should have following details:

- Reference of purchase order and purchase requisition.
- Name of the supplier.
- Details of materials received.
- Quantity as dispatched by the supplier and as found on inspection.
- Quality or specifications as ordered and deviations in the specifications as found on inspection.
- Number of the discrepancy report and its date.
- Date of inspection and reference of documents used in inspection of the material, such as manufacturer part list or drawings.
- Name and designation of the person, who has inspected the item(s).

Material is received at times in a damaged condition. The damage may be repairable or beyond economic repair. The repair cost is recovered either from the Insurance Company or is borne by the supplier/buyer as may be agreed upon. A discrepancy report is also prepared for materials received in damaged condition.

NATURE OF DISCREPANCIES

Different types of discrepancies can be noticed, such as:

- Materials received lesser in quantity, for example five numbers of an item received against an ordered/dispatched quantity of ten.
- Materials received in excess of the quantity ordered, for example ten items received in place of five items ordered.
- Material supplied by the supplier is in conformance with the item ordered, but is an updated design having some changes in the construction. For example, a latest version of a cooler unit received based on the specifications of the old unit installed in the plant had different connections for the pipes and fittings. The user rejected the item on inspection. Later on, on receipt of the clarifications from the supplier, the same was accepted and the discrepancy report was resolved.
- The user rejects the items with changed part number. Supplier changes part numbers due to modifications in the mother machine. In most of the cases, the part with new part number may be exact replacement of the part ordered. Discrepancy report prepared due to different part number is resolved after clarification is obtained from the supplier.
- Material specification does not tally with the specifications as ordered.
- Material dispatched by the supplier but not found in the packet.
- Material of different make is received, for example, an electrical switch of L & T make received in place of English Electric make.

- A different item is dispatched by mistake in place of the item ordered. In place of an item ordered as 'nut and bolt', the supplier supplied only bolt due to wrong understanding of the item.
- Materials intended for another company wrongly dispatched to buyer.
- Material is visibly damaged.
- The material received is in good physical condition but its characteristics are changed during transit or storage and therefore is rejected on inspection.

REASONS FOR DISCREPANCIES

Discrepancy may arise due to various reasons. Some of the reasons are:

- Poor packing. In some cases, the supplier does not follow the industry norms for packing the item under consideration.
- Inadequate markings and directions on the packages, especially in cases of delicate materials.
- Wrong handling of the packages.
- Damage due to use of wrong tools and tackles, or non-availability of proper tools and tackles.
- Accident of the vehicle in transit carrying the goods.
- Damage due to external factors, such as exposure to sun, rain, humid environment, or too cold an environment.
- Poor storage during transit or improper storage in the warehouse of the buyer till inspection is arranged.
- Mistake in identification of the item by the supplier. The supplier may misunderstand the item and dispatches another item in place of the item required by the buyer.
- Mistake by the user in giving specifications. On inspection, the user realizes that he has given the wrong specifications. Even though it is his mistake, he does not accept the item and requests purchaser to settle the matter with the supplier.
- Terms and conditions of purchase order/contract not taking care of the type of packing to be done. The supplier sends the items in cheap and inadequate packing, which may result in either loss of item or its damage.
- Selection of improper mode of transportation. For example, electronic items or delicate materials should be transported by air to avoid exposure to too much handling of the packages. Delicate materials, if transported by road, are exposed to lot of jerks and are likely to be damaged.
- Mistake by the material inspector in inspection, thus creating a discrepancy report.

DELAYS IN INSPECTION

It is also not uncommon to find that the material received is not inspected for long for various reasons, such as:

- The inspection in case of some materials requires testing of the material in a laboratory to establish the quality of the material supplied. The laboratory delays the testing of the material. Sometimes, though the testing is completed, the test report is not finalized.
- If the material is costly or a complicated machine has been received, its packages are to be opened in the presence of the user. Sometimes, the user is not available for inspection either due to absence from duty, or is busy with some other important assignment. This delays the inspection.
- The consignment requires special tools and tackles to open it and the same is not available or is under repair, thus delaying the inspection.
- Delay on the part of warehouse staff in attending to the job.
- Information not given by the warehouse staff to the user to inspect the material.
- The Surveyor of the Insurance Company has not come for joint inspection as expected.

It is very essential that inspection of the material be completed at the earliest opportunity. Any discrepancy, if noticed, is reported to the supplier or to the Insurance Company immediately. It is in the interest of the buyer as well as the supplier to know the discrepancy and its reasons as early as possible and arrange its resolution.

The matter regarding discrepancy is taken up with the supplier to find out the facts and take remedial action in supplying the items short supplied or arranging for the repairs, if it is established that the damage is due to his negligence. In other cases, where the supplier is not found responsible, the matter is taken up with the Insurance Company for settling the insurance claim.

The supplier may or may not take the responsibility of a loss either in quantity or quality, if the discrepancy is not reported to him within a reasonable time. It is for this reason that in important orders/contracts of high value, a time limit is incorporated in the terms and conditions of the order/contract for reporting any discrepancy within the given time limit. If the discrepancy is not reported to the supplier within the stated time limit, he is not responsible to compensate for the loss to the buyer. The same is true with an Insurance Company. If the insurance claim is not raised within a time limit, the claim is rejected on mere technical grounds.

PREPARATION OF DR

(i) The Supervisor, MIR Section is responsible for preparation of discrepancy report (DR). The DR must include the following:

- Technical reasons for rejection, considering the details on the Materials Inspection Notice (MIN) (Appendix 3.3).

- Additional technical details of the required item, where applicable, which may include sketches /drawings /manufacturer's drawings /photographs /samples, etc., to highlight the discrepancy.
- Photographs indicating the condition of the package(s)/material(s) at the time of receipt for showing the discrepancies resulting from poor packing, handling, transportation, etc.

(ii) All DR should bear a number and is to be signed by the Materials Receipt & Inspection Clerk/Inspection Controller, MIR Section and Stores Manager as evidence of checking, verifying, and approval.

(iii) A separate numbering sequence should be maintained for local and overseas discrepancy reports.

(iv) The DR number is recorded by the Supervisor, MIR Section/ Materials Receipt & Inspection Clerk on the MDRR (Appendix 3.1) or the receipt document (if MDRR has not been prepared), prior to passing the document to the Warehousing Section.

PROCESSING AND DISTRIBUTION OF DR

The processing and distribution of DR is done as follows:

- The Materials Receipt & Inspection Clerk files the yellow copy of DR in numerical sequence in either the local or overseas Outstanding DR file, as the case may be.
- The original, green & blue copies of the DR are forwarded to the Stores Manager, who, after review and approval, forwards the DR to purchasing for resolution.
- Once the discrepancy has been resolved, the DR (three copies) indicating the results of settlement is forwarded by the concerned buyer in purchasing to Stores Division.
- The Materials Receipt & Inspection Clerk matches and attaches the yellow copy from the outstanding DR file with the other three copies.
- The Supervisor, MIR Section ensures that a note is made on the DR with the action taken by Stores Division and signed by him and Stores Manager prior to forwarding the same to Inventory Control Section (if requirement is still outstanding), otherwise to the Data Entry Clerk, for entering the data in concerned record.
- The Inventory Control Section raises a new Materials Requisition for Purchase (Appendix 2.2), or cancels the requirement after reviewing with the user/ originator department by initiating a Materials Requisition for Purchase Update (MRPU) (Appendix 2.4).
- The Data Entry Clerk enters the details of the outstanding DR file in the records and clears the DR.
- After entry, the Data Entry Clerk signs the DR and forwards it to Materials Receipt & Inspection Clerk for distribution and filing.

- Distribution of the completed DR will be as follows:
  - Blue copy to purchaser.
  - Green copy to Finance Department.
  - Original & yellow in the settled DR file in sequential order.

HANDLING OF MATERIALS UNDER DISCREPANCY

The material under discrepancy is to be properly marked and stored until it is dispatched to the supplier for replacement or is inspected by the surveyor of the Insurance Company.

Marking and Storage

- As far as possible, the Supervisor, MIR Section ensures that items under discrepancy are retained in their original packing and marked with the DR number.
- Items not stored in their original packing are to be stored either in carton/ wooden boxes or in the open depending on the nature of the item. The DR number should be clearly marked on the box or on a tag attached to the item.
- All items in the DR are moved from the inspection area to a pre-designated area in the main warehouse.
- Electronics cards and other sensitive items that are under DR are marked with the DR number and stored in a steel closet in an air-conditioned room.

Returning the Materials under Discrepancy to Vendors

The Purchasing Division after securing the agreement of the vendor to return the items under discrepancy advises Stores Division to prepare the material for dispatch. Packing, documentation, handling and finally dispatch.

Insurance Inspection

- Wherever an insurance claim has been lodged on items, the items are stored safely until the Insurance Company representative completes his inspection.
- After completion of inspection or survey by the Insurance Company representative and subsequent receipt of DR with remarks or advice from the Purchasing Division, the material is to be disposed of by the Officer warehouse Section.

MONITORING THE DR REPORTS

All the discrepancy reports are listed in a report, which should be reviewed at regular intervals to ensure that all the issues pending in the discrepancy reports are settled either with the supplier or with the Insurance Company by settling the insurance claim.

In the first week of each month the Supervisor, MIR Section ensures that both the Local & Overseas DR Status Reports for the previous month are obtained. This report is printed in duplicate in the DR number sequence.

The information is cross-checked with computer printouts of the outstanding DR File. Any error noted is to be corrected in the computer and on the printout. A copy of the report, corrected as necessary, is forwarded to purchasing for resolving the discrepancies.

DISPOSAL OF ABANDONED DISCREPANCY ITEMS

The abandoned items are disposed of following the procedures as stated below:

- Where vendor has abandoned material and on receipt of disposal instructions from Purchasing, the Stores Division shifts the material from the discrepancy items rack/area to a designated area for storage of items abandoned by vendors. Storage will be in DR number sequence.
- A separate register should be maintained in the DR number sequence for such items.
- Every six months, all these items should be included in the category of surplus items for sale.
- All the badly damaged items or those of a hazardous nature should be disposed of in appropriate disposal areas.

APPENDIX 6.1 DISCREPANCY REPORT

No..................
Plant .... Date ....

INSPECTION SECTION

MRP #	MRP ITEM #	ITEM CODE	
PO #	MDRR # & DATE	INV. #	BUYER CODE ....
Supplier		Ref. Doc. #	MIN #

On inspection of items received against the above MRP & PO following descrepancies were noted:

Item Description — Unit — Qty.

DESCREPANCY PARAMETER	DETAILS AS PER MRP/PO	DETAILS AS PER RECEIPT	REMARKS (attach report if space is not sufficient)

Descrepancies: damaged/defective/short/excess supplied — Incorrect/specify others

MI/IC — Officer/WH

STORES MANAGER

Comments:

....
Stores Manager

PURCHASING DIVISION

Assigned to Buyer: ....

....
Purchase Manager
Date: ....

Remarks for settlement of DR

- ☐ Correct/Short delivered items received — Ref. of Inspection Note: ....
- ☐ Claimed through Insurance
- ☐ Write off approval attached.
- ☐ Incorrect/Excess items to be returned/retained as per PO amendment No......
- ☐ Others

Date: .... Buyer ....

Recommended to settle DR as above	Approved
Date: .... Purchase Manager	Date: .... Stores Manager

Store Division

Comments

- ☐ Item(s) under discrepancy to be returned/retained/disposed off.
- ☐ Item(s) accepted by user after clarifications from supplier.
- ☐ Short/correct supplied items received.

MRIN # ....

MI/IC: .... Officer/WH: .... Stores Manager ...... SRC ....

FINANCE

Supplier
Invoice No. .... Date: ....
Item No. ....

Distribution: Original & Yellow: Stores Division, Green: Finance, Blue: Purchasing

CHAPTER 7

Control of Tools, Surplus, and Scrap Materials

INTRODUCTION

Other than spares, consumables, and raw materials, which are important for production process and plant maintenance, items such as tools/equipment, surplus materials, and scrap materials are also dealt with by the Stores Division. Tools and equipment are needed to perform various jobs of repair and maintenance, without these no plant can carry on its activities.

Surplus materials are materials in the store, which are more than what the user department requires. These materials are an avoidable burden on the stores inventory and should be disposed of to recover the money blocked because of them.

Scrap materials are generated during the production process and maintenance jobs. Some of the stock items, which have exceeded their shelf-life, are not suitable for use any longer and become scrap materials. For example, castable refractory, jointing materials for belt conveyors and cable jointing materials have a limited shelf-life and therefore have an expiry date, beyond which they lose their properties and should be disposed of. Storage of any of these materials occupies costly stores space and involves unnecessary handling, especially during physical verification of the stores items.

CONTROL OF TOOLS

There are varieties of tools. For example:

- tools for mechanical works like spanners, wrenches, screw drivers, hammers, chain pulley blocks, welding sets, bearing pullers and vibrators etc.
- tools for electrical repair works, such as pliers and knifes etc.
- workshop tools
- hydraulic tools like hydraulic jacks

- tools for cable jointing
- tools for electronic repairs
- special tools for typical repair jobs for a specific machine or for a specific application

Use of proper tools for a given application is very essential for the following reasons:

- to complete work in minimum possible time
- to complete the work without damaging the equipment under repair, thus ensuring safety of the equipment
- to do work with less efforts and less fatigue
- to avoid chances of accident and consequent losses
- to provide safe operations and ensure safety of employees
- to carry out difficult jobs, which cannot be completed without the help of tools

Non-availability of a tool can prove to be a very serious and costly affair. A small bolt in a machine if not tightened due to non-availability of the correct size of spanner may result in stoppage of the machine. This will result in production loss.

Tools are issued to the user on demand. Regularly used tools are normally issued to individual technicians, so that time is not lost in attending the repair jobs. Some tools are costly and are frequently required by different working teams. These tools are stored in tool rooms under the control of the user departments. For example, workshop, electrical repair shop, or tyre repair shops may have separate tool rooms to meet their own requirements.

It is necessary that tools be in good working condition at all times for their effective use. Broken or damaged tools are more dangerous than not having a tool. For maintenance of tools, their proper storage, accounting, and upkeep are very essential.

In many cases, even though tools are issued to the user department or to individual technicians, they are not available when needed. It is therefore necessary to do regular physical verification of tools to ensure that tools are available when needed. Sometimes tools are even stolen. Physical verification would help in proper accounting of the tools. Tools, which are not in good condition, should be disposed.

Requisitioning of Tools and Equipment

Normally user departments obtain tools/equipment for their use on loan from the tool room. However, if the tools are required for regular use, they are got either from the tool room or from the Stores Division on a permanent basis.

For making a requisition to the tool room, the user completes Tools Issue/Return Note (Appendix 7.1) and obtains approval of the concerned Department Head and tool room control authority. The approved requisition is submitted to the tool room custodian, who issues the required tools/equipment and obtains the signature of the employee who receives the tools. Details of permanent issue are included in Tools and Equipment Update (Appendix 7.2) by both the Tool Room and receiving Department.

For making a requisition to the Stores Division, User Department prepares Material Requisition for the items (Appendix 2.1, Chapter 2) and obtains appropriate approval from the competent authority to get the same issued.

Receipt and Inspection

The user inspects the tools/equipment upon their receipt. If the item is accepted, a MRIN is prepared after obtaining an asset code from the Finance Department. Items are issued on signature of an authorized employee from the requisitioning department. Discrepancies if any, are dealt with in accordance with the procedures as laid down.

Issue and Accounting of Tools and Equipment

Tools/equipment are issued permanently or on a temporary basis.

Permanent issue of tools and equipment Each department maintains a record of tools and equipment issued to them on a permanent basis with the following details:

- Department reference

  This will identify the individual or section or location to which the tool and equipment is assigned.
- Asset code

  A unique ALPHA-NUMERIC code is assigned to the individual tool or equipment.
- Description

  The full description of the item includes, make, model, size, electrical specifications as applicable, and accessories.
- Quantity

  Total number of each of the assigned items of the same description.

Temporary loans of tools and equipment within a department or division are made at the sole risk of the person to whom they are originally assigned.

Temporary issue of tools and equipment In addition to the above record, the tool room maintains a register of tools and equipment temporarily issued to individual departments, which includes the following details:

- tool room reference number
- asset code of tool/equipment
- brief description
- quantity loaned
- employee number and signature of the employee to whom the tool/equipment is loaned

- date of loan
- date of return
- signature of tool room custodian, acknowledging return
- remarks, to include any details of damage or loss

Tools and equipment are issued on loan basis for a maximum of one week without prior agreement. All tools and equipment, not subject to extended loan, should be returned within one month from the date of loan. If this is not done, the replacement cost should be recovered from the concerned employee.

Reporting the list of tools and equipment On a quarterly basis, each department should submit a report to the Stores Division about the availability of the tools in Appendix 7.3 with supporting documents. Details of all additions and deletions to the Tools & Equipment List is available in the report. The Stores Division updates computer records based on the details received from different departments.

Safekeeping of tools and equipment while an employee requires long leave Prior to an employee proceeding on long leave, all tools and equipment assigned to him should be verified by his immediate supervisor and placed in a secure area for reassignment upon his return. The cost of any tools or equipment damaged or missing due to negligence should be recovered from the employee.

Employee resigns or is terminated All tools and equipment assigned to an employee, who resigns or is terminated, must be withdrawn from him prior to payment of his final benefits. Acknowledgment of the concerned supervisor should be indicated on the employee's check out list. Supervisors who fail to withdraw the assigned tools and equipment prior to an employee's departure will be responsible for replacement of any subsequently discovered missing or damaged tools or equipment.

Spot checks by auditing Spot checks will be carried out by an audit team to ensure availability of permanently assigned tools and equipment, based on the verification lists for the tools as received from Finance.

Maintenance of Tools and Equipment

To ensure that all tools and equipment are properly maintained, cleaned, and in serviceable condition, the user department should conduct periodic tool inspections. Unsafe and poorly maintained tools or equipment should be immediately withdrawn and appropriate action should be taken to rectify the fault. In case, a negligence or wilful default from the employee is noticed, disciplinary action against the concerned employee may be considered. Worn-out/unsafe tools are not allowed to remain in use under any circumstance.

Disposal of Tools and Equipment

When tools and equipment are in surplus of a department's requirements or damaged beyond economic repair, disposal is to be done as follows:

Surplus Tools and equipment, which are in surplus of a department's requirement, should be returned to the tool room on Tools Issue/Return Note and acknowledgment of the custodian must be obtained. Details of the tools and equipment returned should be included on Tools & Equipment Update (Appendix 7.2) by both the concerned department and the tool room.

Beyond economic repair A Repair Requisition/Scrap Declaration should be prepared for any tools or equipment, which have been declared by the appropriate authority as being beyond economic repair. This should be forwarded to the Stores Division with the scrapped tools or equipment for disposal. Details of tools and equipment scrapped should be included in the Tools & Equipment Update by the concerned department.

Inspection & disposal of tools/equipment declared scrap Materials Inspection & Receipt Section, receives, inspects and disposes of the tools/equipment included on the Scrap Declaration.

SURPLUS MATERIALS

Materials, which are in surplus of the requirements of the user department due to excessive purchasing or discontinuation of the use of the item by management decision for any reason, should be identified with the help of the user department. The Surplus items should be differentiated from the insurance items, which are to be stored for any eventuality.

The operational staff hesitates in declaring an item as a surplus item as long as it is possible to use the item in future, even though the need may not occur for a very long period. The operational staff do not want to be questioned for the initial purchase of the items in excess quantity which resulted in the surplus. Surplus materials are good materials and can be used by any other department or any other organization. A good amount of money could be recovered by finding a right source for their disposal. Once it is established that the material is surplus to the requirement of the department or the organization, it should be disposed of as early as possible.

Disposal of Surplus Items

Once the surplus items are identified, the following actions could be taken for their disposal:

i. It should be determined if the surplus items can be used elsewhere in the organization. In case of a multi-unit organization, the availability of surplus items should be informed to all the units to find out, if they could be of use in any way.
ii. A list of surplus items is to be circulated to other similar organizations, which can use such items, so that the value of these items could be recovered to some extent by selling them.
iii. The original supplier/machinery manufacturer may be interested in taking back certain items that are in surplus. Some other customers may be in need

of such items, which are otherwise not in the production program of the manufacturer any more. Good value can be recovered by selling these items through the original suppliers/machinery manufacturers. These days the information about availability of surplus items is provided on Internet so that more customers in need of such items could take advantage of the availability of these items from a source, which may not be within their reach in normal course.

iv. Trading organizations are very good source for disposal of surplus items as they are in touch with various types of customers in need of items not readily available.

v. In cases, where, it is difficult to find a party interested in buying the surplus item, the same can be donated to an educational or technical institute free of cost for the purpose of education or training.

vi. For disposal of surplus material the user department is asked to assess the value, which could be recovered from a sale. An approval of the competent authority for the disposal of the surplus material at the estimated reserve price is obtained. Proposals are invited from interested parties for the sale of the surplus items. In case the offer for the sale is received higher than the reserve price, the surplus material can be disposed of at that price. However, in case no offer is received up to the level of the reserve price, approval has to be obtained to sell the items at a price lower than the reserve price. In case no party is interested in taking the surplus item, it may be decided to dispose of the items as scrap material.

SCRAP MATERIALS

These are rejects from the production process, which cannot be used any more and are to be thrown away. Similarly, old, broken parts, rejects, cut pieces of iron sheets, angle iron, gaskets, insulation materials etc., are generated during maintenance and repair works. These materials are removed from the place of work and dumped in the scrap yard. Some of these materials are very useful for small jobs or can be re-processed for other works. For example, damaged tyres are a good source of heat generation as they can be burnt in a furnace. Batteries, rejected or damaged, can be an useful source; its battery case can be taken out for making the re-conditioned battery. Similarly, shafts can be recovered from scrapped pumps. They are likely to be in good condition for use in repair of other pumps.

Scrap materials become a nuisance if not disposed of. They may further deteriorate and lose their characteristics and create a dirty environment. Some of the scrap materials can be a big health hazard or even a safety hazard, for example, explosive scrap material. Iron pieces in scrap can be dangerous and may result in physical injury to the workmen. Scrap materials, if not disposed of, occupy valuable space. Disposal of scrap material is a continuous process in a Stores Division.

Scrapping Procedure

The Stores Division will declare any stock/inventory item that has exceeded its shelf-life and cannot be used due to deterioration of quality. However, before declaring an item as scrap, a guarantee should be obtained in advance from the user department that the item is not suitable for alternative use.

Assets, Items on Record, Repairable Items

Assets, Items on Record (items that are to be controlled by the individual department, for example, tools, calculators, briefcases, cash boxes etc.) and repairable items, which are confirmed to be beyond economic repair or whose repair is forbidden by the manufacturer, will be declared as scrap on the Scrap Declaration Form (Appendix 7.4). However, it should be ensured that a reasonable attempt has been made to repair the same, except where repair is forbidden due to high cost, non-availability of required spare parts/lack of in-house/outside facilities etc. Items received from the repair and maintenance of plant and machinery, which cannot be used any more in the plant are also declared as scrap.

Handling of Related Spare Parts

Before initiating scrap declaration for an asset which is either irreparable or beyond economic repair, the originating department will obtain a list of parts for the asset in question and confirm to the Stores Division whether these can be used for other assets. In case the spare parts cannot be used, write-off approval may be obtained for the spares along with the assets. It happens very often that large number of spares are in the inventory even after scrapping and disposal of the assets. In some cases, the asset is disposed off but spares are replenished as the team replenishing the spares is not aware of the disposal of the assets. A proper co-ordination is very essential and necessary entries have to be made in all the relevant records. After approval of the scrapping of an asset and writing off the spares, the Stores Division is to be advised to amend its records and arrange disposal of the items.

Preparation of Scrap Declaration

Appendix 7.4 is to be originated by the user department, signed by the Head of the Department and the concerned Workshop Supervisor for the item to be scrapped, and is forwarded to the Stores Division after obtaining the appropriate approvals.

For the item being scrapped directly from the inventory, the Stores Division should prepare Stores Requisition & Issue Note (SRIN) after approval by the Manager, Stores Division and attach it to the Scrap Declaration.

Approval of Scrap Declaration

It is the responsibility of the user or controlling department to obtain approval for scrapping any item in accordance with the delegation of powers, prior to forwarding the Scrap Declaration to the Stores Division.

Scrap Reclamation

All salvageable items are to be recovered by the user department from the items to be scrapped, and returned to the respective stores by initiating a Return Note (RN) (Appendix 4.3). Verification of RN, inspection, and acknowledgment of the salvaged material should be carried out. The approved Scrap Declaration together with all the non-usable items is to be returned to the Supervisor, Materials Inspection & Receipt (MIR) Section for processing and disposal.

Scrap Disposal

The Supervisor, MIR Section, ensures that the scrapped material conforms to the details on the Scrap Declaration, assign a sequential number and after approval by the Stores Manager, mark the item as, "Scrapped vide SD #..." with paint or by attaching a tag. The marked scrapped material, if of ferrous origin (Iron or Steel), is kept in the designated space in the scrap yard together with the other ferrous scrap. Scrapped tools and equipment or assets, which are semi-metallic, will be crushed under supervision of the Supervisor, MIR Section to eliminate any possibility of recycling by anybody. The Supervisor, MIR Section will arrange for disposal of the crushed scrap in the relevant garbage disposal pit according to the type of material, for example, plastics, rubber, wood, etc.

Every three months or as required, the supervisor of the Warehouse Section will review the quantity of ferrous scrap collected in the scrap yard. If it is estimated to be a large quantity, the Stores Manager arranges a sale on "As is, where is, as seen" basis.

Junk dealers may be invited to see the materials in the junkyard and are invited to give quotations for the scrap material. To ensure that the junk dealer does not back out later on, he should be asked to deposit an earnest money, which is to be forfeited if he does not remove the materials before the specified time limit. In case, the junk dealer with the highest bid does not lift the material within the specified time, his earnest money is forfeited and the junk dealer with the next best bid is asked to remove the material with the same terms and conditions.

REFERENCE

Menon, P.G., *Scrap, Surplus and Obsolete Materials Management and O.R. in India*, MMJ Publications, D 409, Defence Colony, New Delhi - 3, 1968, pp 133-145.

APPENDIX 7.1 TOOLS ISSUE/RETURN NOTE

NO.: Date:

Plant/User:	Initiated By:	Recommended By:	Approved By:
Category:	Required By:		
Received By:	Reviewed By:	Issued By:	Entered By:
Employee:		Signature/Date:	

Seq.	Location	Part ID Description	NURM	Bin	Exp.GL No.	AUP Control ID	Qty. UOM	Extended Value US$
							Total VALUE us$	

NURM: New, Used, Re-built and Manufactured

UOM: Unit of Measurement

ID: Identification

DISTRIBUTION: Original: Store Division/Tools Room, Green: Finance, Pink: Originator

APPENDIX 7.2 TOOLS AND EQUIPMENT UPDATE

Date:...

	REFERENCE	DESCRIPTION	ASSET CODE	MRIN # & SRIN #
ADDITIONS				
DELETION				
TRANSFERS				

Department:........ Department Head:..........

APPENDIX 7.3 QUARTERLY REPORT OF TOOLS/EQUIPMENT AVAILABLE IN......

PLANT:	DEPARTMENT/DIVISION:			PERIOD:		QUARTER/YEAR	
LOCATION	DESCRIPTION	SIZE	MAKE	MODEL NO.	ASSET CODE	QUANTITY	DOCUMENT

APPENDIX 7.4 SCRAP DECLARATION

Plant:....

No. ....
Date ....

Originating Dept./Div.	Description of item	Name of Parent Machine/Equipt.	Year of Acquisition	Original Cost	Book Value	Qty.	Item No. WH & Location	Finance Code
	Value of Spares in Stock US$			List is to be attached with details of alternate usage. Otherwise GM's approval for write off of spares is to be attached separately				
	Dept./Div	Initiated by:		Reviewed by:		Recommended by:		Date
Workshop	Reasons for Scrapping:							
	Inspected & Tested By:		Recommended by:			Authorized by:		Date
Approval	Approved By:		WGM		Date	General Manager		
Stores Division	Comments:		Verified By Officer, Warehouse		Authorized By Stores Manager		Disposed By Inspection Controller	
	Qty. Received for Scrapping							

Distribution: Original - Stores Division, Green - Finance, Blue - Audit, Pink - Originator

CHAPTER 8

Storage and Handling Practices of Materials

INTRODUCTION

Various types of materials are stored in the warehouse. Each material has its own characteristics. Some of the materials are affected by environmental conditions, the method of storage, and the time of storage. For example, rubber materials like belt conveyors, tires, and vulcanizing materials are affected by temperature; refractory materials are affected by moisture or humidity; steel items rust in the presence of moisture and air; some materials become deformed, if not stored properly and can not be used any more; some materials lose their characteristics, if not used before the expiry date; some materials are of dangerous nature and special precautions are required in their storage whereas some of materials evaporate, if left open. These factors call for discussion on suitable storage practices for various items. It is not possible to cover each and every item of stores in this discussion; however, some of the important materials, which are commonly in the inventory are covered in this chapter.

STORAGE OF CONVEYOR BELTS

All belting is received in roll form. Fabric belting is received on a central bolted core in a wooden drum or wrapped in synthetic Hessian and bound with steel or heavy-duty plastic tape around the outside lap. Steel cord belting is normally packed in steel reels. The belting should be kept in its original packing until required for installation.

Belting should be stored with the central axis horizontal on level, smooth ground, out of contact with water, oil, solvents, or other corrosive liquids, protected from direct sunlight and at a temperature of less than 20° C if possible.

Belting should be protected from extremes of temperature, humidity, and ozone (as developed by electrical machines).

When extended storage is necessary (e.g. in excess of 12 months) the belts should be stored, if possible, off the ground, suspended through the central core and rotated periodically to prevent permanent deformation.

Belt rolls should be lifted using a square batch bar passed through the hole in the belt core. A spreader beam with suitable lifting chains or cables should be used ensuring that the edges of the belt roll are not damaged.

STORAGE OF BELT SPLICING MATERIALS

General Guidelines for Storage of Belt Splicing Materials

- Store each splicing material in a dark and cool place below 20° C (Indoors) (Fig. 8.1)
- Store the materials required immediately, on racks after opening the packing. (Place A)
- Store the materials required later, in wooden boxes in packed conditions (Place B)

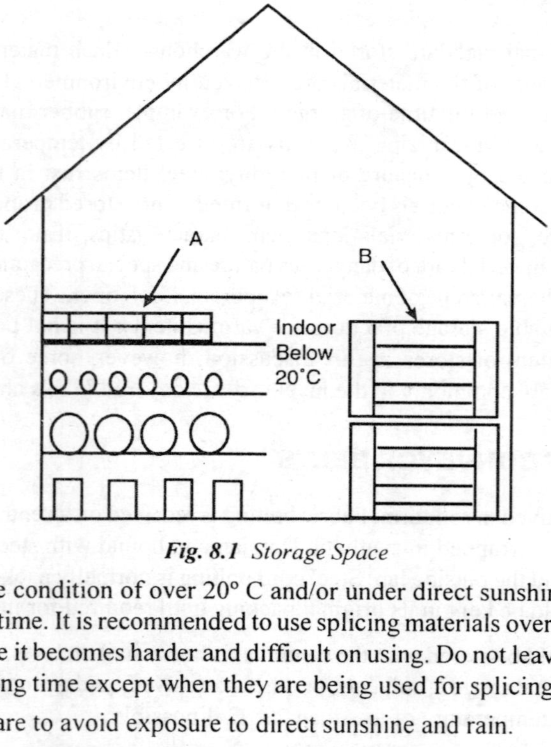

Fig. 8.1 *Storage Space*

Storage condition of over 20° C and/or under direct sunshine could shorten the lifetime. It is recommended to use splicing materials over 5° C (Ambient), because it becomes harder and difficult on using. Do not leave them outdoors for a long time except when they are being used for splicing.

- Take care to avoid exposure to direct sunshine and rain.
- The place used for storage should strictly be kept free from fire.
- Put up a notice "Inflammable" at the storing place and appoint a responsible person to handle them.

- Cement and solvent of splicing materials contain organic materials: therefore, "INFLAMMABLE" mark is attached on the outside of the packing of these materials.
- Belt splicing materials should be away from oxidizing agents. Materials should not be stored together with acid.
- While storing them, classify them into respective materials and store each material attaching a tag, which indicates clearly the description, size, and quantity.
- The maximum permissible storage life is about six months from the date of production, when they are stored in a dark and cool place (below 25° C). The date of production is indicated on each material.
- Splicing materials should be used in order of delivery, that is, use up the old materials first. Old materials should not be stored in the interior of a shelf.
- If the description of material is doubtful, or one is apprehensive of a material being scorched already, never use such a material. A scorch means a state where a rubber material is cured naturally due to its storage for a long period or because of influence of heat. Such a scorched rubber material can never be used for an endless splicing work. Accordingly, it is very important to adhere to the above-mentioned method for preservation for the purpose of preventing a scorch or mixing of one material with another.
- Prepare a ledger for incoming and outgoing materials and keep a record of the description, size, and quantity in detail.
- Check up the description, size, and quantity of each material once a month and materials becoming scorched should be identified.
- Draw attention to a place where splicing materials are placed, even in the course of a splicing work on the spot, and keep materials in a cool shade avoiding direct Sunbeams.
- The materials brought back from the working spot are likely to be ambiguous with respect to their description and quantity. Always attach a new tag indicative of the description, size, and quantity to each material, and scrap out those doubtful materials, if any.

Handling and Storage of Tie Gum

- The tie gum is usable if an uncured sheet of it is easily torn off at the time of stretching it by both hands, however, if it has rubber-like elasticity and the stretched sheet can be restored to its original state, this is an indication of a scorch (vulcanization is progressing) and such a material cannot be used.
- Another method is to wipe an uncured sheet with a small cloth strip moistened with a solvent. In this case, if the rubber dissolves easily and the cloth blackens, the tie gum is useable. But, if the rubber is hard to dissolve and the cloth does not easily blacken, it is evidence of a scorch, and such tie gum cannot be used. Confirmation of a scorch by the above two methods will be helpful in the judgment of scorched rubber in most cases.

Handling and Storage of Cement

If the cement in a can is viscous and can easily be agitated by a brush, it will be useable, however, if it has been gelatinized like jelly or many grains are present in it, this is an indication of scorched cement and the cement cannot be used.

STORAGE OF V BELTS

V Belts should be stored in a cool place at an ambient temperature. They should not be kept flat on the racks or should not be pressed by other heavy objects that may cause deformation of the V Belts. V Belts should be hanged on a cantilever so that their shape is not distorted and there are no kinks on the length of the V Belts.

STORAGE AND HANDLING OF TIRES AND TUBES

In order to avoid premature ageing and degradation of tires, they should be stored in a dark and closed area. If this is not possible, they should be protected from:

- Source of ozone (sun, arc-welding, mercury vapor lamps)
- Ultraviolet radiations.
- Exposure to weather.

The tire should be stored vertically on their treads, one against the other.

Tubes, flaps, and rubber seals must be stored in their original packing, on shelves or in containers, on condition that the surfaces in contact with them are clean and smooth (to avoid risks of tearing, cuts of perforations).

Considerations in Storage of Tires

Various considerations in shortage of tires are:

- atmosphere
- temperature
- lighting
- humidity
- ground
- duration of stocking
- method of stocking

These aspects are discussed here.

Atmosphere

Ozone is one of the main enemies of tires. Its effect is aggravated on tires when put under pressure by stocking. It causes cracks on the surface of the tires.

Air currents are the main source of ozone, but some types of machines also produce ozone, such as :

- electric welding machines
- battery chargers
- electric motors

However, white washed walls (lime washed) rapidly destroy the ozone in the air.

Temperature

Tires should not be stocked at temperature exceeding 40° C. In hot countries, when this temperature is reached, regular and natural aeration should be insured, but tires to be stocked for a period exceeding 5 months should be protected from direct air currents by sheets, tarpaulin, cardboard etc.

Lighting

Sunrays or certain artificial lights such as mercury vapor quartz lamps are a source of harmful ultraviolet radiation.

Humidity

Water inside the tires as well as humidity can cause moldiness of the internal coatings of the tires.

Ground

Any contact of the tires with greasy bodies or with solvents can lead to the deterioration of its performance. Avoid stocking on asphalted surfaces or mud floors.

Duration of Stocking

Age gradually alters the tire's properties and therefore its performance. Tires should not be kept in stock for more than five years.

Method of Stocking

Colored side walls (white, red......) in contact with the black parts of another tire will cause rapid staining (the stain will often only becomes apparent after exposure to light).

The best way to store tires is to place them vertically, one against the other, in rolling position.

Stocking in piles is more harmful. The height of each pile should not exceed 2 meters. Tires should be rotated every 6 months to attenuate its effect.

STORAGE OF REFRACTORY BRICKS

Correct storage of refractory bricks is equally important as their selection for a given duty and correct installation. While certain types of bricks can be easily stored in the open without adversely affecting their properties there are some of these refractory bricks, which have to be kept in dry and well-ventilated areas. Exposure to moisture, entering of dust in the pores of some of the refractory bricks can greatly deteriorate their characteristics and disqualify them from use.

Burnt High Alumina, Alumina, and Fireclay Bricks

Burnt high alumina, alumina, and fireclay bricks are not adversely affected when they come in contact with water or absorb moisture from the environment. Care should be taken to stack these bricks on a levelled dry floor. The bricks should be covered with weatherproof tarpaulins.

Magnesia Bricks and Lightweight Refractory Bricks

Unlike alumina and fireclay bricks, magnesia bricks, refractory lightweight bricks, and all unburnt chemically bonded grades of bricks should, as a general rule, be stored in dry and well-ventilated spaces.

Magnesia-Chrome and Magnesia Spinel Bricks

These bricks are called basic bricks. Basic bricks undergo hydration in contact with water by absorbing moisture. Hydrated bricks show white deposits on the surface and develop cracks, which extend like network on the surface over a period. Bricks, which have developed cracks are not suitable for use any longer and must be discarded.

Layout of the storage area of these bricks should be well planned to provide enough space for operation of the forklift truck, easy access to the bricks, and proper space between different stacks. Bricks should be kept in such a way that the forklift truck can easily reach to the bricks received first. Stacking of the pallets should be such that the labels on the pallets can easily be seen to find the source of supplier, type and size of bricks and the date of their receipt in the stores. Each grade of bricks should be stored together. In case of any doubt, about the quality of the brick, it is preferable to get the bricks tested in a laboratory. The bricks, specially the basic bricks, should be used without long storage following the principle of 'first in and first out'. It is recommended, not to store basic bricks, for more than a two year period.

Precaution in Storage and Use of Basic Bricks at Site

- In case outdoor storage is unavoidable, the storage place should be paved or should consist of a densified permeable and well-drained ground.
- Stagnation of water in the storage area should be avoided. Pallets stored in a wet place carry the risk of ingress of moisture in the refractory material by capillary action.
- Care is taken to cover the bricks with weather resistant, impermeable tarpaulins tightened from all sides to prevent them from being lifted up by strong wind or storms. An unprotected outdoor storage bears the risk of water and moisture penetration with subsequent rapid hydration. However, the best course of action is to store the bricks indoors in a well-ventilated building with a paved dry floor.

- Packing can get damaged during transportation and an unprotected outdoor storage carries the risk of water and moisture penetration with subsequent rapid hydration. Shrink foils exposed to sunshine age sooner or later, become brittle loosing their mechanical strength despite their resistance to ultraviolet radiation.
- Basic bricks should be inspected immediately on arrival. In case some packing is found damaged, such packing should be unpacked, and the bricks found wet, should be loosely piled up in a dry and well-ventilated building to allow natural air-drying. Drying of brick with the application of heat should not be resorted to as this may lead to increased hydration at temperatures higher than the ambient temperature.
- Check again all the undamaged packing after a period of six months of their arrival and subsequently every three months. Few pallets should be opened randomly for visual inspection of the bricks. If a gray or whitish surface (sign of hydration) is observed, all the pallets of the supply should be opened up and inspected. Packing materials of the pallets having signs of hydration on the bricks, should be completely removed and the bricks are to be preserved in open air. Use the endangered bricks as soon as possible. Such bricks may become dusty with time, but the dust has no negative effect on their shelf-life and performance.

It should be noted that storage of basic bricks in open air is less critical than in sealed packing, in which an unfavorable microclimate may have occurred due to some absorbed humidity. This may adversely affect the more sensitive bricks, especially the spinel bricks, due to the moderate and cold climate prevailing.

STORAGE OF MOTORS AND CASTABLES

Mortars and castable refractory should always be stored in a dry and well-ventilated space. Their quality is adversely affected when moisture has ingressed or they get in touch with water. These materials should be rejected and not used in the event of effect of water/moisture and also if these are stored beyond the recommended storage period by the manufacturers. Hydraulically setting castables, which have hardened in the sacks or have become unsuitable with age cannot be used and should be discarded. However, in case where hydraulically setting refractory castables are stored for more than the recommended period of storage but still do not show signs of deterioration in its condition, it is suggested to make a test specimen with the material, before using it on the actual jobs.

Storage Life of Refractory Materials

Storage life of refractory bricks is presented in Table 8.1

Table 8.1 Recommended Life of Refractory Materials

S.No.	Type of Material	Period of Storage
1	Basic bricks in dry conditions and under roof	2 years
2	Fireclay and high alumina bricks	Virtually unlimited

General guidelines for storage life of the mortars, castables, adhesives, and refractory are presented in Table 8.2

Table 8.2 Storage Life of the Mortars/Castables/Adhesives

S. No.	Type of Material	Period of Storage
1	Refractory Motors	24 months after production date
2	Refractory Cements	12 months after production date
3	Refractory low cement castables	6 months after production date
4	Sintered Corrundum based refractory concrete	6 months
5	Mullite based refractory concrete	6 months
6	High-alumina special "fireclay" concrete	6 months
7	Low-iron fireclay	6 months
8	Adhesive based on epoxy resin	6 months

Guidelines for Stacking

Bricks are supplied on pallets and can be stacked up to recommended heights. The safe height of the stack depends mainly on the bearing capacity of the surface, on which the pallets are to be stacked. In case of uneven or paved surface, the stack height should be up to the minimum height range stated in Table 8.3. To avoid damage to the edges of the bricks, the pallets are stacked one upon the other and load is distributed to the entire area.

Table 8.3 Recommended Height of Refractory Pallets

S. No.	Refractory Material	Maximum Stacking Height
1	Basic bricks	2 - 5 Pallets
2	High-alumina and fireclay bricks	2 - 5 Pallets
3	Lightweight bricks	2 Pallets
4	Mortars, mixes	2 Pallets
5	Insulating bricks	2 Pallets

Packing of Bricks

Pallets used for packing the bricks are in two standard sizes such as 800 × 1200 mm and 830 × 1100 mm. Lightweight bricks and fireclay bricks are packed using crepe paper with foil, gray cardboard for horizontal covering, corrugated cardboard for vertical covering in broken joints, and completely covered with 0.175 mm shrink-film wrapping, edge protection hard board/metal sheets, 16 mm steel board including cardboard wrapping (Fig. 8.2). Pallets are provided with identification labels.

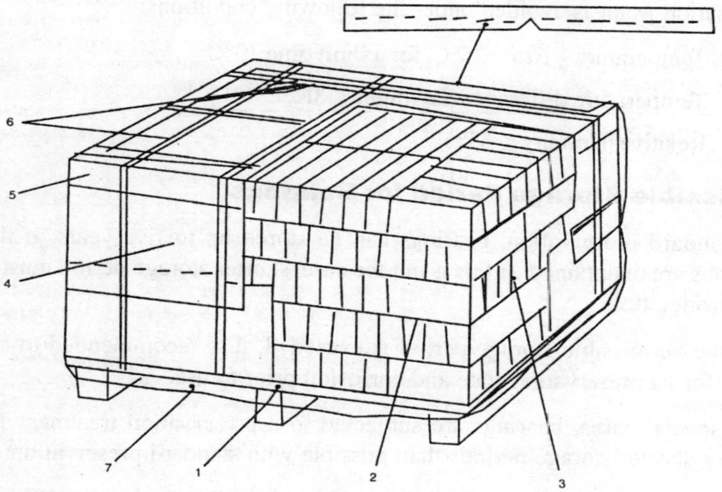

Fig. 8.2 Packaging of Refractory Bricks

1. Standard pallet 800 × 1200 mm, 830 × 1100 mm
2. Grey cardboard horizontal
3. Corrugated cardboard vertical
4. Water-repellant telescopic cardboard with imprint
5. Edge protection metal sheets
6. Steel band 16 mm
7. Shrink-film

Packing of Castables

Castable refractory are packed in multi-wallpaper sacks of 25 kg. Complete pallets consisting of a number of sacks are shrink-wrapped with plastic sheet and sealed against moisture. The original shrink-wrapping should preferably be left enclosing the pelletized sacks for as long as possible to serve as extra protection. Well-sealed steel drums are recommended for packing castables to protect them from high degree of humidity, especially in tropical countries.

STORAGE AND HANDLING OF BEARINGS

Precautions in Storage of Bearings

In shipping bearing, because they are covered with proper anti-corrosion oil and are wrapped in anti-tarnish paper, the quality of the bearings is guranteed as long as the wrapping paper is not damaged. During storage, the bearings must not be exposed to the effects of aggressive media such as gases, mists or aerosols of acids, alkaline solutions, or salts.

Avoid storage in places exposed directly to the sun's rays or placing boxes of bearings against cold walls. Direct sunlight can cause large temperature vibrations in the packages, apart from the harmful effects of UV radiations. The formation of condensation water is avoided under the following conditions:

- Temperature + 6 to + 25°C, for a short time 30°C
- Temperature difference day/night $\leq$ 8K
- Relative humidity $\leq$ 65%

Permissible Storage Period for Bearings

With standard preservation, bearings can be stored up to five years, if the above conditions are maintained. If this is not the case, shorter storage period must be taken into consideration.

If the permissible storage period is exceeded, it is recommended to check the bearing for its preservation state and corrosion prior to use.

In special cases, bearings are subjected to a preservation treatment for either longer or shorter storage periods than possible with standard preservation.

Bearings with shields or seals on both sides should not be kept to their very limit of storage time. The lubricating greases contained in the bearings may change their chemicophysical behavior due to ageing.

Precautions in Handling of Bearings

Since roller and ball bearings are made more precisely than other machine parts, careful handling is absolutely necessary. The following precautions are necessary in handling of bearings:

- Keep bearings and the operating environment clean.
- Handle carefully. Bearings can be cracked and brinelled easily by strong impact if handled roughly,
- Handle using the proper tools.
- Keep bearings well-protected from rust. Do not handle bearings in high humidity. Operators should wear gloves in order not to soil bearings with perspiration from their hands.
- Experienced or well-trained operators should handle the bearings.

STORAGE OF ELECTRICAL WIRES

Single-wire spools can be arranged on the spool holders according to insulation color or cross-section and located with the aid of a retainer clip. The spool holder is provided with pedestal foot topped with a vertical post and is ideal for table or wall mounting (Fig. 8.3)

Fig. 8.3 Spool Holder with a Pedestal Foot

A mobile version of the spool holder can be used with a number of spindles on the cable trolley, which is suitable for holding and unwinding rolls of wires (Fig. 8.4)

Fig. 8.4 Mobile Spool Holder

The coil storage wall panel can be used for storage of a large number of wire coils. The coil storage wall panel can be extended, as required, and is designed for use wherever cable coils, metal strips, wire spools, and other wound products of varying sizes have to be stored in a convenient space-saving manner (Fig. 8.5).

Cable drum storage racks with both mobile and stationary features are also available. The unit consists of prefabricated elements (frame and cross-ties) easily assembled into a well-arranged, space-saving, and extremely practical storage unit. The welded-on spindle mounts accommodate a large number of small and large cable drums. A mobile chassis is fitted with double-stop swivel castors and two idlers rollers, together with a drawbar, to convert the static unit into a mobile unit (Fig. 8.6).

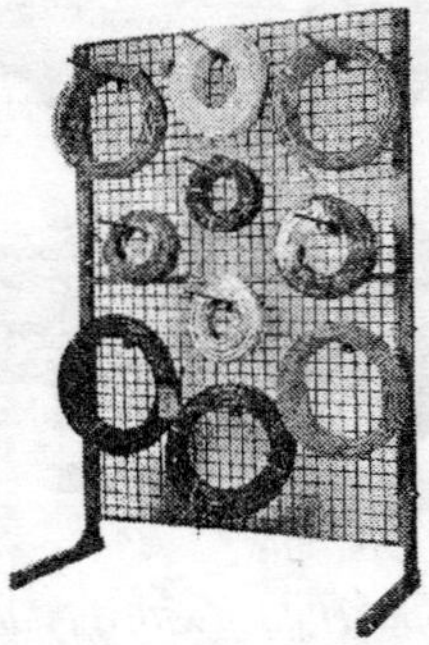

Fig. 8.5 *Coil Storage Wall Panel*

Fig. 8.6 *Mobile Coil Storage Panel*

STORAGE AND HANDLING OF POWER CABLES

Power cables are stored safely on the cable drums. Cable drums can be made of wood or steel. Wooden drums are commonly used. The drum has a hollow shaft for insertion of iron bar. Both ends of the hollow shafts are fitted with flanges for protection of the cable.

Storage

If at any time the drums of the cables are required to be stored for reasonably long periods, the following points are to be noted:

- The site for storage of drums should be well-trained, hard-packed soil, or preferably a concrete surface, which will not allow the drums to sink, causing damage; it is extremely difficult to move drums when they sink into the ground.
- All drums should be stored with the battens intact, and in such a manner as to leave sufficient space between them for air circulation. Check and tighten tie bolts on the drums at regular intervals.
- Tier stacking of drums is not recommended. In no circumstances must the drums be stored 'on the flat, that is, with flanges horizontal (Fig. 8.7). Use proper stopper to prevent the drums from rolling (Fig. 8.8).

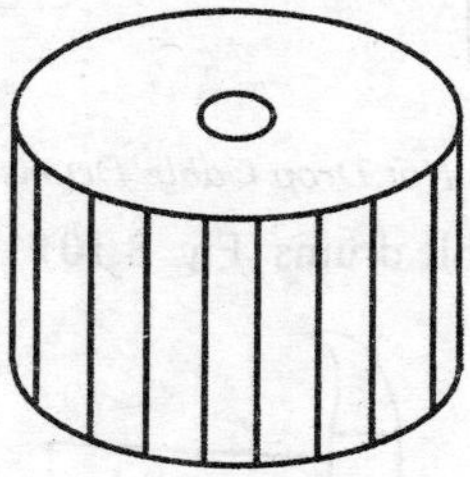

Fig. 8.7 *Do Not Lay Drums Flat on Their Sides*

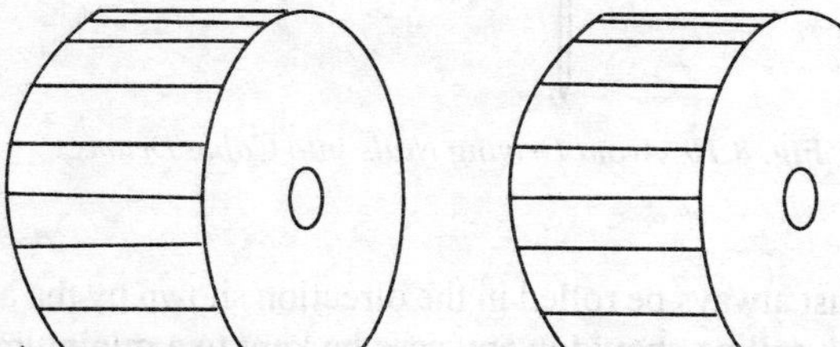

Fig. 8.8 *Use Proper Stoppers to Prevent Drums from Rolling*

- All drums during installation (i.e. when the battens have been removed) should be 'scotched' so that there is no danger of the flanges of drums coming into accidental contact with the unprotected cable on other drums. The cables should not be left unprotected.
- Cable ends must be sealed with end-caps during storage and transportation.

Handling

Damage to cables can occur due to the incorrect handling to which the drums and cables may be subjected, causing breakdown of the drum flanges and in exceptional cases, movement of the drum barrel takes place. Once this breakdown of the drum occurs, the cable is immediately exposed to damage.

Under no circumstances should a drum be rolled off a vehicle on to a cushion of sand, tarpaulin etc. (Fig. 8.9). This action could crumple the flanges and barrel of the drum, driving splinters and/or nails into the cables.

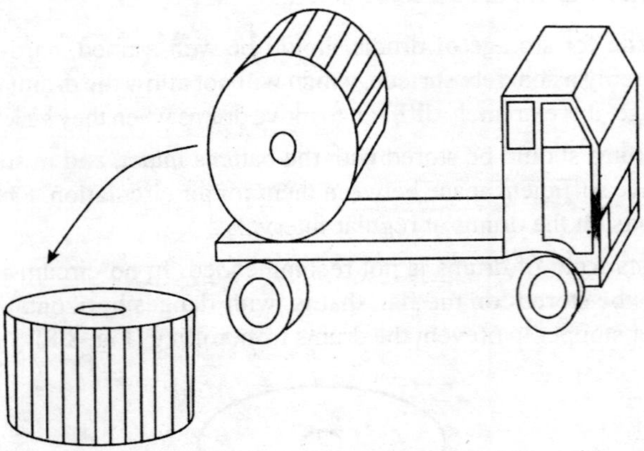

Fig. 8.9 Do Not Drop Cable Drums from Trucks

Avoid driving nails into cable drums (Fig. 8.10)

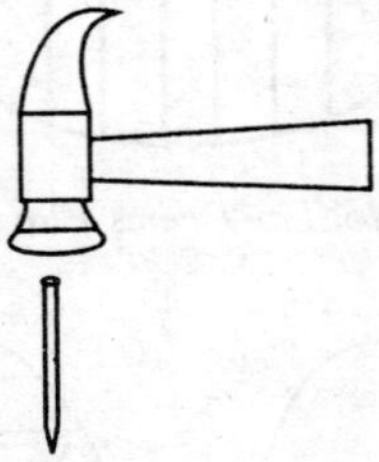

Fig. 8.10 Avoid Driving Nails into Cable Drums

Rolling Drums

Drums of cables must always be rolled in the direction shown by the arrow painted on the flanges, but such rolling should in any case be kept to a minimum.

Turning Drums

The best way to turn a cable drum is to roll it on to two well-greased thin plates or boards about two feet square. The plates can then be used as a turnable and the drum can be rotated in the desired direction. The practice of using an iron bar under the bolt head is regarded as extremely dangerous to the operator and is detrimental to the drum.

Lowering or Lifting Drums

When drums are moved from one level to another, for example, lorry to ground, wharf to ship, etc. lifting and lowering gear must always be used. When drums are lifted from the upper layer of a tiered stack, care should be taken to ensure that no movement of the bottom layer occurs so as to cause collapse. Drums, whether loaded or empty, and too heavy to be manipulated, should always be slung; they should never be dropped.

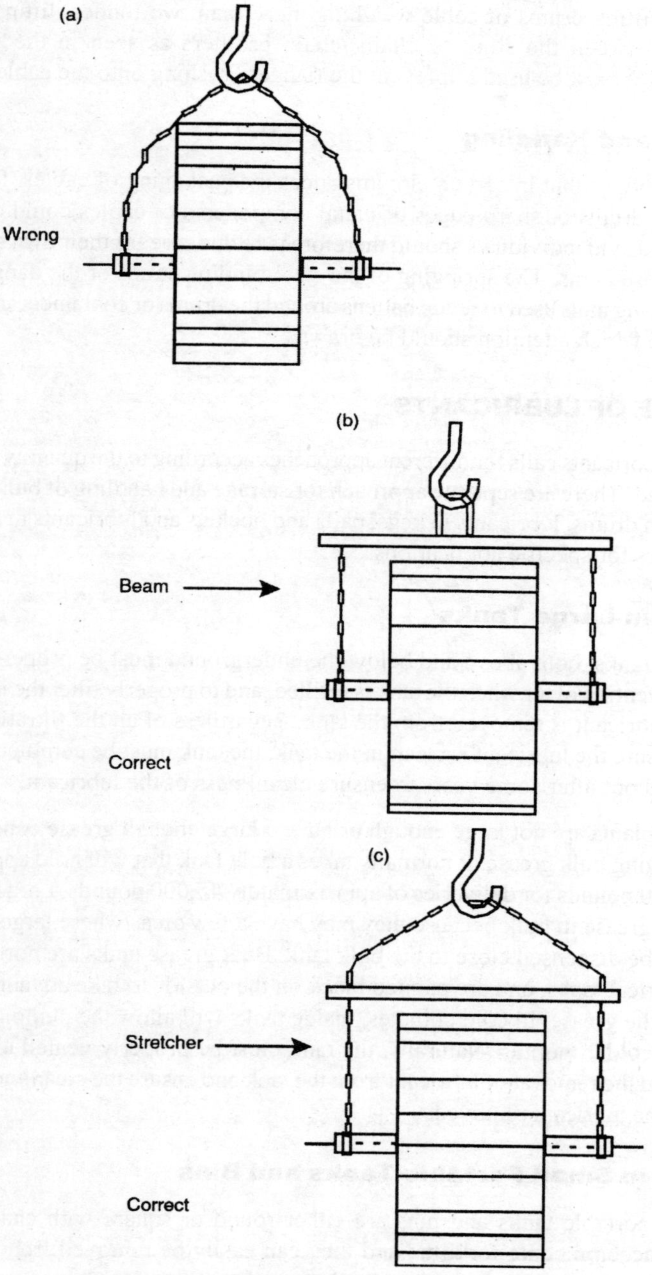

***Fig. 8.11** Lifting Cable Drums using a Crane*

While lifting drums of cable for loading, spindles must always be used in conjunction with crane slings, chain 'brothers' or lifting beams (Fig. 8.11(b)). On no account must any drum be lifted by other means, that is., by using claw-grabs, wires slings, etc.

When lifting drums of cable weighing more than two tonnes, lifting beams or stretchers between the sling or chain, chain brothers as seen in the illustration (Fig. 8.11 (c)) must be used to prevent the flanges crushing onto the cable.

Packing and Handling

It will be obvious that in certain circumstances the packaging of cables, for example large heavy drums or sharp edges of metal components of cables could constitute a safety hazard, and individuals should therefore take due care for their own safety while handling these items. The springing of the steel-binding straps or the dangers arising from projecting nails used to retain battens around the drums or containers are particular examples to which attention should be drawn.

STORAGE OF LUBRICANTS

Storage of lubricants calls for different approaches according to the quantity of lubricant to be handled. There are separate approach for storage and handling of bulk lubricants, lubricants in drums, lubricants in kegs, pails and buckets and lubricants in special-size of containers for specific applications.

Storage in Large Tanks

Large bulk tanks, both above and below the underground must be properly vented to handle the venting of air when the tank is refilled, and to properly filter the incoming air when the lubricant is removed from the tank. Regardless of all the filtration and care taken to ensure the lubricant is clean in the tank, the tank must be completely emptied and cleaned out after some years to ensure cleanliness of the lubricant.

Many plants are not large enough or have a large enough grease consumption to warrant buying bulk grease. It normally takes a bulk tank that will hold approximately 60 to 80,000 pounds for deliveries of approximately 45,000 pounds. Large plants may like to buy grease in bulk because they may have a few areas where large volumes of grease can be dispensed close to the bulk tank. Bulk grease tanks are normally above ground vertical tanks, and are painted black on the outside to take advantage of solar heating of the grease. In cold climates, inside tanks will allow the pumping of grease during the colder months. Naturally, the tank must be properly vented to handle the addition and the removal of lubricant from the tank and ensure the cleanliness of the air replacing the lubricant removed.

Storage in Small Portable Tanks and Bins

The small portable tanks and bins are either round or square with channels at the bottom to accommodate forklifts, and they can easily be removed from the storage yard to the points of applications. As the small tanks or bins get empty, they are returned to the lubricant supplier and refilled.

The small tanks and bins are on loan from the supplying lubricant distributor. Normally breather vents are permanently installed in the top of the bin so that the air, which replaces the lubricant removed, is clean. The bins for different lubricants are painted a different color for ease of identification within the plant to reduce the possibility of misapplications.

Outside Storage of Drums of Oils and Greases

Drums of oils/greases, stored outside, should be covered if possible. This can be done with a covered open-air shed (Fig. 8.12), plastic sheeting, or drum covers. Plastic sheeting tends to be a nuisance because they must be removed and then replaced after drums are distributed and drum covers, which are just plastic or metal caps over the drum, tend to sail away in a windstorm. Drums are normally stored on pallets and should be rotated so that the bungs are parallel to the bungs on the drums next to it. This way a 2-by-4 piece of wood can be inserted under the bottom edge of the drum (Fig. 8.13), parallel with the bungs to prevent water from collecting around the bungs.

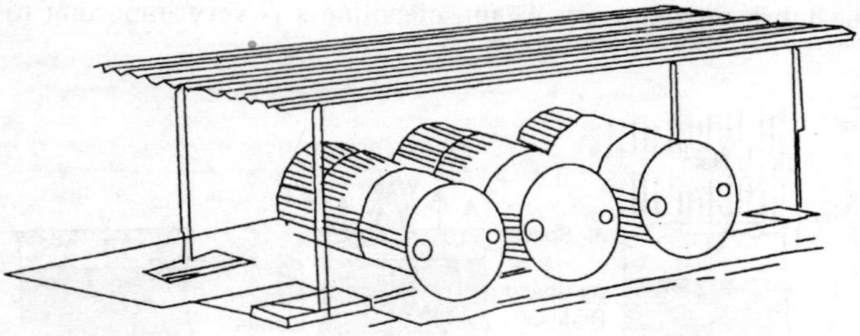

Fig. 8.12 Drums Stored in Covered Open-air Shed

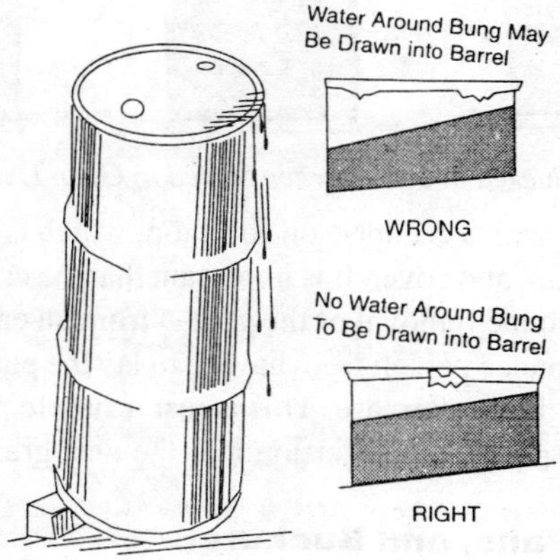

Fig. 8.13 Wooden Piece Inserted At the Bottom Edge of the Drum

Bungs on oil drums are not waterproof. If the drum is allowed to remain flat on the ground and it rains, the water will collect on the top of the drum. As the sun warms the lubricant in the drum, it will expand, and then it will cool and contract in the evening and suck the water right past the bungs and into the lubricant (Fig. 8.14).

Storing drums on their side is a good way to prevent water from entering the drum but one-third to one-half of the drums will leak lubricants from the bung unless the seal is first removed and the bung is tightened right down. Drums stored on their sides should rest on wooden rails to keep the drum off the ground.

Inside Storage of Drums of Oils and Greases

Drums stored inside a building may be stored flat or in stacked racks, whichever is available in the plant. They can then be easily moved with a drum hand truck forklift individually or by the pallet to the place of application.

Two kinds of drum valves are inserted into the small or large bung openings of the drum. The size will be determined by the normal amount removed from the drum. The drum is then elevated so the distribution container can be inserted below the valve. Although many consumers just loosen the vent bung to allow air to replace the lubricant removed, a filter vent should be inserted into the vent bung to ensure that filtered air replaces the lubricant removed. Again, cleanliness is very important to machine longevity.

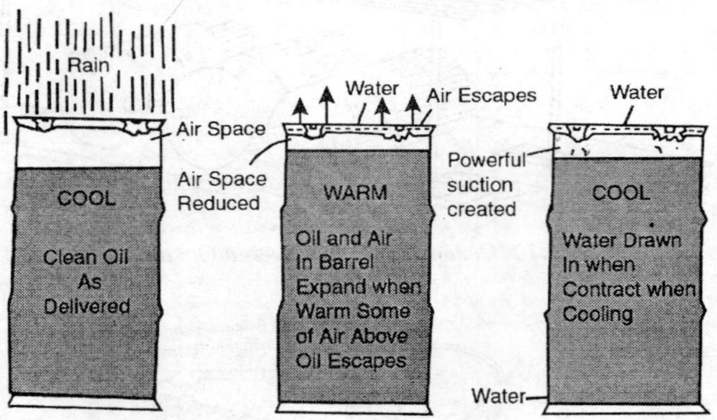

Fig. 8.14 Water Sucked in Drums when Stored in Open During Rainy Days

Grease drums come with a crimped-on solid top, which is normally removed and replaced with grease pump, and cover. It is important that the crimped cover of the new drum be removed prior to the removal of the grease from an empty grease drum. This will preclude the maintenance person from having to lay the pump on the floor prior to inserting it into the new drum of grease. This is just a simple procedure to ensure the pump does not get dirty prior to its insertion into the new grease.

Storage in Kegs, Pails, and Buckets

The next smaller container is a 120-pound keg, or a quarter drum, as it is sometimes called. They are normally used for grease or automotive gear oil. The next size container, and a fairly common one, is a 5-gallon pail or bucket of oil or a 35-38 pound container of grease. The oil has a crimped-on top with a pop-up pour spout for easy transfer or application. A grease keg or pail has a solid crimped-on lid, which is removed, to instal a grease pump and cover. The pump is then used to dispense the lubricant into grease guns or into the point of application. Containers smaller than a pail are uncommon in an industrial plant, construction site, or mine.

The trend is toward plastic pails today, which can be cleaned out and used for other purposes in the plant. Pails of cutting oils are very handy to have for cutting fluid operations where the machine operator is responsible for keeping the cutting fluid level up during the day.

Storage in Special Sized Container

With bulk, drums, kegs, and pails covered, the need for any other small sizes are not there, but there are exceptions.

Relatively small requirements for forklift motor oil or some small air compressors can be handled very nicely with a case of quart bottles. Motor oil is easy to handle and dispense in a container of this size.

Special greases for use in specialized applications can be made available in 14.5 oz cartridges, which comes 10 tubes per carton or 60 tubes to a master case. Cartridge grease is also very convenient for maintenance personnel to carry in back pockets to refill a grease gun as they proceed on their maintenance route if refilling the grease gun from a pail is impractical. When climbing on top of an overhead crane to grease bearings, carrying a spare tube or two is the most efficient way to carry more grease.

Storage of Greases for Roller Bearing

The storage conditions for rolling bearing greases are :

- Temperatures + 6 to + 40° C, if possible room temperature,
- Closed, filled original containers.

Permissible storage periods for rolling bearing greases:

- 2 years for lubricating greases of consistency class > 2,
- 1 year for lubricating greases of consistency class < 2.

For these periods, rolling bearing greases can be stored at room temperature in closed original containers without quality loss.

The storage time cannot be regarded as a rigid limit. As compounds of oil, thickener, and additives, rolling bearing greases may change their chemicophysical properties during storage and should, therefore, be used soon. At careful storage, that is, observing all conditions described, low room temperature, full and airtight containers, most rolling bearing greases can be used even after five years if minor changes are accepted.

Higher temperatures and only partly filled containers should be avoided because they promote separation of the base oil from the grease should be inspected chemicophysically for alterations.

When opened containers are to be kept in storage, the grease surface should, in any case, be smoothed, the container closed airtight and stored with the hollow space on top.

STORAGE OF INDUSTRIAL GASES

Industrial gases, which are commonly used in most industrial units include the following:

- Oxygen (O_2)
- Acetylene (C_2H_2)
- Nitrogen (N_2)
- Argon (Ar)

The gases are used for various types of welding works in an industrial unit. Handling and storage of industrial gases is an important activity, as these are hazardous, have fire potential, and some of them are toxic. Storage of industrial gases is greatly influenced by their characteristics.

General Guidelines of Handling and Storage of Industrial Gases

- Identify the gas in the cylinder before use.
- Cylinders must be stored and preferably utilized in a vertical position.
- Cylinders must be stored in a well-ventilated place.
- Cylinder storage in places of ambient temperature above 50° C must be avoided.
- Flammable gases like Acetylene and oxidants like Oxygen must be separated by a minimum distance of 20 Feet and by dividing wall of minimum 6 Feet height with a fire rating of at least one hour.
- Cylinders should not be stored with flammable items like fuels and oils etc.
- Cylinders should not be stored with corrosive items like acids and other similar chemicals
- Cylinder storage in a corrosive environment where cylinders are exposed to corrosive vapors must be avoided.
- Keep cylinder away from sources of heat and flame like radiators and furnaces.
- Storage of cylinders in damp and wet surfaces must be avoided to prevent bottom corrosion.
- Storage should be planned so that cylinders are normally used in the order that they are received from the supplier.
- Smoking and other sources of fire must be prohibited near cylinder storage area.
- Stored cylinders must be protected from access to unauthorized individuals.
- Storage of cylinders in places where any heavy object may fall on them or where they may be subjected to severe shocks should be avoided.
- Empty and full cylinders must be stored separately.
- Gas withdrawal from cylinders should be only through approved regulators.
- Never attempt to increase cylinder pressure by external heating.

- Do not transfer gas from one cylinder to another.
- Maintenance work on cylinders should not be done by anyone except approved personnel.
- Do not drop cylinders.
- Always close the cylinder valves after use.
- Always fix caps when cylinders are not in use.

Storage of Oxygen

- Avoid contamination of gas cylinders, cylinder valves, regulators, fitting etc.
- Don't permit cylinders to come into contact with any electrical circuit.
- Don't smoke in close proximity to pure Oxygen.

Handling of Acetylene

- In storage and transportation of Acetylene cylinders, care must be taken to avoid any damage to the bottom fusible plugs.
- Always keep Acetylene cylinder in upright position weather in use or in store, full or empty.

Handling of Nitrogen and Argon

- Handle high-pressure cylinders with caution. A broken valve or rupture in a high-pressure cylinder can cause a serious accident.
- Don't lift cylinders by its caps.

STORAGE OF EXPLOSIVES

There are four considerations in the storage of explosives:

- Security
- Safety
- Prevention of fumes, which could be hazardous to health
- Government Regulations

Precautions in Storage of Explosives

Various precautions in storage of explosives are:

- Explosives must be stored with strict observance of the government regulations. Storage places must be maintained in good and clean condition. The general security of the area must be maintained. Keys must be kept safely so that unauthorized persons cannot obtain them.
- Explosives must be stored in such a manner that they are not subjected to shocks, tearing, undue heat, or other stresses likely to cause them to explode or burn unintentionally or to deteriorate to a dangerous condition.

- During storage and handling, explosives should, where possible, be kept in the manufacturer's packing. Cartridge explosives in an inner cover should only be separated from the cover immediately before use.
- Lighting and ventilation in storage places should be of such a nature that there is no risk of ignition or explosion through heating or electric current.
- Explosives must not be stored with other materials. Follow necessary procedures for the cleaning and maintenance of the storage area.
- Except keeping in and taking out of the explosives, no other work should be carried out in storage room. In case any other work is to be carried out, the stored materials must be emptied and the area cleaned out before such work is started. Unpacking of any crate should be done at a place away from the magazine area.
- Easily legible and conspicuous notices with words 'NO SMOKING-EXPLOSIVES' must be erected at the approaches to and within the storage area.
- There should be local exhaust ventilation of storage places in addition to good general ventilation.
- Workers should practice good personal hygiene, for example, always washing hands after handling explosives.
- Those handling and transporting explosives must remember that they are dealing with dangerous materials.
- Personal protective equipment (gloves and uniforms) should be supplied and used.
- Employees handling and working with explosives should be medically examined prior to employment. Emphasis should be on Cardiac disorders, Hypertensions, and Neurotic disposition.

CHAPTER 9

Computerization of Warehouse Activities

INTRODUCTION

Warehouses store a large variety of items. The number of items in the warehouse of an industrial unit is normally very large and may range from 20,000 to 100,000 depending upon the size of the plant, type of plant, machinery installed, and nature of manufacturing process. Making entries of receipt, issue, temporary issue, and return of materials generate lots of data, which are very difficult to handle manually. Manual handling and retrieval of data does not meet the present day requirements of industrial units, which in most cases work with automatic plants and machinery.

Handling of bulky files manually is very difficult, inconvenient, time-consuming, and involves lots of man-hours. Retrieval of information is even more difficult from manual files. Sometimes, the data and information is lost in the manual files, and decisions are taken without considering all aspects of the issue on hand. This affects and quality of decision taken. Today, Computer Based Information System (CBIS) plays a very important role in handling, processing and retrieval of large data, and converting the same with ease into useful information for decision-making. Most of the Computer Based Information Systems are integrated information systems for material procurement, warehouse management, and inventory control. Some of the latest software packages like SAP and BPCS are very comprehensive packages. In addition to warehouse management, inventory control, and procurement support, they encompass other organizational activities like:

- Demand Management Support
- Sales Management and Control Support
- Distribution Resources Planning Support

TASKS FOR COMPUTERIZATION IN WAREHOUSE ACTIVITIES

Almost all the activities of warehouse can be computerized, they include the following:

- Maintaining stock balance of all the items in the stores.
- Replenishment of stock items.
- Report on material usage.
- Inventory costing and valuation.
- Preparing materials requisition for purchase.
- Review of status of materials requisition for purchase.
- Updating materials requisition for purchase.
- Inventory receipts.
- Direct issue record for materials issued to user departments.
- Handling of discrepancy reports.
- Records of resolution of discrepancies.
- Spare parts management.
- Inventory control, fixing minimum level, maximum level, safety stock, economic order quantities, lead time for various materials etc.
- Performance evaluation of vendors.
- Management reports.
- ABC analysis.
- Consolidation of data.
- Maintaining historical data of receipts, issues, and usage.
- Checking the finished work for mathematical accuracy and typographical errors.

It is not as if the above activities cannot be carried out manually but the computer does them very easily, quickly, and accurately.

BENEFITS OF COMPUTERIZATION

A computerized system can be beneficial to a Stores Division in many ways. Many of these benefits result in considerable savings. These savings occur in the following general areas:

i. Reduced inventory cost
ii. Reduced operational/administration costs
iii. Increased productivity in store-keeping and inventory control
iv. Other benefits

Reduced Inventory Cost

An automated inventory control system will make a very positive contribution towards inventory reduction through such results as:

- Lower lead times through faster processing.
- Economic Order Quantity: Economic order quantity is the quantity, which takes into account all the relevant costs associated with a particular procurement and not just the costs of the materials. By balancing the frequency of ordering with the cost of carrying inventory, total cost of materials can be reduced without affecting the unit cost charged by the supplier for the material.

Because of the number of calculations involved in this process and the frequency of ordering new materials, the manual system with its limited resources finds it unable to support this technique fully.

- Arranging for the material's arrival when it is needed, not before.
- Identifying orders for materials that have engineered cutoff dates for withdrawal from use.

Reduced Operational/Administrative Costs

Clerical costs Computerization not only lowers the direct clerical cost, but also makes the day-to-day job of the inventory/warehouse staff more satisfying through greater variety of work and lesser need for constant routine. Productivity and morale of the personnel also rise.

Because of the significant increase in productivity made possible by automation, more work can be achieved in future with the same or fewer number of people. This offers potential savings from less employment with proper allocation of resources.

Eliminating duplicate information Like inventory, information is expensive to store especially on a manual paperwork system. Store-keeping and inventory control need to maintain records of the same data on duplicate files. An example of this is the stock item's file, stored once by part number, once by location, once by manufacturers/suppliers, and so forth. There may be similar other cases also. Computerization helps in elimination of such requirements and provides the facility to get the information quickly.

Data errors Computerization gives opportunity for fewer data errors in the following four ways:

i. Eliminates duplicate files.

ii. Reduction of key-punching, by use of codes to represent parts description, location and so on. On receipt of the code, the system looks up the information relating to that code in the database. That information is only entered once and the source of error is removed.

iii. Using a database, responsibility for data accuracy can be assigned to the user who knows what should be entered. That person can spot errors before the information is finally passed to the system more often than someone who does not understand the information being entered. For example, specifications of stock items can be checked by the user department to make sure that the item is described fully and all the relevant information of the supplier, name of the manufacturer, item code of supplier's part list, drawing number etc., are entered in the system.

iv. Elimination of data duplication: Information once entered by an user, is not supposed to be re-entered by another user.

Lower expediting costs The system can provide the inventory control team information on the stock level of critical items, raw materials, and expedite deliveries that are due to be made in any predetermined time period, such as next week, the remainder of the month, or whether it is past the date for delivery. In case of excessive consumption of critical items, review helps in advancing the procurement action to enable building up the stock again well in time. The computer records, showing the stock level and any outstanding quantities on order, help in getting the items replenished on time. In case of a likely shortage, the suppliers are asked to deliver early or use a faster mode of transportation, even if it is at a higher cost, such as airfreight in place of seafreight.

Lower shipping charges It becomes routine to have timely delivery of materials with more effective selection of source and greater efficiency. This reduces shipping charges by reduction or elimination of:

- Rush orders
- Partial shipments
- Air freight
- Special messengers/special deliveries

Reduced costs of forms With an on-line system much information is passed between the user and the system on an interactive basis, both through the keyboard to the system and via the screen (and occasionally the printer) to the user. This reduces the need for numerous forms and reports, which are required in a manual system.

Improved Personnel Productivity

This is a real area of benefit from an automated store-keeping and inventory control system. For example, simplification of replenishment of stock items, improved interdepartmental communication, fewer unexpected problems.

Improving interdepartmental communications This can happen in two ways:

i. Through the on-line interactive inventory control system, callers to the inventory controller can get their information more quickly than before.

ii. Availability of information through integrated application makes it possible for specific departments to access the required data. For example, knowledge of current specifications, stock position, quantities on order and outstanding or goods under inspection helps those departments to themselves access the data for information they need. They would not even need to contact the inventory control section. For example, the maintenance department may see the stock level of spares on their terminal itself or can know the delivery status of parts ordered.

Improved planning Better planning leads to fewer unexpected problems. An automated system contributes to better planning with:

- Review of stock levels that gives a comprehensive picture of stock levels, usage pattern, and delivery status.
- More planning and efficiency in the expediting process.
- More accurate order release dates, with up-to-date lead time information from the supplier.

When problems do occur, the inventory control staff have immediate access to the information needed without having to wade through paper files of stock levels, item codes, requisitions, and extensive lists. So paper work is reduced drastically.

Job satisfaction This is a proven area for increasing productivity. By reducing clerical content of jobs, increasing variety, increasing responsibility, developing the new, modern skills with the aid of computerization, job satisfaction is increased and with it employee morale and productivity.

Other Benefits

There are other benefits, too, that are not always as visible or measurable as a reduction in 'inventory value'. These include:

- Segregation of various types of inventories. For example, spares, consumables, stock items, non-stock items and direct issue items etc.
- More accurate information used for controlling inventory by reviewing non-moving and slow moving items.
- Timely information for replenishment of inventory. Automatic replenishment review helps in quick results and decision.
- Quick information about spares in stock for machines, which are to be replaced, disposed of or written-off.
- Information about obsolete items, generated as a result of disposal of equipment and selling the spares to the supplier.
- Disposal of overstocked items, keeps the inventory low.
- Information of expiry dates of various items avoids their spoilage.
- Improves efficiency of shop floor functions and operations.
- Inter-linking of a spare in different locations helps in reducing inventory.
- In case of multi-unit organizations, items of high-value can be kept at one place reducing inventory value.
- Improved warehouse management that is, tagging of parts and areas within the stores.
- Helps in better procurement process.

APPROPRIATE SOFTWARE FOR STORE KEEPING AND INVENTORY CONTROL

Having considered the requirements of the Stores Division, the next step is to select appropriate software. The alternatives are:

- A software package
- A general purpose program
- Custom made programs

Each alternative has its own part to play, its own advantages and disadvantages, and should be given due consideration. This is a crucial decision and should not be rushed. Correct choice of software is very important.

Alternative I Software Package

A software package is one, which an organization has produced to meet what it sees as the requirements of customers in general. The strong advantage of using a software is that one just requires to buy the package, have it demonstrated, read the manuals, and get started. It's usually just that easy.

A package, as opposed to a general-purpose program, contains not only the programming and documentation but also a set of instructions to the user. This is the difference between a software package and some general-purpose software like a spreadsheet or a database.

In a reasonably standard store's environment, one is likely to find a fit between actual software requirements, and what the software organization has estimated about the requirements of the customer. However, the major disadvantage of a software package is that it might not do just what the customer wants it to do. This is because store-keeping and inventory control requirements of one customer will be different, to a greater or lesser degree, than that of another organization or company. For example, if a system does not have a formal parts-numbering system, then a package based on parts numbers would not be much good either.

In the same way, a less serious disadvantage is that the package might in fact do more than what would ever be needed. The reason is that, for the software organization to have as large a market as possible for its product it will have to be useful to as many different store-keeping and inventory control environments as possible. This means that it could have all kinds of extras built into it, any one of which could be useful to someone. But not many of them will be useful to everyone. Out of 20 or 30 such features, five may be applicable in some case. In this case, the disadvantages lie in two areas. For one, the package will cost more, probably a lot more. Secondly, and more importantly in the long run, it will be more complicated and therefore more difficult to use.

Alternative II General Purpose Programs

As implied by their name, these programs are ones that help manage the information in a specific way. They differ from software packages in that the user does the specifying, whereas a package is already programmed to handle the data in a predetermined way.

There are many programs for general purposes. The ones that can be used for store-keeping and inventory control, fall into four categories:

i. Database managers
ii. Spreadsheets
iii. Communications
iv. Word Processing

Generally, a database manager is used to support the transactional system, a spreadsheet is used for decision support, communications software is clearly dedicated to linking computers, and word processing is an aid to personal productivity.

Database managers The basic premise is that the parts of information, such as part number, description, etc., is kept on one database file. Issue of materials is kept on another file. Many sophisticated database managers on the market today allow creation of a Materials Requisition for Purchase (MRP), combining the input information such as:

- What is the stock of an item in the inventory?
- What is the outstanding quantity from purchase orders placed?
- What is the trend of consumption for the item?

Then they print out a Materials Requisition for Purchase (MRP) having all the information.

The database manager will also store this MRP information onto its own database file for future reference. Once all the open MRP's are on the file in this way, it would be in a position to extract information. For example, one can ask—"What are the specifications of this part?" or "How much should be the maximum and minimum quantity of this item and what is the present stock of the item?" or "How many MRP's were prepared in a particular month of this year?" However, although database managers can perform calculations on the data, it will not be very sophisticated as compared to the analytical abilities of a spreadsheet program.

Spreadsheets Spreadsheets on personal computers are electronic versions of the standard paper spreadsheets. But they contain a lot of electronic advantages such as automatic calculations of totals, handling of complex formulas, using look-up tables, and many other useful features. This ability to handle a selected amount of information and perform calculations, comparisons, look-ups, and sorting allows them to be used for many decision support applications.

The amount of information needed for any decision support application (such as optimum order quantity) is not large. The data can either be entered into the spreadsheet as it is required, or, in some cases, the same information is extracted automatically from database files through a sufficiently sophisticated database manager.

In this case the user would be combining the data-handling power of the database manager, as it manages the transactional information, with the facilities for analysis provided by the spreadsheet. That is done by taking the required spreadsheet data directly off the database files of the database manager and storing it on another file in a spreadsheet format.

Once the information is in the spreadsheet, it can be used for analysis under the rules and formulas previously set up by the user in the spreadsheet itself.

Communications This area of personal computing is now immensely popular. There are many types of hardware and software available to choose from to enable one computer to communicate with another one, for example, communication between Stores Division and Maintenance Department or between Stores Division and Finance Department, and so on.

Word processing As with communications, this popular branch of personal computing has many software packages available. They all process words, and the choice comes down to factors such as individual features, ease of use, after sales support, and price.

Integrated software Some newer software packages available today allow the user to pass easily from one general purpose application to another, all within the context of one integrated program.

Alternative III Custom-made Programs

If it is desired that turnkey set of disks should start to automate store-keeping and inventory from the first day in the same way as done today, then the software written for the needs of the organization is to be obtained.

There are enough programmers in the market today who will do it for the organization at a price. Clearly, customized software is more expensive than general purpose software.

Choice for the Best Option

The best option depends on the requirements. The approach to select the software is, however, crucial. The advantages and disadvantages of each approach are presented in Table 9.1. The following factors can be used to compare various database managers when making a selection for the best option.

i.	List price	US$............
ii.	Menu Driven	Yes/No
iii.	Custom Menus	Yes/No
iv.	Custom Entry Screens	Yes/No
v.	Sophisticated Reports	Yes/No
vi.	Pass Word	Yes/No
vii.	Multiple Sort Fields	Yes/No
viii	Files Open	Max. Number
ix.	Records/Files	Max. Number
x.	Fields/Record	Max. Number

xi. Character/Record Max. Number
xii. Character/field Max Number

Table 9.1 Software Selection Review

S. No.	Software	Advantages	Disadvantages
1	Software Package	a. Customer requirements are built in. b. Customer gets going quickly once selected. c. Less expensive than custom-made approach. d. Upgrades from the supplier as they release them.	a. May not fit customer's requirements fully. b. Change of format may not be possible. c. Might not be able to add parts to it. d. Might do more than needed.
2	General Purpose Software	a. Can do what the customer wants it to do. b. Inexpensive	a. Customer may not know how to use it. b. Difficult to use for sophisticated or complex applications.
3	Custom-Made	a. Customer gets what he needs b. Customer can start as soon as the software is ready	a. Expensive b. Takes time

CREATING A DATABASE FOR TRANSACTIONAL TASKS

Creating a strong automated store-keeping and inventory control system needs to set up the database files for various applications. Some of them are mentioned here and they are used for the following applications:

- Accept Materials Requisitions (MR), and use them to generate Materials Requisitions for Purchase (MRP).
- Determine the quantity to be procured.
- Generate open MRP and amend them for cancellations, new quantities, revised specifications and so on.
- Print out the MRP ready for forwarding to the Purchase Division, with copies for internal use.
- Allow expediting by identifying MRP that are getting close to, or have passed, the due dates of materials required.
- Accept receipt of the goods, which includes matching the receiving notes with the purchase order and reconciling quantities received.

All the above tasks are called transactional, because they perform the routine administrative transactions involved in store-keeping and inventory control activities of the organization. These transactional tasks require relatively large amount of data stored on separate files. These files may already be in use, whether they are on a computer or a similar type of manual system.

To start with, time and effort is required to either transfer existing manual files onto the new computer database or to create them directly onto the database if they are new.

There are a number of key database master files that the system needs for performing transactional tasks. They are:

- Location file
- Commodity codes
- Parts/Item master file
- Units of measure
- Vendor Master
- Currency code and exchange rates

Locations

Materials are stored in different warehouses of the company located at different places in the plant. Location files will identify the parts with the warehouse, where the parts are stored. List of warehouses in an industrial unit is given in Table 9.2.

Commodity Code

The inventory is divided into commodities having items of similar nature. For example, some of the commodities in the inventory can be classified as:

- Automotive Parts
- Building Materials
- Bearings
- Castings
- Electrical items
- Lubricants
- Forgings
- Mechanical items

Each commodity can be further classified into sub-heads. For example, bearings can be classified as Roller bearings, ball bearings, Journal bearings etc.

Different codes are assigned to each commodity for the purpose of computerization.

Table 9.2 List of Warehouses

S No.	Warehouse Code	Warehouse Description
1	A	Mechanical, Electrical and General spares
2	B	Raw Material Yard I
3	C	Raw Material Yard II
4	D	Raw Material Yard III
5	E	Electronic Items
6	F	Automotive Spares
7	G	Open Yard-Oil and Lubricant
8	H	Heavy Equipment spares
9	J	Stationery and Clinic
10	K	Laboratory
11	L	Explosives
12	N	Open Yard – Heavy Items
13	M	Kitchen Utensil and Furniture
14	P	Packing Materials

Item Master File

This is the list of all the items that are currently being purchased on a regular basis. If the organization already has a parts-numbering system, that is the one to use here.

The item master file contains the following basic information:

1. Parts number- like the supplier code; this will be a unique identification of the part. It may be alphanumeric, but pure numeric is preferable.
   A non-structured code is typically a sequential series to which individual parts are assigned as they come up. In this case the code itself will not reveal anything about the part that has been assigned to it. On the other hand, a structured code is one for which the part itself will determine, to some degree or other, what its part number will be.
2. Part description - the name of the part.
3. Unit of measure - kgs, pounds, cubic meters, liters, gallons, etc.
4. Average Prices - Average of the previous and the current prices.
5. Commodity code - for performing analysis of purchases by commodity code, selection of suppliers by the commodities they can supply such as casting, steel mill products, rubber parts, chemicals, etc.
6. Engineering reference - for relating back to drawing numbers and other engineering requirements. This list is the minimum needed for an item master file. It simply allows the performance of transactional tasks.

Unit of Measure File

Different units of measurements are used for different purposes. For example, unit of stockkeeping will be different from the unit of order, sales unit, and delivery unit. These are explained as under:

- **Stocking Unit of Measure (SUOM)**: This is the base unit of measure and is the lowest unit in which stocks are managed. A conversion factor is normally specified. Quantities, which are entered in other unit of measures, are converted into the base unit.
- **Purchasing Unit of Measure (PUOM)**: Unit of material purchased.
- **Unit of Issue**: Unit of materials issued from warehouse/stores. Goods issued and physical inventory transactions can be entered in this unit. Usually issue is done by the Stocking Unit of Measure.
- **Sales Unit**: Unit of materials sold.
- **Delivery Unit**: The delivery unit is made up of a number and a unit of measure.

Vendor Master

The Vendor Master contains the following data:

(i) General data
- Name
- Address
- Vendor ID
- Phone & Fax Number
- Postal Code
- State Code
- Country Code

(ii) Purchase data
- Terms of payment
- Supporting terms
- Shipping terms
- Contact person (Name, Designation)
- Minimum order value

(iii) Account data
- Payment terms
- Payment method
- Accounting clerk
- State Tax ID

Currency Code

Currency codes describe the currency used by the buyer and the exchange value to the currency used by various international vendors with whom the company is dealing. A currency code is assigned to each vendor for his currency. The purchasing price is converted to his currency at the appropriate exchange rate at the invoice reconciliation time. The information in the currency code file includes:

- Data
- Base currency value
- Foreign currency
- Exchange rate

Creating the Necessary Fields

Whenever practical, a code should be used for a field rather than for a complete entry. This is the case for part, stock balance, and usage. The part comes from the Item Master file and is linked to the MRP file by the relationship set up between the item code and item description. When the MRP is printed, the system recognizes the item code and goes to the item description by itself because the database is set up that way (using its relational capabilities).

Need for Relational Database

Although the master files are separate, most of the tasks performed require information from other files. It should be ensured that the database software is able to work comfortably with more than one master file at a time.

To do this requires a special kind of database software known as a relational database manager, as opposed to the less sophisticated file manager type. The database is the file of data, whereas the database manager is the application software that uses the database.

A relational database manager can be used to manage separate database files to perform one task. Linking the related fields together on the separate files does this. The links are established at the time of creating the files and this requires advance planning.

For example, the open MRP file contains the item code. This is the same code that identifies the stock balance, and is found on the stock file as well. If these fields are linked, then a relational database manager can "look" at the open MRP file and see the item code. It then uses that to go to the stock balance file to get the rest of the information on the stock balance with that code. Then it combines that data to print out information both from the open MRP file and the stock balance file at the same time. This is what happens when a MRP is printed.

For the purpose of replenishing the stores items, the key links are:

i. Item code on the Item Master file to the stock balance file.

ii. Part number on the open Materials Requisition for Purchasing file to the item master.

iii. Materials Requisition (MR) number on the open Material Requisition file to the open Material Requisition for Purchase (MRP) file.

iv. Part location.

Most of the early software packages for use on a personal computer were non-related, that is they could only handle one open file at a time. This was largely due to capacity restraints on personal computers at that time. Although by using them one could perform some database management applications, they were closer to file managers than database managers.

Today, there are several packages that are true relational database managers. Store-keeping and inventory control today need a relational database manager.

Setting Up the Data

This requires careful preparation to be most effective, no matter what master file is being created. In particular, the database file needs to be complete, well-defined, and accurate. For any of the files, the first step is to know exactly what data is going to make up the record.

While defining the overall layout of any set-up master file, only the necessary data should be included. Files designed should be complete in the sense that all types of data are built into the file structure and not that all the records are input into file.

It is not sufficient to simply describe the name of the field for each file on the data entry forms. The database also needs to know how many characters (maximum) will be allowed for that field.

For example, you may decide that the maximum part description can comprise 120 characters. This does not mean that all part description must be that long. It also does not mean that, once defined, all names must be that long. A balance has to be kept between the number of characters and size of the file. Choosing a large number of characters for the part description may increase processing time.

For the database software to do its job efficiently, the file should be so structured that each field is allocated the maximum number of characters whether or not any individual entry is of the maximum length. Using some abbreviations for descriptions of the part can control the number of characters for the part's description.

Since changing the design of a file already set up can be quite difficult, if not impossible for some database programs, it is very important to get these decisions right the first time. This requires judgment on not only of the current requirements but also of likely future requirements. That will ensure that the whole file set-up does not become obsolete within the first few years or so.

Another consideration when defining the file is a field, which may contain numbers and numeric symbols such as decimal points and minus signs.

SETTING UP USER'S OWN INVENTORY CONTROL DATABASE SYSTEM

The preliminary stages for setting up own inventory control database systems are:

i. Forms definition:

The data is put into the system by using "forms" on the screen. The forms are designed according to own requirements and are saved for repeat use.

ii. Data collection:

This means:

- knowing where to go for the data
- whether the data found is useful
- making sure that it is accurate
- filling in any gaps
- ensuring that it stays accurate

iii. Menu creation:

The database software should allow one to set up own menus, which are simply screens designed to offer choices of tasks to perform. Menu-driven systems are among the easiest to use.

iv. Report definitions:

Layout of the reports designed, to see that the information held in the system is set up and saved for future use.

v. Security:

A good database manager package allows building security checks, such as passwords, into the system to prevent unauthorized users gaining access.

Forms Definition

The transactional system operates off a relational database software package. In order to get data in and out of the system, the input forms have to be designed and they will appear on the screen for access. In this sense, forms mean the layout of the input fields on the screen as they would appear to the person inputting the data.

Defining the forms includes both specifying the layout and - for such data entry field - specifying what type of data can be entered into the field. The option of using other data entry features will also be available, such as calculated fields, range fields, and others.

Number of forms As many number of forms can be had as required. Some need to be specified at the outset. Others may not be needed until the system is in its second year, till a history has been built up. A new form can always be added, or an existing one can be deleted.

Initially, at least one form for each database file will be needed for the first entering of the data. This form may also be used for making further changes to the data, or a separate form may be designed for this. Since most of the data does not change, having a separate form containing only the fields, that are likely to be changed will be quicker and simpler. Ease of use is the major factor in any design consideration with respect to running the system.

Defining the field selection This involves deciding what fields need to go into the forms for each of the major files - item master and commodity code master.

It should be ensured that the field selection gives all the information needed from the system for the present as well as for future needs. Advance planning should be done for data requirements. However, the form should not include more information than is necessary. There is a tendency to include too much. The form should be kept as simple as possible.

Define the field characteristics Each field can be defined as being alphabetic (letters only), alphanumeric (letters and numbers) or numeric (numbers only). It should be specified whether the numeric fields should be in monetary format, date format, number of decimal places allowed, and a range.

Entering the range, where applicable, is useful because it helps data accuracy. The system uses the range information to check whether a new number being entered can be allowed.

A field can also be calculated. This means that the value of the fields can be derived from a formula entered for the purpose which links absolute values and other numeric fields together mathematically. For example, on the MRP file, the maximum level and minimum level of an item can be arrived at by the formula.

A field can also be sequenced, which means that the system will automatically increment that field as a new record is created. An obvious application for this is the generation of MRP numbers, where the system allocates a new MRP number as being the next in sequence. A field can contain a default value.

Setting up relationships Another area of vital importance in the definition of data entry forms is relationships. For this purpose a separate form is required, which allows linking data fields together between files. For example, working out maximum and minimum quantities require information on average yearly consumption and the lead-time from different files.

The look up relationships can also be used to eliminate data entry errors. This is done by the system verifying an entry as and when it is made. For example, when creating a new MRP, the item code as entered may not be existing particularly if it is mistyped when entered. The system will check back to the item master file to confirm that the item code in fact exists if an appropriate look up has been set up. The same can be done for all other codes such as part location and commodity codes etc.

Defining the layout Once all the fields that go into the form have been identified, their characteristics specified, and the look up and other relationships set up, then the final step is to lay out each individual field position on the screen. The forms are now ready for entering the data.

Data Collection

Collecting good data Good data means that a particular piece of information, or group of data, is going to be useful. Similar data may be very important in one context but in another context it may be useless. Good data has to be valid. The Inventory Controller may know the correct specifications of a particular item. But the old records for that item description are out-of-date and no one bothers to change the document till someone knowledgeable realizes that it has to be changed. Data collection is not a one time process. Once the system starts managing the information, it has to be kept up-to-date. The data in the system is expensive. Its accuracy is vital to the operation. Therefore if there is change in information, such as an item description, the system has to be informed about it. The only way to be sure that this will happen is to have a clear policy, understood by everyone, that spells out how this should be done. It is better to delegate all data accuracy responsibility to one person, we should be notified of any change in information. Alternatively, the responsibility should lie with several people, one for item master data, one for receipt file, one for issue file, and so on.

Creating instead of collecting It may be that the data needed does not exist. In that case, it should be created. Perhaps the manual system never needed a location code. But the new system does. This is the opportunity to not only define what the code will look like, but also to see whether all the location data is relevant to the needs of the Stores Division.

Data should be updated regularly. For example, the location code, part description etc. should be updated, additions being made for new items and deletions made for items that are no more in use.

Menu Creation

The selected screens are known as the "menus". Screens which present the user with a selection of functions to be performed from that point in the system are created. Any one of the functions, when selected, will bring the corresponding form to the screen for utilization. The selected database software package will describe how this is done in its documentation. Each package is different.

An example of a menu would be file maintenance. Assuming that there are three master files (item master, location master and receipt master), a menu could be set up, that gives the choice of what file to update. It may look like the box below.

File Maintenance

Select 1, 2, 3, or 0

1. Update item master file.
2. Update location master file.
3. Update vendor master file.
0. Return to main menu.

In this way, the user has only a limited choice of functions, that can be performed from this point in the system, that reduces the opportunity for a possible wrong selection of functions. Also, reducing the selection to one keystroke cuts down the time taken while using the system. Such menus are safe, easy to use, and fast.

Menus are structured so that they can be built within other menus. By organizing system's functions into groups and putting each group into its own menu, an operating environment that is almost as good as a complete transactional system made for the requirements is created without the need for programming.

Reports Definitions

The database is capable of accepting all the data put into it, keeping track of the open MRP status, and not revealing any thing about the data it has accumulated.

For accessing any data, the procedures for same have to be followed. The reports are defined in advance in the required format. Any needed information can be accessed and seen on the screen at any time.

Other than data accuracy, good design and definition of the reports from the system are probably the most important aspects of the transactional system.

Accessing records using the database software Most database managers allow the user to go into the database files with a report query. The software pulls the records needed for the reports, formats them, and prints out the finished products. It is to be ensured that the selected database software has a report generation capability.

Querying and formatting Database software, has a query language, which allows one to:

a) Collect the data needed
b) List any fields from the records
c) Perform calculations on the field if chosen, including statistical operations
d) Order or group data to several levels

On a query, the selected data can be used either in a selected standard format or the one designed for the purpose.

Using the reports The database package has a reports menu that contains these items for selection:

0. Exits
1. Run a one-time only report
2. Run an existing report
3. Define a new report
4. View an existing report
5. Modify an existing report
6. Delete an existing report

Through Option 3, a new report is created that can be used more than once. The system asks the user to give the report a name by which it be recalled later. Then the report query is defined, the format is created, and the print style is specified.

At a later time, Option 4 can be used to look at the format specified in an existing report, and modify it or delete it using Option 5 and 6 respectively if necessary.

Option 2 allows one to run the report and gives an on-screen list of the names of all existing reports, which can be chosen from it. Once the selection is made, the report is produced.

User-defined formats The position where the information is to be put can be indicated on the screen. The information can be data from the database files, or user's own text, or calculated data from numeric file data.

For data fields, the system shows the maximum field length that could be taken up by that field. That way, no two pieces of data can occupy the same part of the report. The user can have his own text (headings, notes, and such) placed anywhere on the screen. Numeric fields can be created using arithmetic or numeric data fields, such as summations of the same field over a group of records, sums of different fields in the same record, division, multiplication, and so on.

This is a very versatile part of database software. With just a little creativity, reports can be designed in such a way that they serve the purpose of information management without depending on programming.

Security

The information in the database is vital. If the system is successful, the Stores Division will have eliminated the need for large files of paper. The data will be in the machine. Some of this data will be sensitive. Any good database software will allow inserting security measures in the form of passwords, which prevent anyone having access to the data without their having the right password. Passwords can be controlled.

Also, as well as preventing unwanted scrutiny of the data, it is just as important to know that no one can enter new data, or change existing data, unless they have access. One disadvantage of electronically stored information is that a change can be made surreptitiously. Then it is just about as impossible to be sure that a change has been made, let alone know what the change was, what the original data was and so on.

Adequate password protection should be ensured by proper security checks installed in the system. In particular, ensure that the software gives the desired protection before buying the same.

Another form of data security is preventing data files being corrupted by accident. Once the files are created, they are subject to potential mishaps, such as fire, physical damage, being overwritten by other software, power failure in the middle of an updating session and so forth. All these can ruin the files.

One way of protecting the system against this is to backup the data files frequently. The frequency of data file backup can be decided by the user. Many organizations make copies of their stores receipt file every day, and most certainly at least once a week.

In this way, if a file needs to be replaced, the backup copy is used to over-write the bad file. Then any transactions that took place after the copy was made are re-entered to bring the restored file up-to-date.

INTERNAL COMMUNICATION

Data can be exchanged in any type of form— numbers, pictures, reports, programs, and spreadsheets. In fact, anything that can be stored on a floppy disk can be transferred down the telephone lines to another personal computer.

For store-keeping and inventory control, the applications are especially significant. For example, link open MRP files with files in another department such as Maintenance Department to see which materials have been ordered.

The application of interdepartmental linking is the most difficult. But if developed successfully, it can bring substantial benefit to the whole organization.

Transfer of data through computers offers a lot of advantages such as speed, accuracy, less manual effort, less paperwork, and less duplication of common data.

Prime examples of other departmental functions that can share data with Stores Division are, among others:

- Purchasing
- Production Planning
- Accounts Payable
- Maintenance Department
- Quality Control

Networking

Linking computers together is networking. The simplest form of networking is one in which a number of so called "dumb" terminals are hooked up to a main central computer. These terminals can receive and transmit data to and from the computer, but cannot process any data by themselves.

The next most powerful networking environment is one in which independent computers are attached to one mainframe. Like dumb terminals, each computer can communicate with the host computer. In addition, they can process their own data too in this environment; the local computers are sometimes referred to as "smart" terminals.

The most powerful networking arrangement using personal computers is where a group of computers linked to each other without a central, or host, computer. In this case, not only is each computer a smart terminal, but also each computer can share data with other computers in the system.

Because of this facility, there is no need for a massive central database of information. Each terminal communicates only with other terminals in other departments as required. This kind of networking is more difficult to instal than a straight stand-alone personal computer system.

Stores and Purchasing

Up-to-date knowledge of inventory information benefits every buyer. It helps buyers in the following ways:

- To keep a check on the quantities being called for on MRP
- To be alert if the quantity looks unusual
- It also gives the buyer latitude when deciding on the actual quantities shown on the requisition,
- It gives better understanding of the rates at which materials are being used.

In addition to the current on-hand inventory levels, the "inventory information" also includes history of usage, current inventory goals, such as target stock, minimum stock levels, maximum stock levels, economic order quantities, and so on.

The usage history of an item enables a second check to be done on the requisition quantities. For example, if a part had been used at an average rate of 50 per month, and was usually being ordered in monthly quantities, then a requisition for 5000 items clearly looks unusual, it being a 100 months supply at current consumption rates.

The time taken to check out the query on usage history on the screen is drastically reduced as compared to the time in making phone calls and/or going to see the appropriate person making the requisition to confirm the quantity.

Sometimes an item is available at a very low price for a short period of time. In such circumstances, the buyer would generally want to buy more than the requisition quantity in order to maximize savings. If the buyer knew quickly through the screen, what the current inventory levels are, and what the maximum inventory level has been set at, then he could make his decision on how much to buy to take advantage of the special situation.

Stores and Production, Maintenance and Finance

Lots of information is transacted between Stores Division and Production, Maintenance and Finance Departments. The Production Department can have direct access to the stock levels of various raw materials. The Stores Division can see the production plans on the screen of the terminal for controlling the inventory of raw materials.

The Maintenance Department can have access to the stock levels of various spare parts and can see the specifications of various items directly from the screen.

The Finance Department can see the status of inspection reports for settling supplier's invoices. It can also see the status of Discrepancy Reports resolved.

LEADING STORE-KEEPING AND INVENTORY CONTROL PACKAGES

There are number of software, which can meet the requirements of store-keeping and inventory control. For example:

SAM	:	Holderbank, Switzerland
R/2, R/B	:	SAP AG
Oracle Application	:	Oracle Corporation
People Soft	:	People Soft
Baan IV	:	BAAN Company
Marshal	:	Ramco Systems
BPCS	:	Systems Software Associates
MFG/PRO	:	QAD

All these software have similar features except for some additional features in one as compared to the other. The features of one of the leading packages "Computer Assisted Materials Management (SAM) are presented in brief here:

Computer Assisted Materials Management (SAM)

A general diagram of SAM is presented in Fig. 9.1. The SAM package has eight Store Modules as under:

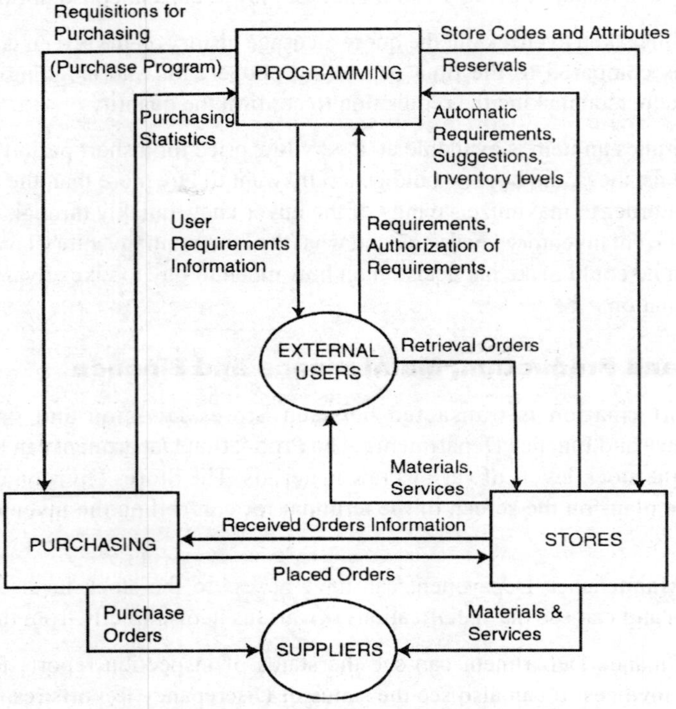

Fig. 9.1 SAM General Diagram

SRINIVASAN B

- Materials Entries
- Materials Retrievals
- Database Maintenance
- Reports
- Tools Control
- Inventory-Taking
- Value Adjustments
- Closing Processes

Table 9.3 Stores Module Function Description

S. No.	Module	Function
1	Materials Entries	This function allows registering all the transactions for entries of materials and services into the stores, which can be purchases, returns from users, borrowers or repairs. A quarantine process is available for those items requiring quality control previous to the acceptance.
2	Materials Retrievals	This function registers and controls all the outputs of materials from the inventory, being consumptions, loans and repairs, refusals to the suppliers, or sales. For the case of consumptions, the value of each one is calculated using a Last-In-First-Out process and is charged to the corresponding user or cost center.
3	Database Maintenance	This is a service function to define the data entities relevant to the stores operation, like the data in the Inventory Master file, material attributes, and location in the stores. This allows preserving the integrity and consistency of these data. Also, it is an available set of sub-functions to control the obsolete items in the inventory.
4	Reports	In this function can be integrated reports relative to inventory control, stores operation, and statistics addressed to different entities in the company including middle and high-level management.
5	Tools Control	This is a sub-system intended to control in a centralized way, the inventory and usage of tools pertaining to all the activities in the plant – specially maintenance – in order to keep as low as possible the costs related to tools and to generate profits from the complete use of this resource.
6	Inventory Taking	This function is to control and correct periodically the registered inventory stocks by updating them with hand-taken counts.
7	Value Adjustments	Through this function it is possible to update periodically the value of stocks in hand, in order to adjust it to the variations in the market prices due basically to inflation.
8	Closing Processes	This is a service function which performs all those operations required at the end of the day or month, to update historical data to transfer data to accounting or other systems, to backup important database files, and to prepare them to start a new operation period.

Table 9.4 Stores Module Menu Structure

S.No.	Module	Menu Structure
1	Material Entries	Entries by purchase. Entry by devolution from user. Entry forms lending. Entry by repairing.
2	Material Retrievals	Output by consumption. Output by refusal to supplier. Output by lending. Output by selling. Output for repairing. Output from direct charge.
3	Database Maintenance	Inventory Master file. Attributes file. Commercial description file Cost center file. Obsolete Parts Processing. Expenses accounts.
4	Reports	Stores inventory reports. Stores operation reports. Stores revaluation reports.
5	Tools Control	Control of handouts and refusals. Control of deductions. Control of tools.
6	Inventory Taking	Inventory Taking. Analysis of deviations. Authorization of adjustments. Inventory adjustment.
7	Value Adjustments	Revaluation of inventory. LIFO process.
8	Closing Processes	Daily closing process. Monthly closing process.

REFERENCES

1. Michiel R. Leenders et al, *Purchasing and Materials Management*, Richard D, Irwin Inc., Homewood, Illinois 60430, 1980 (Seventh edition), pp. 61 – 115.
2. Heinritz, Stwart F et al, *Purchasing Principles and Applications*, Printice-Hall Inc., Eaglewood Cliffs, N.J. 07632,1981, pp. 601 – 628.
3. Greens, James H; *Computer-based System, Production & Inventory Control Handbook*, pp. 23 – 12 to 23 – 33.
4. Bennet, William R., and James R Davey, *Data Transmission*, McGraw-Hill Book Company, Newyork, 1965
5. Dearden John, *Computers in Business Management*, Dow-Jones and Richard D. Irwin, Inc., Homewood, III., 1966.
6. Muth, J.F., and G.L. Thompson, *Industrial Scheduling*, Printice-Hall, Inc., Eaglewood Cliffs, N.J., 1963.
7. Popell, Steven D., Computer Time Sharing, *Dynamic Information Handling for Business*, Printice-Hall, Inc., Eaglewood Cliffs, N.J., 1966.
8. Savas, E.S., *Computer Control of Industrial Processes*, McGraw-Hill Book Company, New York, 1965.

CHAPTER 10

Performance Evaluation of Stores Activities

INTRODUCTION

Efficient operations of Stores Division is one of the most important factors in maintaining high operational efficiency as well as achieving high productivity in an industrial plant. Productivity of a plant can be increased if materials of the right quality are made available in the right quantity at the right time and place. This would mean that there is neither a shortage of materials nor an excess of inventory. Further, materials are stored properly so that they are available when needed and their quality does not deteriorate during storage. Attempts are made to standardize the materials by reducing variety. Obsolete materials are removed from the inventory. In spite of its best efforts to provide efficient services, the Stores Division is often criticized for various shortcomings that are observed in its day-to-day operations.

CRITICISM OF STORES DIVISION

The Stores Division is often criticized for various reasons, some of which are genuine problems faced by the users and could be overcome by proper planning and organization. Some issues are difficult to resolve due to limited resources at the command of the stores. The main areas of criticism are:

- Poor inventory control
- Improper store-keeping
- Improper tools management
- Delays in inspection
- Poor record keeping
- Inefficient operational control

Poor Inventory Control

- Maximum and minimum levels are not maintained properly.
- Normal items of regular consumption such as brooms, brushes, lubricants, batteries, tyres etc., are frequently out-of-stock. If such easy-to-procure items are out-of-stock, how can the stores manage the availability of the items which are difficult to purchase?
- Replenishment of materials is not done with efficiency.
- Inventory value is too high.
- Many of the items have wrong specifications and the specifications are not updated regularly.
- There are a number of obsolete items in the stores.
- There is no control over the slow moving and non-moving items.

Improper Store-keeping

- Materials are not stored properly, which results in spoilage. For example, V Belts are kept in the racks instead of hanging them on a bracket or a cantilever. Ball and roller bearings are not greased and wrapped in special paper for safekeeping. Tyres are stored flat on the ground instead of being stored vertically. Steel items are stored on the ground instead of storing them on the stands specially fabricated for the purpose.
- Materials are not arranged in an orderly manner in the stores.
- Important and costly materials are stored in open yards. Exposure to sun, moisture, and rain during long storage affect these materials adversely. The quality of these materials deteriorate and sometimes they become unsuitable for further use.
- Materials are not stored safely. There are cases of thefts.
- Some items are found at two different locations.
- Items stored in more than one store are not linked.

Improper Tools Management

- Proper tools and tackles not available for unpacking and packing the packets.
- Tools and tackles stored are not in working order.

Inefficient Operational Control

- The Stores issue timings are not adequate. The users find it difficult to get the materials issued in the limited time for which stores are open for issue. Repair works are delayed due to non-availability of the items in case of unforeseen breakdowns of machines.
- The Stores take an unduly long time in issuing the items requisitioned.
- Trucks bringing the materials have to wait for long before they are allowed in the stores for unloading of the materials.

- Items received in the stores are not accounted for sometimes.
- Physical verification of store items is not done regularly. The quantity of items in the records may be different from that of the actual quantity on the racks.
- Items with limited shelf-life remains on the shelves even after the expiry date.

Delays in Inspection

- Delays in inspection of items received in the stores. Timely information is not given to the user for inspection of the items.
- Mistakes in counting the quantity of the materials and in some cases even in correct identification of the items.

Poor Record Keeping

- Records are not up-to-date. Retrieval of information takes too much time.
- Stores records are not reliable. It takes a long time to establish the correct status of the stock.

Delays in Reporting

- Reports on Critical items are not submitted to the management on time.

PERFORMANCE EVALUATION

In order to improve the performance of the Stores Division and to reduce the criticism from other departments, it is essential that the performance of the Stores Division is evaluated regularly with respect to its various activities and corrective measures are taken in time.

Advantages of Performance Evaluation

Performance evaluation helps in the following:

- To increase the efficiency of the warehouse.
- To improve the productivity of the Stores Division.
- To induct a professional approach in various areas.
- To identify the weak areas for improvements.
- To continually identify strong areas, for further maximization of benefits.
- To create a competitive environment for improving the working of the Stores Division in comparison to other departments of the organization, as well as the stores Division of other organizations.
- To maximize the utilization of existing resources of materials, men, and facilities.
- To modernize the working of the warehouse and induct the latest technological developments in its functioning.

Inventory-carrying cost is a hidden cost, which has an impact on the product cost. Inventory is essential to carry on production activities even though it does not add to the value of the product. Control of various activities including control of inventory is possible by comparing the performance with some yardsticks. These yardsticks may already exist for the industry or for similar organizations. In certain cases, the yardsticks might not have even been developed. Often, these yardsticks are not fully identified. In the absence of any yardstick for the industry or for similar organizations, company yardsticks should be developed for evaluation of its performance in various areas.

PERFORMANCE INDICATORS

The yardsticks for various activities are termed as Performance Indicators (PI). Review of Performance Indicators, working out the values of Performance Indicators, and evaluating the performance of the Stores Division in the context of Performance Indicators is an important and continuous activity and should be done as per schedule. Performance Indicators should be representative of the concerned activity.

Performance Parameters (PP) and Performance Indicators (PI) can be developed for the following domains:

- store-keeping as a service function
- quality assurance
- cost reduction
- inventory control

A number of PP and PI under each domain of performance evaluation are used for evaluation purposes. Different levels of management need to focus on different PI. Table 10.1 and Table 10.2 list out various Performance Parameters (PP) and Performance Indicators (PI) under each domain of performance evaluation of the Stores Division and show their relevance to different levels (top, middle, and lower) of management.

Attention given by top, middle and lower levels of management is different to different Performance Parameters (PP) and Performance Indicators (PI). 'Store-keeping as a service function' draws attention of all the three levels of management. In some cases more attention is given by the lower level of management as compared to other levels, whereas in some other cases the middle and top level of management give more attention. Routine activities draw more attention from the lower level of management. Stock levels of major materials draw more attention from the top level of management, whereas consumption of materials draws more attention from the middle level of management.

Performance Parameters (PP) and Performance Indicators (PI) relating to 'Quality Assurance' get more attention from the middle level of management.

Cost reduction and inventory control domains constantly get the attention of the top and middle management levels. These are the most important domains in the performance evaluation of warehouse activities.

PARAMETERS TO BE EVALUATED

Very often a question arises, whether all the Performance Parameters (PP) (Table 10.1) and Performance Indicators (PI) (Table 10.2) are to be evaluated. The answer is yes, but the Stores Division may not be in a position to generate information for evaluation of all the Performance Parameters/Performance Indicators. A large number of PP and PI often necessitate the warehouse personnel to carry out this work also in addition to the routine work on hand. The result is that the Stores Division limits the evaluation of its performance to some important parameters only. Stores Managers are often heard complaining about the followings

Table 10.1 Parameters Used by Different Levels of Management for Evaluation of Performance

Sl. No.	Performance Evaluation Domain	Performance Parameters		Management Levels		
				Top	Middle	Lower
1.	Store-Keeping as a Service Function	1	Major materials stock report			
			• Raw material 1	•		
			• Raw material 2	•		
			• Raw material 3	•		
			• Fuel	•		
			• Explosives	•		
			• Packing materials like bags	•		
		2	Consumption of A items and B items	•	•	
		3	Purchase Requisitions prepared			
			• Routine		•	•
			• Urgent		•	•
			• Total		•	•
		4	Consignment received			
			• From foreign suppliers			•
			• From local suppliers			•
			• Total			•
		5	Issue Notes prepared		•	•
		6	No. of items issued			•
		7	Notes on deterioration, obsolescence, pilferage, etc.	•	•	

2	Quality Assurance	1	MRN Processed			
			• Stock items		•	•
			• Direct issue items		•	•
			• Total		•	•
		2	Discrepancy Report prepared		•	•
		3	Items in Discrepancy Report		•	•
		4	Discrepancy Report resolved.		•	•
		5	Items accepted			
			• Stock items			•
			• Direct items			•
			• Total			•
		6	Items, whose specifications are updated.		•	•
3	Cost reduction	1	Savings by change in specifications.		•	
		2	Savings by standardization.		•	
		3	Stores-handling cost.	•	•	
		4	Losses in stores.	•	•	
		5	Reduction in inventory levels.	•	•	
		6	Reduction in variety.		•	
4	Inventory control	1	Investment in:			
			• Raw materials	•	•	
			• Spare parts	•	•	
			• Consumables	•	•	
			• Packing materials	•	•	
			• Total	•	•	
		2	Inventory increase or decreasing during the month, especially in case of raw materials and major materials.		•	

		3	Inventory turnover (By commodity classification).		•	
		4	A list of category A and B items, where lead-time for delivery has changed or is likely to change in the near future.		•	•
		5	Machine down-time due to shortage of materials.	•	•	
		6	Revision of production schedule due to shortage of materials	•	•	
		7	Total materials, including raw materials stores, components, and the other items, used in the process of manufacture	•	•	
		8	Total work in progress.		•	
		9	Finished Goods.	•	•	
		10	Inventory overall turnover.		•	
		11	Manufacturing materials turnover.		•	
		12	Value of scrap		•	•

Table 10.2 Performance Indicators Used by Different Levels of Management for Evaluation of Performance

Sl. No	Performance Evaluation	Performance parameters		Management Levels		
1	Domain Store keeping as a Service Function			Top	Middle	Lower
		1	No. of purchase requisitions		•	•
		2	Average no. of purchase requisitions prepared (routine)/ month.		•	•
		3	Average no. of purchase requisitions prepared (routine)/employee/ month.		•	

		4	Average no. of purchase requisitions prepared (urgent)/month.	•	•	•
		5	Average no. of purchase requisitions prepared (urgente/mployee/month.		•	•
		6	No. of requisitions delivered on time as percentage of the total number of requisitions.		•	
		7	Average no. of items (routine) in Purchase Requisitions/month.		•	•
		8	Average no. of items (routine) in Purchase Requisitions/ employee/month.		•	
		9	Average no. of items (urgent) in Purchase Requisitions/month.		•	•
		10	Average no. of items (urgent) in Purchase Requisitions/employee/mo nth		•	
		11	Average no. of inspection reports for stock items processed/month.		•	
		12.	Average no. of inspection reports processed for stock items/employee/month.		•	
		13	Average no. of inspection reports for direct issue items processed/month		•	
		14	Average no. of inspection reports processed for direct issue items/employee/month.		•	
		15	Average no. of inspection reports for total number of items processed/month.		•	
		16	Average no. of inspection reports processed for total number of items/employee/month.		•	

		17	Area of storage space used as percentage of the total space available.		•	
		18	Service indicator: No. of demands met in time Vs Total no. of demands received (%)		•	
2	Quality Assurance	1	No. of items, whose specifications were updated vs. total number of items in inventory (%)		•	
		2	No. of Discrepancy Report vs. total number of inspection Reports (%)		•	
		3	No. of items in Discrepancy Reports vs. total number of items inspected (%)		•	
3	Cost Reduction	1	Stores-handling cost as percentage of total value of stores received and issued	•	•	
		2	Losses in stores as percentage of total value of stores received and issued	•	•	
		3	Inventory-carrying cost indicator: Total cost of holding inventories vs. Average value of inventory (%)	•	•	
		4	Savings by change in specifications vs. average value of inventory (%) .		•	
		5	Reduction in inventory levels vs. average value of inventory (%)	•	•	
		6	Reduction in variety vs. number of items in inventory (%)		•	

4	Inventory Control	1	Value of inventory as a percentage of turnover.	•	•	
		2	Value of inventory as a percentage of assets.	•	•	
		3	Machine down-time due to shortage of materials vs. available production hours (%)	•	•	
		4	Number of times the production schedule was revised due to shortage of materials.		•	
		5	Value of inventory per employee in Inventory Control Section.		•	
		6	Total materials, including raw materials, stores, components and other items used in the process of manufacture. (Expressed in terms of a month or a day's consumption)	•	•	
		7	Total work in progress. (Expressed as of month's production).	•	•	
		8	Finished Goods. (Expresssed as of month's cost of sales).	•		
		9	Inventory overall turnover ratio: Sales to inventory ratio = Sales at sales value/ Total average inventory.	•		
		10	Manufacturing materials turnover ratio: Inventory as number of days of consumption.	•		
		11	Work-in-progress ratio: inventory in days of production at production cost.	•	•	

		12	Finished goods ratio: inventory in days of sales at cost.	•	•	
		13	Service indicator: No. of demands met in time vs. Total no. of demands received (%)		•	
		14	Stock-out indicator: No. of items not met in time vs. Total no. of demands received (%)	•	•	
		15	Spare parts indicator: Value of spare parts inventory vs. Value of capital cost (%).	•	•	
		16	Value of spare parts inventory vs. total production (US$/ton).	•	•	
		17	Value of scrap left over vs. value of scrap disposed of (%).			•
		18	Discrepancies in stock taking as percentage of no. of items checked.		•	

- too many papers to handle
- very long procedures
- too much disturbance to normal work
- too many visitors taking up valuable time
- too many unscheduled urgent requisitions
- shortage of staff
- unprofessional staff
- untrained staff
- inadequate space for properly organizing the warehouse activities

It is reasonable that a beginning is made to evaluate only a few of the Performance Parameters and Performance Indicators. The PP and PI may be selected under each domain of performance evaluation, for which data is easily available. For example, reports for number of purchase requisitions prepared, number of items covered, number of issues made, number of inspections done, number of Discrepancy Reports prepared, number of stock items in the inventory can be prepared without any problem. Gradually, the base of the PP and PI should be enlarged. Proper formats should be developed to generate the required information. Evaluation of Performance Parameters and Performance Indicators will require information from within the Stores Division as well as from other departments. Details about production data and materials substituted etc., are required from the Production Department. Details of machine downtime will be available from the Maintenance Department. Cost figures with their breakups are required from the Finance Department. The information on all these aspects is organized in a period of one to two years from the start. Thereafter, a flow of information is established and performance evaluation activities become a regular activity of the Stores Division.

All the Performance Parameters should be analyzed properly and the relevant Performance Parameters and Performance Indicators are reported to different levels of management, that is, the top, middle and lower levels of management.

Performance evaluation activity should be assigned to one of the officials in the Stores Division. Normally this responsibility is given to the Supervisor, Records Section, who would generate various reports for review by the respective levels of management.

HOW IS PERFORMANCE EVALUATION CARRIED OUT

The first step in the performance evaluation activity is to structure the scheme of performance evaluation and obtain the approval of the management. As time progresses, necessary improvements, enlargements, modifications or deletions are carried out to meet the requirements. Proper reporting formats should be designed to present the information on time and in the form as required.

As some of the parameters depend upon information from other departments/ divisions/sections, it is necessary to follow a time schedule for reporting by each department/division/section. It must be ensured that the data or information is received on time from each source. The Supervisor, Records Section should follow a strictly scheduled program, and completes the analysis and presents his report to the management without delay. Timely preparation of reports is important, otherwise the very purpose of the exercise would be lost.

WHEN TO EVALUATE PERFORMANCE

Performance evaluation timing and frequency depends upon the requirements of the various levels of management. At lower levels, A monthly reporting is desirable, whereas at the middle level, the frequency of reporting can be three months for some parameters and 6 months for some others. Similarly, the top level of management may require different reports at different frequencies such as monthly, quarterly or yearly. As one goes up in the management hierarchy, the management pyramid tapers down. The same is true with the information arising out of the performance evaluation exercise. The information from performance evaluation should be structured in such a way that the top level of management get only the necessary and relevant information. There is no point in loading the top level of management with too much data or information. The report to the top level of management should be concise, to the point, reliable, clear and timely.

LESSONS TO BE DRAWN FROM PERFORMANCE EVALUATION

Every performance evaluation report whether, monthly, quarterly or yearly brings out issues about the working of the division and its various sections and identifies areas of possible improvement. Any deviation from the norms should be critically examined. Reasons for the deviations should be closely studied and suggestions for corrective action should be made. Based on these suggestions, the views of involved departments, divisions, sections, or even individuals should be obtained. Thereafter, directions are given about changing the practices and procedures wherever necessary. In case a need is felt to review the policies and procedures, corrective action should be taken without delay.

Every performance evaluation report provides an opportunity to the management to review its policies and procedures, so as to match them with the needs of the competitive business environment, technological scenario, and national and international policy changes. This is one of the most important roles of the performance evaluation of warehouse activities. The role is even more crucial, as the warehousing activities affect both internal as well as external activities of the department and have a decisive impact on the ultimate results, that is, the profitability and productivity of the whole organization. Performance evaluation has thus become the most important management tool to bring about any change for improvement.

CHAPTER 11

ISO Standards and Warehouse Activities

INTRODUCTION

Appropriate quality suitable for a given purpose is considered as the right quality. Therefore, the cost of an item and its quality go hand in hand. A high-quality item will cost more whereas a low-quality can be obtained at a lower cost. An item may be produced by more than one manufacturer conforming to the same standards, yet the quality of one may be superior to the quality of the other with a substantially higher cost. Higher quality may be preferred in some cases, even at a higher cost. Organizations have realized the importance of the quality assurance program.

Systems, programs, policies and procedures are, therefore, developed to achieve the required quality of the final product. Implementation of quality systems, programs, policies and procedures assures the quality of the product.

ISO STANDARDS

The ISO 9000 series consists of five documents, which are:

- ISO 9000: Quality Management and Quality Assurance Standards, the guidelines for selection and use.
- ISO 9001: Quality System, Model for Quality Assurance in Design/ Development, Production, Installation, and Servicing.
- ISO 9002: Quality System, Model for Quality Assurance in Production and Installation.
- ISO 9003: Quality system, Model for Quality Assurance in Final Inspection and Test.
- ISO 9004: Quality Management and Quality System Elements Guidelines.

ISO 9001, ISO 9002, and ISO 9003 are the main quality system documents and are models for quality assurance. The focus of these standards is on the documentation of operational techniques, managerial activities and controls to meet the expectations and requirements of the customers. These standards are not specific industry oriented but are generic in nature and are therefore applicable to all industrial sectors.

ISO 9000 and ISO 9004 standards are in fact guidelines only. The ISO 9000 set of guidelines is for customers/buyers and suppliers to select an appropriate quality assurance model as relevant to a particular contractual relationship. ISO 9004 provides the set of guidelines to develop and implement the quality management system.

NEED FOR ISO STANDARDS

ISO standards are something more than a model for quality assurance. ISO standards provide an opportunity to improve the management system and managerial style of functioning, and they can help an organization to reduce its internal cost/or increase its efficiency. In fact, the adoption of ISO standards is seen as an opportunity to develop a Total Quality Management concept. Adoption of ISO Standards are useful to any organization as its implementation results in number of advantages such as the following:

- leads to team effort
- encourages collective commitment
- creates clear understanding
- improves communication
- prepares a base for total quality management

REGISTRATION FOR ISO CERTIFICATION

Registration should be obtained for one, two or all the three quality assurance models only, that is, for ISO 9001, ISO 9002 and ISO 9003. ISO 9001 standard is the most comprehensive of all the three models for quality assurance. It consists of twenty paragraphs as detailed in Table 11.1.

Paragraph 10 deals with Inspection and Testing covering the following aspects:

- Receiving Inspection and Testing
- In-process Inspection and Testing
- Final Inspection and Testing
- Inspection and Test Records

Paragraph 15 deals with handling, storing, packing and delivery. Paragraph 16 deals with Quality Records. These activities are the normal activities of any Stores Division. Inspection and testing in the context of Stores Division refers to the receiving inspection and testing of all incoming materials received from the suppliers against purchase orders or contracts.

WAREHOUSE ACTIVITIES AND QUALITY ASSURANCE

The quality of a product is directly linked with the materials used in its manufacturing. The warehouse plays an important role in many ways in any quality assurance program. Material's specification is important so that the materials of the desired quality only are procured. The quality of the materials is checked through inspection. Laying specifications and maintaining the quality of the incoming materials through appropriate inspection are important factors in the quality assurance program.

Quality assurance is greatly dependent on the Quality System Management. The Stores Division should develop systems and procedures for various activities of handling, storing packing and delivery of materials for building up a healthy Quality System Management. Documentation is another important area towards maintaining quality assurance.

Table 11.1 Paragraphs Covered in ISO 9001

Paragraph Number	Title of the paragraphs
1	Management Responsibility
2	Quality System
3	Contract Review
4	Design Control
5	Document Control
6	Purchasing
7	Purchaser Supplied Products
8	Product Identification and Traceability
9	Process Control
10	Inspection and Testing
11	Inspection, Measuring, and Test Equipment
12	Inspection and Test Status
13	Control of Nonconforming Products
14	Corrective Action
15	Handling, Storage, Packaging and Delivery
16	Quality Records
17	Internal Quality Audits
18	Training
19	Servicing
20	Statistical Techniques

Quality system records should be developed to provide an information system, which would guide in formulation of specifications, updating specifications, inspection of materials, and also help maintain systems procedures for the warehouse activities.

Materials can be divided into three categories:

- Materials, which directly become the part of the product. For example, raw materials are converted into the product after the manufacturing process. It is necessary to maintain the quality of raw materials for maintaining the quality of final product.
- Materials, which do not become part of the final product, but have an influence on the quality of final product. For example, quality of fuel, that is, coal/diesel/gas affects the manufacturing process in a cement plant and thereby the quality of the product, that is, the clinker. Similarly, the quality of lubricants and oil, or important spares and components decides the smooth and uninterrupted operation of the plant and machinery. Interrupted operations adversely affect the quality of the product being manufactured, and in some cases may result in spoilage or even wastage of the product due to its poor quality.
- Materials, which do not influence the quality of product being manufactured but are needed to produce the items. For example, tyres and tubes are required to run the vehicles, they are required as support facilities for carrying out plant operations. The quality of these items is also important for efficient operation of the plant, yet it is not part of the Quality System Management.

Specifications

Specifications are very important for describing an item correctly and fully. The specifications of the materials should be developed, approved, reviewed and updated to procure materials of the desired quality.

A quality assurance program is aimed to achieve quality in all the materials purchased. Special emphasis will however be on those materials, which form part of the product, that is, raw materials.

The Stores Division plays a key role in getting inputs from the user department, Quality Control Department and Purchase Division for finalizing the specifications. It also ensures that the specifications are complete and all related documents such as parts lists with part number, photographs, drawings, samples, and details of mother equipment are available to provide any clarifications to suppliers for correct identification and supply of the items. Systematic development of specifications enables one to take care of all the characteristics or properties essential in the materials being purchased, which will ultimately result in producing the desired product.

The Stores Division attempts to encourage competition and to make sure that specifications are not tailored to any particular product and conforms to the established commercial and industrial standards, to the extent possible.

Formulation of specifications The Stores Division follows a definite pattern during formulation of the specifications, which acts as a guide to the writer of the specifications preventing oversights, loopholes, or omissions. A set pattern is also easy for the user looking for the needed information.

The following elements of specifications are kept in view while finalizing of the specifications:

- Reference to the standard specification is made.
- A statement of the various types, grades, classes and sizes of materials is given in the specifications.
- The statement pertaining to the use for which the material or equipment is intended.
- A statement of the kind of materials and workmanship required in a fabricated item is covered by the specification, and also of any special method of production or manufacture that is required.
- Non-essential quality restrictions are avoided. Quality restrictions create difficulties in procurement and adds to avoidable cost without adding to utility and value.
- General requirements common to all types, grades and classes of the materials covered.
- Detailed requirements peculiar to each type, grade, and class in the specification.
- Inspection and test procedure to be used and the stage/location for the inspection in determining the quality of materials.
- Instructions for packing, labelling, printing, logos, color combination, marking on the shipments etc.

Methods of specifications The Stores Division normally uses following methods of specifications:

- Use of brand name
- Use of a sample
- Formal specifications
- By drawings

The Stores Division keeps all the control samples in a systematic manner with all related information for quick reference. The supplier's catalogues are properly kept for any reference. All drawings are kept safely with details of drawing numbers, name of the items, name of the machine including the name of the manufacturer.

Updating the specifications The specifications are kept updated with full information of any change in the supplier, the user, design personnel, inspection personnel etc. In case of any revision, the new specification is given a new number and effective date, with the notation that it supersedes a particular previous one. As a precaution, all outstanding copies of the outdated specifications are recalled and destroyed. A record is kept about all persons or departments to whom copies of specifications have been issued, and wherever copies are sent out to vendors for bidding or ordering purposes.

Materials Inspection

Inspection of incoming materials received from the suppliers has three important components:

- Physical inspection is the quantity inspection and checking the dimensions of the item.
- Visual inspection, that is, checking the physical condition of materials received.
- Chemical analysis or testing for other parameters such as hardness, density, ductility, thermal expansion etc., to establish the desired characteristics of the material. These tests are conducted in the testing laboratory of the organization. In some cases, the materials samples are sent to Expert Testing Organizations for carrying out the tests. The facilities for such specialized tests may be available with these Expert Testing Organizations only.

Raw materials are consumed in large quantities on a regular basis as compared to other materials. Raw materials form a large portion of the cost of the product. Every care is taken that the quality of the raw materials is controlled right from the point of its mining. The quality is further checked at the dispatch point and at the receiving point or at plant. The test results of raw materials should be representative of the whole quantity of the raw materials rather than that of the few samples taken for testing. For this purpose, detailed procedures are developed for collecting samples from different lots of supplies. Large number of samples are collected and a representative sample is prepared to represent the whole quantity.

The raw material quality control plan includes the following:

- Sampling and testing frequency chart of raw materials
- Controlling parameter and action plan for raw materials
- Sampling methods
- Testing methods
- Raw materials selection and acceptance criteria

Any loose end in the quality control plan and procedures is likely to affect the ultimate test results. In some cases of raw materials, the cost of the materials is dependent on the quality of the material received. Therefore, inspection of raw materials is of great importance from the point of view of the cost involved as well as the fear of rejection of the material, in case quality of raw materials does not conform to the specifications.

The procedures for sample collection, sample preparation, and testing is developed by standard organizations or by research institutions after lot of research and statistical analysis. The test procedures and methodologies are specific to each material.

Care is further taken to keep controlled samples for a predetermined period of time for purpose of re-testing in case of any doubt or for a need for reconfirmation of the results. The comprehensive testing procedures involves lot of effort and money, and ensures the quality of the material.

Inspection of materials has been discussed in detail in Chapter 3 'Receipt and Inspection of Materials', in this book, which deals in great detail with the process of inspection of materials received in the stores.

After completing the inspection, the next step in quality assurance will be preparation of Discrepancy Report, if any. Discrepancies are to be resolved before using the materials.

Handling, Storing, Packing, and Delivery

Handling, storing, packing and delivery in the context of ISO 9001 refers to development of the documented procedures, which guarantee proper handling, secure storage designed to prevent damage or deterioration of the product, packing which conforms to specified requirements and delivery procedures which maintains the integrity of the product after final inspection. All incoming materials should be received, inspected, accepted if conforming to the specifications and stored properly. The materials are issued to the users on request. There should be proper management systems to take care of all the stores operations. The Stores Division develops systems and procedures

Table 11.2 List of Procedures in Stores Division

Main Activities	Title of Procedures
Requisitioning and replenishing of materials	Replenishment of stock items
	Requisition for new/out-of-stock items
	Processing and approval of Materials Requisition for Purchase
	Amendments/cancellations of Materials Requisition for Purchase
	Updating, status, follow-up and control of Materials Requisitions for Purchase
Receipt and inspection of materials	Handling of control samples
	Recording of additional/new specifications
	Reporting and handling of discrepancies
	Receipt and inspection of materials
	Materials returned by User Department
Warehousing operations	Security, safety and maintenance
	Issue of materials
	Stock taking
	Control of Tools, surplus materials, and scrap materials

including their documentation to assist in total quality management system of the organization. A representative list of various procedures for a Stores Division is presented in Table 11.2. The list will be different for different organizations. The importance of each procedure and their procedural details will depend on the type of the industry or organization. In case of some companies, storage may be a very important activity, whereas in other cases it may not be so important. Instead, packing and handling may be more important.

Quality Records

Proper record keeping, maintenance, and their retention are part of quality assurance program. The quality records in the context of Stores Division may include the followings

- Procedures (Table 11.2)
- Detailed specifications of various items
- Inspection reports
- Discrepancy reports
- Test reports
- Details of approved period of retention of various documents.
- List of formats used in store-keeping activities (Table 11.3)

Table 11.3 List of Forms Used in the Stores Division

S. No.	Title of the Form	Appendix Number
1	Materials Requisition (MR)	2.1
2	Material Requisition for Purchase (MRP)	2.2
3	Material Replenishment Report (MRR)	2.3
4	Material Requisition for Purchase Update (MRPU)	2.4
5	Material Dispatch and Receipt Report (MDRR)	3.1
6	Dispatch and Receipt Note (DRN)	3.2
6	Material Inspection Note (MIN)	3.3
7	Direct Issue Stores Voucher (DISV)	3.4
8	Materials Receipt and Inspection Note (MRIN)	3.5
9	Stores Requisition & Issue Notes (SRIN)	4.1
10	Inventory Adjustment Form (IAF)	4.2
11	Return Note (RN)	4.3
12	Discrepancy Report (DR)	6.1
13	Tools Issue/Return Note	7.1
14	Tools/Equipment Updates	7.2
15	Quaterly Report of Tools/Equipment Available in ……	7.3
16	Scrap Declaration (SD)	7.4

Record keeping is an important aspect of ISO 9001 Standards. Most of the organizations have a good to fair record keeping. However, it should be ensured among other things that the location of all records is identified, that pertinent records are up-to-date, reviewed as need be, as well as properly archived and retained for a predetermined period of time.

STORES DIVISION ACTIVITIES IN CONFORMANCE TO ISO 9001

Development and implementation of systems and procedures relating to various activities of the Stores Division is necessary for Quality System Management. It is necessary that the various elements of ISO 9001 are understood properly and implemented to achieve the quality of the final product in the most efficient and economic manner. This calls for good housekeeping, well-laid procedures for receiving , inspection, storing, issue and handling of materials in the stores. To ensure that all the procedures and practices being followed are in conformance to ISO 9001 and that every thing is in order, a checklist should be prepared. The checklists differ from case to case and should be tailored to suit the requirements of each organization. A checklist for such an examination is given below.

Checklist

- Do you have a procedure for finalization of specification?
- Who are involved in finalization of the specifications?
- Are part numbers, drawing numbers, and specifications updated?
- Do you have a procedure for updating the specifications?
- Do you have a procedure for testing of raw materials and other important materials?
- Do you maintain records indicating that the materials have passed the inspection tests with defined acceptance criteria?
- Do you have separate storage space for controlled samples?
- How are discrepancies recorded and resolved?
- Do you keep non-conforming products identified separately?
- Do you have a program for stockchecking?
- Do you have procedures for receiving, inspection, handling, storage, packing and delivery of materials? Give details of procedures finalized.
- Do you have a system to review and updating of the procedures?
- Do you have a procedure to handle control samples?
- Have you a list of Quality System documents with their locations identified?
- When purchased products needs to be released for urgent use in production or maintenance, are they identified and recorded?
- Do you file your Quality Records?

REFERENCES

1. James, L. Lamprecht, *ISO 9000, Preparing for Registration*, Marcel Dekker Inc., 270 Madison Avenue New York, New York 10016, USA, 1992, pp. 3,22,23.
2. Raghu N. Kacker, "Quality Planning for the Service Industries", *Quality Progress*, August 1988, pp. 39 – 42.
3. Carol A. King, 'A Framework for a Service Quality Assurance System', *Quality Progress*, September 1987, pp. 27 – 32.
4. Walter Willborn, *Quality Management System: A Planning and Auditing Guide*, 1989.

CHAPTER 12

Warehouse Location, Layout, and Facilities Planning

INTRODUCTION

Efficiency is the ratio of input and output. However, with the same input, there can be different outputs. It can be more or even less. If there is higher production with the same resources as compared to the earlier production, the plant is said to be working with higher productivity. A plant may be operating efficiently without any breakdown or shut down yet it might be giving a low production as compared to the previous year, which might have even witnessed frequent power cuts or breakdowns of the plant. This represents a case of low productivity of the plant. In another case, a plant may be employing much less manpower but may produce much higher as compared to the production of another plant of the same capacity and technology. This is a case of high productivity. Even though efficiency and productivity are two different things, they are linked to each other. A plant cannot be productive without being efficient, but the same is not true in the reverse case. For example, employees in a department may be working very hard and be very busy throughout the day, but their efforts may not be producing the commensurate results. This may be due to lot of wasteful work being done by them. Eliminating the wasteful work may improve the output with the same efforts and increase the productivity of the department. Thus, it is not enough to have high output—an indication of high efficiency—but the criteria is to have high productivity by achieving higher output with the same or even less resources.

Efficiency and productivity of a plant mainly depend on the working of various departments in the plant, which are directly involved in the production activities. Departments, which are not involved directly in the production activities but provide services which are equally important for the efficiency and productivity of the plant. The Stores Division is one of the most important divisions serving the needs of all the departments in the plant and influencing the efficiency and productivity of the plant, which greatly depends on four important factors as detailed below:

- Number of stores and their sizes
- Location of the stores
- Layout of the stores
- Facilities provided in the stores

Selecting the required number and proper size of the stores, their locations, layout arrangement, and facilities contribute greatly to the productivity of stores operations and their efficiency. A proper planning, execution and maintenance of the facilities in the stores go a long way in maintaining the efficient operations of the Stores Division, which ultimately results in higher productivity of the plant.

NUMBER AND SIZE OF STORES

The number and the size of each store depend upon the nature of plant activities and size of the plant. A large manufacturing plant needs a variety of materials for its production and maintenance activities. Various factors, which determine the number and sizes of stores, include the following:

- Number of items to be stored.
- Types of items stored, that is raw materials, spares for repairs and maintenance, oils and lubricants, explosives, chemicals, and electronics items etc. Each type of item needs a different types of storage facility.
- Shape of the materials, that is big boulders, lumps, powdery materials, liquids, or gases.
- Physical and chemical characteristics of the materials.
- Effect of heat, cold, rain, moisture, wind, snowfall, humidity, sun etc., on the materials. Some materials cannot be exposed to sun, water or cold.

These factors have a bearing on the number of stores and their sizes. Sizes of stores also depends upon the present needs of the plant as well as the future projected requirements. Enough scope should be kept to accommodate more number of items at a later date due to expansion or diversification of production activities. A small-sized store may be enough to meet the present requirements, but space should be earmarked for future expansion at the time of finalization of the plant layout itself. As an illustration, the details of various stores and the area of each store in a large cement plant are given in Table 12.1.

A large number of stores is not a desirable feature, but easy operation is the most important factor in deciding the number of stores. Efforts should be made to keep the number of stores as low as possible without sacrificing the efficiency of operations.

LOCATION OF STORES

Stores should be located at convenient places near to the place of operations. For example, raw material yards should be very close the materials preparation activities of the plant, that is, near the crushing section or grinding section. In case a number of raw materials are used in manufacturing the product, the raw material - which is used in maximum quantity should be located close to the production facilities. Raw materials used in small quantities can be stored farther away. This will help in saving on handling operations and the cost involved therein. A separate store may be there for quarry operations or for the Transport Department. Explosive stores and oil storage tanks should be in a separate and isolated place for safety reasons. The Main warehouse is normally very close to the workshop, mechanical and electrical repair shops. The finished product storage should be near the packing plant. Similarly, packing materials store should be close to the packing plant. Some of the stores are under the direct control of the operational departments. For example, raw material stores are normally under the control of Production Department, who would provide regular information to the Stores Division for keeping the records up-to-date. These arrangements are made keeping in view the overall efficiency of the plant.

Table 12.1 List of Stores and Their Areas in a Large Cement Plant

S. No.	Name of store	Area		Other details
		Description	Size	
1	Main Warehouse	Ground Floor	1875 m^2	18 racks of varying number of shelves and different sizes.
		First Floor	1120 m^2	63 Racks, Size 728L × 65D × 285H cm. (6 Shelves per rack).
		Total	2995 m^2	
2	Refractory Stores	Store # 1	1400 m^2	No. of Pallets : 2900
		Store # 2	165 m^2	No. of Pallets : 500
		Store # 3	175 m^2	No. of Pallets : 215
3	Explosive Stores	Store # 1	90 m^2	No. of beds : 6
		Store # 2	90 m^2	No. of beds : 6
		Store # 3	50 m^2	No. of beds : 10
4	Lubricant Store		750 m^2	700 Drums of 208 liters
5	Gasoline Storage Tank	Main Station	30,000 liters	1 Underground Steel Tank
6	Diesel Storage Tank	Main Station	2 × 30,000 liters	Underground Steel Tank
		Quarry Workshop	50,000 liters	Underground Steel Tank
		Power Station	1000,000 liters	Over ground Steel Tank
		Locomotive Shed	2,500 liters	Over ground Steel Tank
		Deep Wells	30,000 liters	Over ground Steel Tank

7	Store	Gas Cylinders	52 m²	Up to 150 cylinders
8	Yard	Open Storage (Fenced)	21,000 m²	
9	Yard	Scrap (Unfenced)	9,600 m²	
10	Yard	Empty Drum (Unfenced)	8,000 m²	
11	Raw Materials	Gypsum	6,500 m²	22,500 m³
		Bauxite	18,240 m²	36,500 m³
		Iron Ore	6,500 m²	13,000 m³
12	Furniture Store		225 m²	
13	Laboratory Store		50 m²	
14	Auto Parts Stores		110 m²	15 racks
15	Quarry Stores		250 m²	30 racks
16	Paper Bags Stores	Ground Floor	500 m²	
		First Floor	300 m²	
		Second Floor	500 m²	
		Third Floor	500 m²	
17	Clinic Store		6 m²	
18	Electronic Item Stores		10 m²	
19	Reconditioned Appliances Stores		30 m²	

Normally stores are located away from the main entrance of the plant, where visitors or customers are frequently coming to the plant. Stores are normally located near the side or rear entrance so that waiting trucks have no problem of parking space. Normally, the area near the store is not as clean as it should be near the main entrance of the organization. This makes it more important to have a separate entrance for the storage area.

Efforts should be made to locate the stores near the rail-line and highways to facilitate receipt and dispatch of materials and reduce handling cost and labor. Wind direction is another important consideration in location of stores for raw materials. If all the sides of the storage yard are open, lot of material in powdery form will fly away with the wind thus causing loss of material as well as creating environmental pollution. Proper selection of site for raw materials storage can eliminate many future problems.

LAYOUT PLANNING OF WAREHOUSE

Layout planning is one of the key issues for efficient operations of the warehouse. Layout will differ from one warehouse to another, depending upon the available space, type of items stored, number of items, and nature of operations. However, in normal situations, some of the points to be considered in layout planning are:

- Receipt and issue section should be as close to the main entrance as possible, to enable easy receipt and issue of materials. Outsiders, like truck drivers, should not enter the warehouses and should deliver the goods in the receipt section.
- Inspection bay should be arranged near the receipt section. This would help in minimizing the handling and movement of the materials. Inspection of the incoming materials is faster as materials are quickly transferred to inspection area.
- Warehouse issue counter should be away from receiving and inspection area. The user representative should be able to get the materials issued without any problem. Issue activities of the materials should not be affected by the activities of receipt and inspection. The issue counter should be in a covered area, so that the staff do not have to stand in the sun or rain while getting the materials issued.
- There should be separate rooms for keeping the accepted materials, separately from the rejected materials that are to be returned to the suppliers.
- The office of the Stores Manager should be near the entrance to keep an eye on all the persons coming in and going out as well as on the incoming and outgoing materials. Entry of unauthorized persons to the stores is greatly restricted through a proper watch by the Stores Manager.
- Heavy castings and components like pumps, compressors, and motors etc., should be kept on the ground floor, which should have concrete flooring. This will require less effort and time in unloading and keeping the materials properly in the store. This will reduce the possibility of any damage to the material in handling during shifting the materials to the upper floors if they were to be stored there.
- Light materials should be stored in racks on upper floors. Attempts should be made to use three-dimensional space to the maximum extent possible by storing the materials in racks and closed storewells.
- Materials, which are likely to be affected by exposure to sun, humidity or rain, should be stored in a covered area.
- Materials of attractive nature, which are prone to be pilfered or stolen, should be kept in a more protected area, not within easy reach of any outside staff.
- There should be enough space for movement of materials and men in the storage area. The forklift trucks and trolleys should be able to move easily.

- The materials should be arranged in the storage area in such a way that minimum movement of the material is involved in the storage area. The materials, which are received/issued frequently should be near to the receipt/ issue areas; whereas materials, which are received /issued occasionally, should be stored away from receipt/issue sections.

The layouts of main warehouse (Figs. 12.1 and 12.2), open storage yard (Fig. 12.3), and scrap yard (Fig. 12.4) in a cement plant are shown as an example of layout arrangements. There can be different layouts for the same items depending upon the site-specific conditions and requirements.

PHYSICAL FACILITIES PLANNING

The following guidelines are important in planning the facilities:

- Stores should be properly lighted to avoid any dark spots or shadows, which can be a source of accidents. Attempts should be made to allow natural light to the maximum extent possible.
- Proper ventilation is very essential in the stores. Exhaust fans should be provided at appropriate places, especially in areas, where bad smell can affect normal working or can damage other materials. For example, areas of belt conveyors, rubber materials, and chemicals are likely to give out a bad smell during storage. Chemicals may get spilled over on the floor during handling, storage, or physical verification of items in the stores.
- Storage area for liquids like chemicals, oils etc., should be of concrete or cemented with a slope for provision of washing, in case of spillage of materials on the floor.
- Stores should be provided with an adequate capacity EOT Crane for unloading of the materials from the truck as well as loading of the materials onto the trucks.
- Sufficient clearance above the crane and on the sides should be provided for efficient operations and maintenance activities of the facilities.
- The warehouse entrance door should have a collapsable and electrically operated door to facilitate easy closing and opening of the door. There should be a separate door for entry or exit of persons walking in or out.
- Door width and height should be enough to enable trucks with materials to enter the warehouse for unloading.
- Height of the warehouse shed should be about 6 meters to enable operations of chain pulley block for loading and unloading of the materials.
- Stores should have computer terminals at appropriate places for record keeping and retrieval of information quick.
- Some of the store areas should have controlled conditions. For example, electronic spares should be stored in an air-conditioned area.

- Compressed air is required for filling air in tyres of the vehicles or for cleaning purposes. In some cases, compressed air is required for testing purposes.
- Open yards and scrap yards should be evenly floored without any raised or deep areas. Parts of the open yard should be cemented to avoid stagnation of water. It is specifically important in storage areas of steel items.

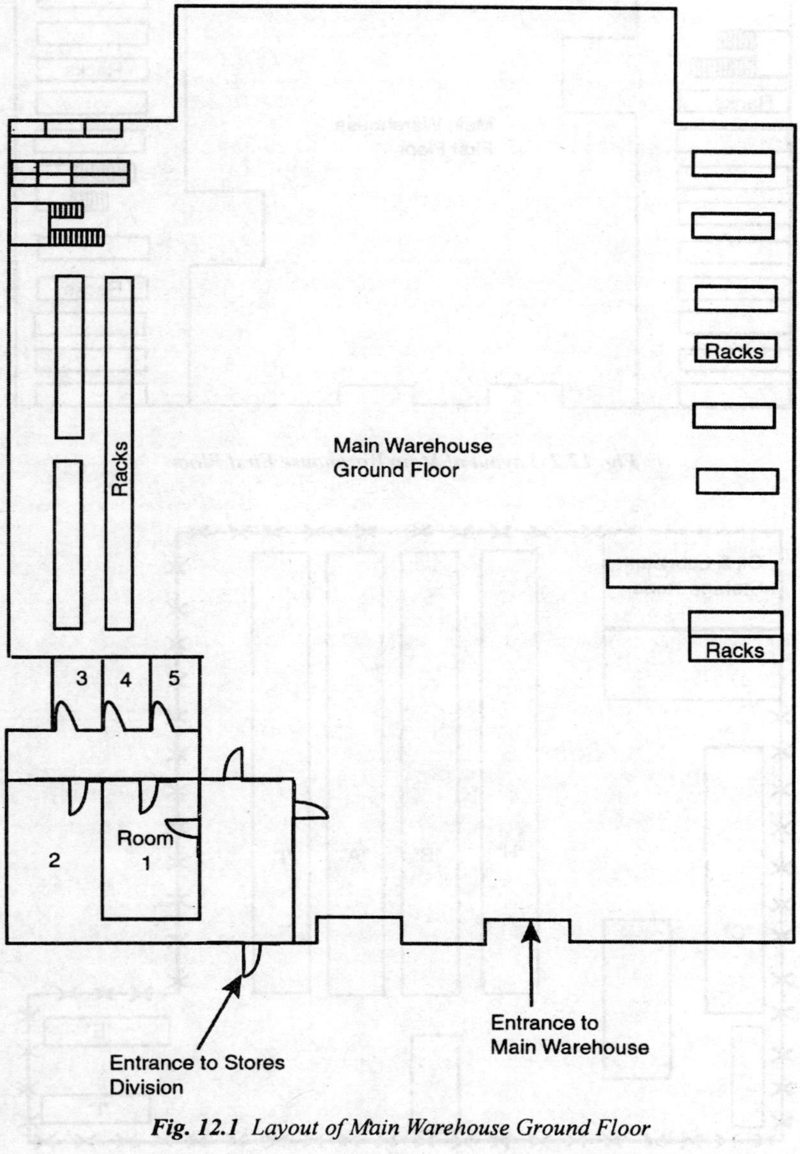

Fig. 12.1 Layout of Main Warehouse Ground Floor

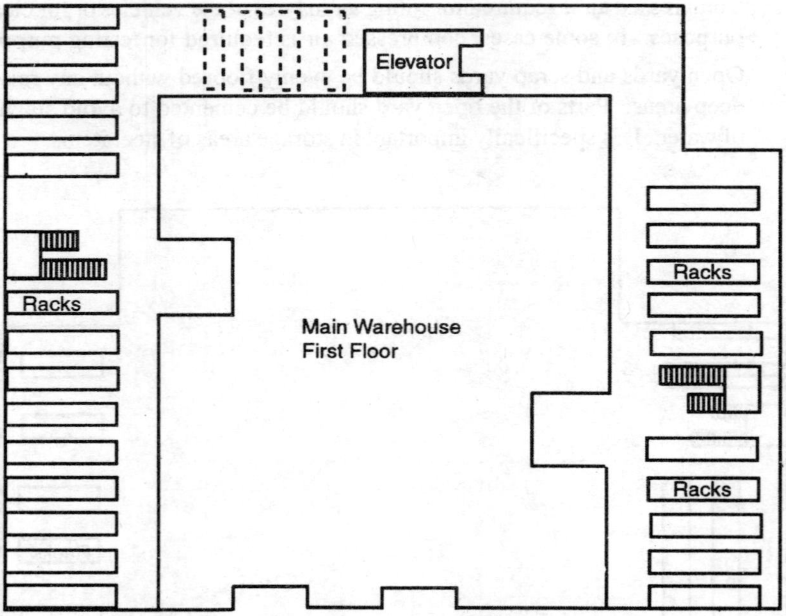

Fig. 12.2 Layout of Main Warehouse First Floor

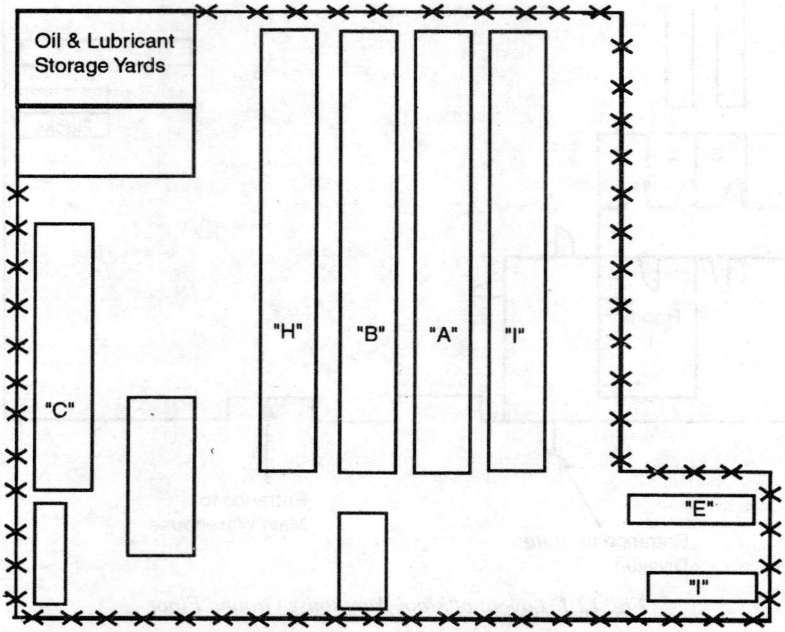

Fig. 12.3 Open Storage Yard

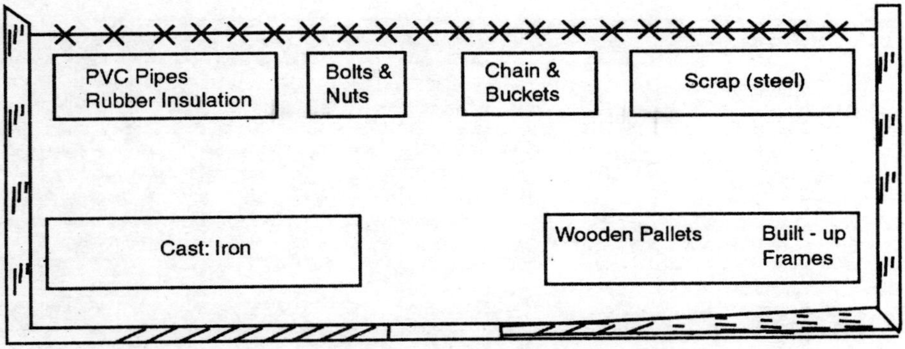

Fig. 12.4 Scrap Yard

- There should be sufficient number of tools, tackles, and equipment for handling of materials. The capacity and specifications of the tools, tackles, and equipment will vary from case to case. Some of the equipment, tools, and tackles commonly used in the stores are:• EOT Crane, 5/10 Tonne capacity, 10 Meters height
  - Hydraulic jacks, 1/2 Tonne capacity
  - Dump trucks, 2 Tonnes capacity
  - Wheel barrows
  - Trolleys
  - Forklift trucks, 2 Tonnes capacity, diesel/battery operated.
  - Damaged tires used for providing cushioning support for heavy materials during unloading
  - Iron Bars
  - Slings and ropes
  - Chain pulley blocks
  - Hammers
  - Spanners
  - Pliers
  - Wooden blocks
  - Pallets, wooden/steel

CHAPTER 13

Warehouse Security, Safety, and Maintenance

INTRODUCTION

A warehouse in an industrial unit has a large variety of items. The number of items in the warehouse is also very large, which may range from 50000 to 100000 in some plants, depending upon the nature and size of the plant. The value of the inventory in the warehouse may be millions of dollars. Many of the items in the warehouse are of attractive nature and are likely to be pilfered by the store staff, or by those who come for getting the items issued from the warehouse. Warehouses are also not free from thefts.

Besides security of items, some of the items need a suitable physical environment for their safety. For example, rubber items should not be exposed to sun or heat. Chemicals are to be stored away from the metallic parts as the chemical fumes may adversely affect the metallic components with corrosion. Similarly, refractory materials are to be kept in a dry space free from moisture. Any ingress of moisture will damage some of the refractory materials, making them unsuitable for use. Electronic components are to be stored at low temperatures as they are likely to be damaged above 50° C. Some of the materials are sensitive to dust. For example electrical contacts are likely to have a flashover in presence of dust and moisture. Different materials require different type of care to keep them safe and to ensure that they retain their characteristics even after a long storage period.

Some materials have a limited shelf-life, for example, cashable refractors, medicines, some chemicals, cable jointing materials and jointing materials for the conveyor belts. A close watch has to be kept in storage of such items and they are to be consumed before expiry of their life.

Safety of people is as important as the safety of materials. The Warehouse staff have to handle various types of items, for example, very heavy castings, big items, sharp-edged materials, chemicals, and explosives. They must use protective gadgets and follow safe working practices to avoid getting physically injured.

Fire is a big threat to stores. The warehouse should be protected from fire hazards. Any accidental fire can result in huge losses of materials.

Explosives are to be stored and handled with special care to ensure that nothing untoward happens during their storage and handling.

All these factors call for high order of systems design for warehouse security and safety. To ensure physical security and safety of materials in all the stores, the guidelines discussed in the following sections should be implemented and strictly followed.

SECURITY

Entry to Warehouse

- The entry to the warehouse/storage area should be controlled through a single door/gate, and no unauthorized person should be allowed inside the warehouse/storage area. This will plug the possibilities of pilferage of materials.
- Vehicle entrance gates in the main warehouse should be kept locked and opened only for receipt/issue of bulky items. If the gates are kept open, anybody can come in and go out with the materials without any difficulty.

Management of Warehouse Keys

- Keys of all the warehouse/storage areas should be kept in safe custody under the control of the Stores Manager.
- The store keys should be assigned to storekeepers permanently stationed at stores. Where no storekeeper is permanently assigned, the Officer, Warehousing Section will, as required, issue store keys to authorized persons and should record receipt and return in the Key Issue Register. The Key Issue Register should have up-to-date entries at all times.
- All keys other than those permanently assigned must be taken back at the end of the workday and kept under safe custody.
- Explosive/dangerous material's stores keys must be kept in a separate steel box controlled by the Officer, Warehousing Section, and issued only to the concerned Storekeeper for receipt/issue of explosive, when necessary.

Closing of Warehouse

- The Officer, Warehousing Section is responsible for ensuring that, prior to his departure, all warehouse/storage area doors/gates are properly secured. The door locks should be sealed properly with the signature of the Stores Officer with date and time of closure.
- Names of the persons who are required to work after the working hours and on holidays for issue of materials in an emergency should be pre-planned and

be informed to all concerned. In case the duty chart is not needed in advance, only authorized persons should be allowed to open the stores as and when needed.

- Any damage to locks/keys must be immediately reported to the Stores Manager, who should report the loss of the keys to the Security Officer and arrange replacement of locks on an urgent basis.
- Attractive items are to be kept in secured areas/locked cabinets. A close vigilance should be kept for attractive items such as bulbs, pen, erasers, small tools, cells etc.

Issue to Authorized Persons

Material is to be issued to authorized persons only upon presentation of completed and approved Store Requisitions and Issue Note (SRIN) (Appendix 4.1).

SAFETY IN OPERATIONS

- The Warehouse personnel must wear work gloves, safety helmet, and safety shoes during material handling. Acid resistant gloves and goggles should be worn for extra safety during handling of chemicals.
- A periodic check should be carried out to ensure that preventive maintenance is carried out on material handling equipment and overhead cranes installed in the main warehouse and other storage areas. These facilities must be tested at regular intervals for safe working load and safe working conditions.
- Instructions for proper use of material handling equipment should be available to all concerned. In fact, all the staff should be properly trained in the use of these facilities.
- Only authorized persons and operators under the supervision of the Officer, Warehousing Section, should be permitted to operate crane or forklifts for material handling inside and/or outside the warehouse and stores.

SAFETY FROM FIRE

- 'No smoking/fire hazard' signs should be displayed on all warehouse/stores entrance doors/gates and at prominent places inside the warehouse/stores, and must be strictly observed.
- Fire extinguishers should be placed, with the approval of the Safety Section, at strategic locations inside the warehouse/stores.
- Warehousing Section employees must be aware of physical location of Fire extinguishers in their respective stores and must know how to use them.
- The Officer, Warehousing Section should periodically inspect the fire-fighting equipment and immediately report any deficiency to the Stores Manager, who should take immediate corrective action in conjunction with the Safety Section.

SAFE WORKING AREA

During unpacking of crated material, working area must be cleared and free of wires, nails or strapping materials, etc.

Special care is to be taken in handling chemicals. In case of spillage, the affected area should be immediately cleared in accordance with instructions of the Manufacturer/ Safety Section.

Electric/gas welding should not be permitted inside the Warehouse/Stores area, except in case(s) of emergency repair, when it will be carried out under the strict supervision of the Officer, Warehousing Section in coordination with the Safety Section.

MAINTENANCE OF STORES

Once in a month all storage areas should be inspected for security and safety of materials and the following must be ensured:

- Wire fences around explosive stores/dangerous materials and open storage yards must be in good condition.
- Ventilators/Louvers in the main warehouse and explosive stores must be clean and free of obstructions.
- Passage lanes inside the warehouse/storage areas are to be properly marked for movement of material handling equipment.
- Material should be properly placed in storage bins with locations clearly marked and area must be clean and tidy.
- Electrical wiring in the warehouse/other storage areas should be properly secured without any damage to outlet/switches and all lights must be functional.
- Illumination level in all the warehouses/storage areas should be good.

STORAGE OF MATERIALS

- The Officer, Warehousing Section should inspect and arrange cleaning and preservation of all stored materials at least once in a year or even more frequently as required.
- The manufacturer's instructions should be strictly followed and care should be taken to avoid scratching of surfaces during cleaning and preservation.
- Rubberized parts should be preserved as per manufacturer's instructions and, if necessary, stored in a cool place.
- Electronic spares should be cleaned and preserved properly.
- Chemicals should not be unpacked for inspection. However, in case(s) where signs of deterioration are apparent, the user department/Safety Section should be contacted for advice.

- In case where material deterioration is suspected/observed, the user department should be contacted for inspection and/or functional test of the item to ascertain if its serviceability has been affected.

REVIEW OF SHELF-LIFE

All items having a shelf-life must be tagged indicating date of receipt and expiry date. To ensure maximum utilization of materials before expiry, for example, vulcanizing materials and castles refractors, the Officer, Warehousing Section should periodically review such items and prepare a list with details of the items and their corresponding expiry dates. This information is to be relayed by the Stores Manager to the user department to ensure timely utilization of the material. Special attention should be given to materials whose remaining shelf-life is less than three months.

Part II

Inventory Control

CHAPTER 14

Inventory Classification and Strategies

INTRODUCTION

All the inventory items in an organization are classified into groups of materials, which are very similar to each other from the point of view of technical considerations. Inventories can be broadly divided into three categories. They are:

- Regular inventory items for production activities
- In-process inventories
- Finished goods inventories

Classification of the inventory in different categories should be such that it helps various activities such as stock control, purchasing, receiving of materials, storing, accounting, and codification.

ADVANTAGES OF CLASSIFICATION OF INVENTORY

There are a number of advantages resulting from classification of inventory of the Stores Division and they are discussed here.

Stock Control

- Identical materials are classified in different classes with stock control cards. Review of all the stock items such as raw materials, spares, consumables etc., is easily done separately for each class.
- Requisitions are prepared separately for different classes of items to take effective procurement action.
- Effective budgetary control is managed by classifying items under various heads and sub-heads.

Purchasing

- Separate inquiries can be issued for different classes of items.
- Limited number of the right sources assists in efficient purchasing. Offers are received from the right sources.
- The vendor's catalogues of one class of inventory items can be kept together for pooling of the information in the most effective manner.
- Price lists of each class of inventory items are kept separately.
- Pooling of similar items in a class enables obtaining very attractive prices.
- Pooling of orders for similar nature of items in a large purchase order helps in reducing number of purchase orders and thus reduces purchasing effort and cost.

Storing Materials

- Classification helps in keeping similar items together in the store.
- Receipt and issue are posted correctly in the bin cards with the help of the class and code number indicated on the goods receipt note.
- Duplication of items of similar nature is reduced with proper classification.

Accounting

- Budget heads are allocated based on classification of inventory items. Receipts and issues are easily linked with the correct budget heads.
- Entries for goods, receipt notes and requisitions are done on the correct cards.
- Budgetary control is easy with the classification of items in separate classes as each class is focussed separately.

Codification

- Classification helps in logical codification of all the items in the inventory.
- Classification helps in mechanization of records.

REGULAR INVENTORY ITEM

In a production unit, regular inventories can further be divided into more categories for effective operations and control and they are:

- Capital equipment: Production machinery and other machines that are either used in manufacturing activities or are supportive to the production functions
- Tools
- Furniture
- General Stores
  (i) Spare parts
  (ii) Consumables

- Inflammable Stores
- Chemicals
- Raw Materials
- Scrap Materials
- Packing Materials

Capital Items

It is essential that all the capital equipment's be properly accounted for. Normally capital items are issued in the name of the nominated official(s). Each capital equipment should be properly recorded in a record referred to as "Asset Register". The details should contain name of the manufacturer, his address, telephone/fax/telex no, year of purchase of the equipment, nameplate details with list of recommended spares, initial cost, present worth etc., for future reference. In some cases, even after replacement of capital equipment, spares continue to remain in the inventory even though they are no more required. This increases the number of obsolete parts in the inventory. It should be ensured that upon disposal of any capital equipment, the related spares should be examined very carefully. Spares, not required for future use, should be deleted from the inventory. Some of the spares may be useful for other units still in operation or for some other models of the same equipment in the company. The concerned technical personnel should examine the spares in the inventory and decide upon their retention or disposal. The views of the manufacturers of the equipment should be obtained about the spares and the recommended spares should be retained in the inventory.

Tools

It is well known that tools play an important role in the efficiency and productivity of an organization. Without tools, it is impossible to repair, install, or dismantle equipment. It is not only the availability of the tool which is important, but also the availability of proper tools for the job, that is essential. For example, a hydraulic puller for bearing may be much better than a mechanical puller for bearing. The same is true for other tools also. A number of special tools are stored to meet the requirements of special applications.

Furniture

Different types of furniture are used in an organization. As in the case of capital equipment, furniture is allotted to an individual who is normally the user. Some of the items of furniture are maintained for general purpose. These are under the control of the Administration Department. The new entrants are issued the furniture according to their functional requirements. Company norms are also established for different levels of officials. As many consider furniture a status symbol, there is a tendency to grab better furniture at the time of new purchases or when some senior official spares the furniture. Addition of furniture of a new design increases the variety of furniture. It becomes difficult to distinguish one item from the other as both items may have the same name. For example, chairs with minor difference in design, size, or appearance.

Proper codification helps in clear identification of each item and each item should be accounted for in the inventory. The responsibility of maintaining the inventory of furniture normally remains with the administration. In some organizations, this responsibility is given to the Materials Department or the Stores Division.

Each furniture is numbered and its location is written on the furniture and a record of this is kept in a register. Annual verification of inventory of furniture is essential. It is essential that broken furniture is either repaired or condemned and removed from the inventory.

General Store

The General store has spare parts and consumables as inventory items. These inventory items are regularly in demand for maintenance and operational requirements of the process. Spare parts management is a very wide area in itself and is dealt with in detail in Chapter 19. Consumables, like oils, lubricants, gases etc., are essential for plant maintenance and operation, and efforts should be made to ensure that there are no stockouts.

Chemicals and Inflammable Store

Both these categories of inventory items are important for production activities. They should be in enough quantity to avoid any stock out. At the same time, excessive storage may result in deterioration of their quality and even may result in total loss. These materials are also safety hazards. Therefore, greater care is necessary in controlling their quantities.

Raw Materials

Raw materials are the most important of all the inventory items. Firstly, the production is directly affected due to shortage of any raw material. Secondly, the consumption of raw materials is so large that the cost of raw material directly affects the cost of the product. The top management controls raw material inventory.

Packing Materials

Packing materials are of great importance as they are required for packing the goods produced. Like raw materials, packing materials are controlled and monitored very meticulously. Any shortage of packing material directly affects the production process. Excess of packing materials increases the inventory. Packing materials are stocked in terms of a few week's requirements, say for six to eight weeks. Top management should check the stock level regularly to monitor the inventory of packing materials.

Scrap Materials

Scrap materials are generated during the process of production and / or from repair activities. They are termed as junk and normally stored in one place and are not accounted for as other items are. Some junk materials are useful for future repairs and should be segregated and kept aside. Other materials are usually disposed of in lots.

IN - PROCESS INVENTORIES

Materials or semi-finished goods lying on the shop floor or in stores for temporary storage before being used in a production process are known as in-process inventories. For example, raw metal in a process plant like cement plant is an in-process material, which has been produced by processing a mix of raw materials. Similarly clinker is an in-process inventory for producing cement.

Why is In-process Inventory Necessary

In-process inventories are always an integral part of any production process. They are there for various reasons. Some of them are:

i. There is a time-lag before a raw material or semi-finished product can be used from one stage of production to the next stage of production. This results in in-process inventories. Efforts should be made in such a way that the in-process materials have to wait for a minimum period before its consumption. This requires strict management control.

ii. Lack of planning in production operations results in accumulation of inventories at certain stages. This may be due to the fact that the next stage may not be ready to use the in-processed inventory. Balancing of material processed with the available production capacity is important for balancing the production at every stage. The problem of imbalance in the production capacity of different sections may arise in one or two stages only out of the many stages. To control this and to ensure that the in-process inventory is kept at a minimum, each production operation should be carefully monitored so that each stage is efficient and balanced.

iii. In-process inventory may also result due to shortage of one of the raw materials in the stock. This may be due to delayed procurement, delayed supply, of material by supplier or transportation delay/failure. Shortage of material affects other proceeding operations and in an increased in-process inventory.

iv. Faulty management decisions cause an excess of in-process inventories. A management decision to stop production of one product halfway to produce another important product results in an excess of in-process inventory of the earlier product.

v. Delays in in-stage inspections of various in-process inventories do not allow continuous production and creates more in-process inventories. At times, inspection is carried out by an external agency, like the surveyor or the customer's representative, who do not arrive in time for the inspection. The delay in inspection causes interruption in production and results in an excess of in-process inventories.

vi. In certain complicated production processes, a large number of sub- assemblies may have to be kept for the production process. This cannot be avoided for certain processes. It should be noted that in-process inventories are as important as raw materials and finished goods for avoiding any loss.

Factors Influencing the Level of In-process Inventories

Some of the factors, which should be considered in deciding the level of in-process inventories are:

i. Realistic requirements of each item or semi-processed items for the production process should be worked out carefully to avoid any shortage or excess. The requirement should take into consideration various uncertainties, like delay in customs clearance formalities in case of imported items or delay in the production process itself.

ii. Acquisition cost, inventory-carrying cost, quantity discounts, and follow-up costs should be considered while deciding on the level of in-process inventories.

iii. Investment needed and availability of funds for the size of inventory needed.

iv. Cost of maintaining and controlling the in-process inventory.

v. Space availability for storing the in-process inventory is a very important aspect. In some of the plants, space restrictions do not permit storing of in-process inventory beyond a certain limit. Single or multiple handling of material is an important consideration. Double or multiple handling of materials should be avoided since the handling cost becomes part of the product cost.

vi. Other considerations such as pollution control aspects, upkeep of factory premises, affect on sales etc., should also be considered.

Strict Monitoring of In-process Inventories

In-process inventories deserve the attention of the top level of management. The top level of management should keep itself abreast with the stock of in-process inventory and should have reports on bimonthly basis or quarterly basis. The report should state the available stock of the in-process inventory in terms of number of days production.

Any excess should be reviewed and the receiving quantity should be controlled. Reasons for increasing in-process inventory should be examined and corrective action should be taken immediately. Low level of in-process inventory should be attended to with more urgency to avoid any production hold-ups. The Materials Department is responsible for keeping the top level of management informed about the status of the in-process inventories. While monitoring the level of in-process inventories, it is desirable to involve a team of representatives from the Production Department, Finance, Engineering, Quality Control, and Marketing/Sales.

FINISHED GOODS INVENTORY

Finished goods occupy a substantial share of the total inventory in an organization. The Production Department and Marketing Department prefer to have large quantities of finished goods so that the market demands can be satisfied easily. However the Finance Department always wants to reduce the stock of finished goods so that money is not blocked. Keeping optimum level of finished goods is very essential for best utilization of the funds. During recession in the market, demand is low. The competition among the suppliers forces them to sell their product(s) at rock bottom prices, which directly affects their profit margin. Stock level of finished goods of perishable nature or of goods having a limited shelf-life should be controlled very strictly. As the expiry date of perishable goods or goods with limited shelf-life such as food products and medicines approaches, they are sold at even lower prices than their cost. The objective is to recover the money to the maximum extent possible before their total rejection.

The size of the finished goods inventory greatly depends upon the nature of business. Individual items of inventory will have different level of inventories. A marketing company may be able to sell an item in demand quickly after its receipt. However, in case of another item in low demand or unsteady demand, the company may have to stock the item for long to meet the requirements as and when they arise. Seasonal production or seasonal requirements also influence the inventory levels.

Factors Influencing Finished Goods Inventories

Various factors which are important and influence the finished goods level are:

- Demand
- Batch production
- Multiple warehouses
- Imports
- Distribution network

Demand Market demand for each product depends upon the nature of the product. For example, sale of cement may be at a low level during the rainy season as construction activities will not be at the same level as in other seasons. Refrigerators, air conditioners, and desert coolers have great demand in the summer season as compared to other seasons. Similarly there is a great demand for room heaters and geysers in the winter season. The same is true for woollens, blankets etc. which have a great demand in the winter season. Books are in great demand at the time of opening of colleges and universities whereas the demand for them may be very low through out the remaining period of the year. Season's greeting cards have a large demand in the relevant season only, whereas birthday/marriage/thanksgiving/congratulation cards would have a demand uniformly distributed over the year. The demand for such items can be forecasted with accuracy to a certain extent.

The level of inventory of items, which undergo frequent changes in design and models should be monitored very closely. This applies to electronic goods, computer software and hardware, where design and features of each model undergo fast changes. If proper control is not kept, such items may be lying in stores thus blocking valuable money.

Certain items are linked with fashion, specially garments and jewellery items. However, the demand for certain garments is so stable that they withstand various changes in the fashion.

There is yet another category of demand which is related to some unpredictable situations, such as earthquakes, floods, wars, accidents, or epidemics. These situations create sudden demands; both short term as well as long term and influence the inventory levels as well as the strategy for stocking them.

Thus demand plays a key role in the level of inventories. Changing economic health of the country, social system, and developmental works are all linked to the finished goods inventory level.

Batch production Certain products are more suitably produced in batches since they cannot be kept beyond a certain time-period. This is very common for medicines, which have an expiry date. Moreover the production facilities have a limited capacity, hence one product is produced at one time in a batch. After producing a required/planned quantity only, the second product is produced. Such items have to be in the stores for a long period at times. An economic batch size should therefore be worked out keeping in view all the related parameters, which directly affect the finished goods inventory level.

Multiple warehouses Big companies may have a very large network of warehouses through out the country or even spread out in a number of countries. Each warehouse will have to meet different demands as each location would have a different market. This would depend upon the type of clientele, different weather conditions from one place to another, different level of industrial activity in different regions, and different social systems prevailing at each location of the warehouse. This would greatly influence the inventory level of finished goods in different warehouses. On the basis of market surveys in the region of each warehouse, appropriate inventory strategies could be developed.

Imports Some industrial products require raw materials and also parts that have to be imported. This is due to the fact that particular raw materials of acceptable grades are available in certain parts of the world only. For example, cement grade bauxite, a raw material for making cement is available in few countries only, like Australia, India, and Italy etc. In certain economies, the government imposes restrictions on imports and controls the import of goods. Companies producing the products involving imports manufacture the goods much ahead of the actual market demand. This results in excessive stock of the finished goods inventories. A well-calculated strategic decision is called for while controlling such factors in the overall management of the finished goods inventory.

Distribution of finished goods There should be a balance between the production, storing, and sales of the finished products. The modes of distribution should be commensurate to meet the requirements of the sales department. In some cases, a road transport system is required for distribution. In other cases, rail, air, or sea transportation is adopted. The adoption of a particular transportation mode or a combination of many depends upon the territory, transport facilities available, and volume of business. Any delay in transportation arrangement will cause piling up of the finished goods inventory.

STRATEGIC CONSIDERATIONS IN THE CONTROL OF FINISHED GOODS INVENTORY

The stock of finished goods requires a very close control. Too much stock incurs a large inventory-carrying cost and is a burden on the selling price. The inventory-carrying cost eats away part of the profit margin. At the same time, the stock should be such that it should be able to meet the customer's requirements not only during normal situations but also during periods of distress requirements. One of the factors contributing to a customer's satisfaction is short delivery period. Various issues, which are important in controlling the finished goods inventories, are:

- Market research
- Recommended stock level of finished goods
- Meeting the sudden increase in demand
- Economy of production
- Control on obsolete parts
- Control on in-transit inventory
- Interdepartmental co-ordination

Market Research

Market research plays a very important role in the control of the finished goods inventory. The marketing department should be in constant touch with their customers to be aware of their demands, their plans of projects or production plans etc. Both national and international scenarios affect the demand. Natural calamities like cyclones, floods, earthquakes, forest fires do have an immediate effect on demand. Similarly, a war between two countries, sanctions imposed against some country, or even increase in the energy prices, affect the business environment. Their demand forecast should be based on scientific analysis and study rather than on thumb rules.

Recommended Stock Level of Finished Goods

Based on past experience and evaluation of pattern of dispatch, the management should lay down norms for stock level of finished goods. A recommended level of finished goods should be established in terms of stock for a given period, for example for one month to two months or any other range. Monthly, quarterly, half yearly, and yearly reports should be given to the management regularly for continuous review.

Meeting the Sudden Demand

On the basis of unexpected emergency situations or an unforeseen demand due to various reasons discussed under the title "Market Research', the finished goods requirements should be reviewed and any changes needed should be incorporated quickly. This may be required in both cases when the demand for a finished product increases or decreases. The management should be alert to sudden changes in business environment. For example, a flood situation may suddenly create a demand for boats, medicines, tents etc.; increase in oil prices may put a lot of pressure on the prices of almost all daily consumption goods, which may adversely affect the financial health of the country and thereby the construction activities. This will result in a sudden drop in the demand for construction materials.

Economy of Production

Economy of production is a very important aspect in controlling inventory. However, when the sale of an item is slow, it may not be prudent to stick to the concept of economic batch production as this may result in excessive finished goods inventory. It is necessary to optimize the total costs. In this regard, the extra unit cost involved in producing an uneconomic batch should be compared with the inventory-carrying cost. In case the inventory-carrying cost is higher than the extra unit cost of batch production, the concept of economic batch production is not to be followed.

Controls on Obsolete Parts

In certain items, technological developments are so fast that earlier models become obsolete after a few years. Electronic items and computers are glaring examples of this category of fast-changing technologies. The manufacturers/suppliers, in order to satisfy their customer's future requirements, try to keep spares of various models as long as possible. This creates a situation wherein a large number of obsolete parts are in the inventory, which become a burden on the finished goods inventory. It is true that there is a responsibility on the part of the manufacturers/suppliers to meet the requirement of their customers, so that they are not forced to make new investments in the latest models. But there is a limit, beyond which the company should not go. The top level of management should decide up to what extent such obsolete spares should be kept in the inventory.

The obsolete parts inventory should be controlled taking customers in to confidence and informing them about the period beyond which the parts would not be available. Their future requirements could be assessed and provided for. Instead of keeping spares, it is preferable to keep drawings and where these are not of confidential nature, the drawings may be given to customers who may experience difficulties at some later date. Thus the customer's goodwill may still be enjoyed by giving them the tool for making spare parts, and also advising them about the type of spares, that need to be carried. This approach may achieve the desired balance in reducing the inventory of obsolete parts and at the same time protect the interest of the customers.

Controls on In-transit Inventory

For certain commodities, goods take a long time before they reach the final destination. This is due to the route and interlining of one mode with other modes of transportation. For example, if transportation by special rail wagons which are custom-made for the goods to be transported is involved, a lot of waiting time is involved by the time it comes back or until a new wagon is provided for loading of goods. Thus one has to study the round-trip-time in such cases so that the same should be reduced to the maximum extent possible. There are various factors, which should be considered while working out the round-trip-time. For example, in case of transportation of milk though insulated road tankers, one should study the type of roads, density of traffic, time of continuous drive of the vehicle by the driver, and repair facilities on the way for repair of the vehicles. Proper planning could optimize the round-trip-time, which may help in reducing the in-transit inventory to a great extent. The management must arrange for a scientific study and analysis for such factors to obtain the best results.

Interdepartmental Coordination

Control of finished goods should not be left to only one department. Other departments too contribute to the process of inventory control. It is customary to give the control of finished goods inventories to the sales department as they are ultimately in direct contact with the market. But, this department, at times, has a tendency to stock as much as is necessary to fully meet the customer's anticipated demands. The projected demand by the sales department has been found to be more than the real demand and thus results in overstocking of inventories. In some organizations, the finished goods inventories are under the control of the Materials Supply Department. Since this department is not directly involved either in production or in sales, it takes an independent view without any bias. In any case, the control can best be done by close interaction between Sales, Production, and Materials Supply Department. The management should ensure that all the concerned departments interact regularly with each other to control the finished goods inventories so that the advantage of interdisciplinary approach is not lost.

CHAPTER 15

Codification

INTRODUCTION

Codification is used to describe an item in short, thus avoiding the necessity of a long statement every time the need to describe the item arises. Codes are very useful for the following reasons:

- Every one finds a similar meaning in identifying an item with the help of a code.
- The same item may be available under different names. A code eliminates the possibility of duplication in names.
- Items with different features but for same purpose can be differentiated easily. For example, a ball pen with ordinary refill will have a code different from that of a ball pen with jotter refill.
- A code helps avoid long descriptions in Purchase Requisitions.
- Entries in bin cards, stock control cards, and account records are made easily with codes. Moreover a code helps in a uniform method of entry.
- Entries in receipt and issue documents are made easily with accuracy in the appropriate records.
- Codes are necessary for mechanization of records through computerization of activities.

METHODS OF CODIFICATION

One can adopt different methods of codification. They are:

- Numerical code
- Mnemonic code (using alphabets)
- Consonant code
- Alpha-numeric code

Numerical Code

Different systems have been used for codification with numericals. A seven-digit system or ten-digit system (Kodak System) have been widely used for codification. All numerical methods of codification seek to describe the item by using groups of numericals to describe the general class to which a part might belong, such as electrical, plumbing, pipes, and fittings etc. The next two characters may describe subgroups such as switches in electrical, valves in plumbing, and steel pipes and fittings under pipes and fittings. The next two characters may narrow down to the unique description of the part it describes.

A seven-digit codification system is used as follows:

XX	X	XX	X	X
Class	Subclass	Description of the materials	Size	Minor variations

In the ten digit Kodak system the structure of the code is as follows:

XX	X	XX	XX	XX	X
Class	Subclass	Kinds	Type	Size	Minor variations
Raw	Metal	Steel	Stainless	Sheet	6 mm thick
Materials			Steel	$4' \times 3'$	

Numerical codification systems focus on the material and ignore the purpose for which the item is used. Quite often, the same part is known by several names depending on its use. Codification eliminates such duplication of names, which may arise because of various uses of the same materials.

Mnemonic Code

Mnemonic codes uses alphabets to describe the items. Since there are only 26 alphabets, there is a limitation in giving codes to classes/subclasses more than 26 in number. A combination of alphabets is used to describe items, but very soon overlapping meanings are represented by these codes. For this reason, mnemonic codes are not well adapted to machine data processing methods.

Mnemonic codes are normally used for identifying relatively short lists of items coded for manual processing where it is desired that the items be recognized by their codes from memory.

Consonant Codes

Consonant codes also use alphabets, either singularly or in combination. In this system, abbreviations are used, which are selected in such a way that sounds like the item to be described. In this system initial letter is retained, but all subsequent vowels (including W and Y) are dropped. Codes developed in this way are unique to the item. While consonant codes can be used for any type of data item, it is more commonly used for coding long names and addresses.

The main advantage of this coding system is the ease with which the new items could be coded. Any body with a little practice can code the items by consonant code. Some of the examples of the consonant codes are:

TPT	Transport
MAT	Materials
PLN	Planning
MNTC	Maintenance
EB	Electric Circuit Breakers
ED	Electric Power Distribution
FK	Flanges-non-metallic
FM	Flanges-Metal

This coding system is used where the number of items to be coded is less. However, as the number of items increases, it becomes difficult to differentiate between items, as the same code is likely to be given to two different items as they may sound similar. This may result in mistake in identification of the items. For example, code FM is used for Flange-Metal. This code also sounds like Ferro-metal. Human errors in typing codes with similar combination of alphabets are more likely such as FLS and FSL. Further, codes starting with the same alphabet create more confusion until the written document is referred to, which can be very time-consuming. For example, FM stands for Flange-Metal but FB stands for Fasteners (Bolts).

Alpha-Numerical Code

This system uses combination of alphabet with numerical for codification. Alpha-numerical codes are used to maintain the lists of individuals or company names, usually their account names. This coding system can have a suitable number of characters say seven or nine or any other number as required.

Elements of a Good Codification System

The codification system should meet the requirements of the organization. Each organization is different from other in many ways such as the prevailing systems, extent of modernization, automation/computerization, and future plans.

A good codification system should serve the needs of purchasing, warehousing, computerization of inventory levels and financial analysis, and should help in controlling procurement delays, stock out situations, repetitive small orders, wrong sourcing of enquiries, and order quantities. It should help further in revealing patterns of consumption, setting order priorities, classification of total expenditures, and serve as an important decision making tool. The code should also be linked with the existing machine code, stores locations code, item description, and inventory levels.

Code structure The size of code depends upon the size of the organization, type of activities, and whether the system is to cater to a single unit organization or multi-unit organization. The number of characters to be used depends upon the type of information desired to be presented through the code. A small organization may satisfy its needs by adopting a seven-character codification system. A medium size organization may be well served by a nine/ten character codification system. A large organization or a multi-product or multi-unit organization may require a still larger system to cover various aspects. The latest software packages for Materials Management activities have up to 18 characters for an item code. The large number of characters provide a greater flexibility in covering as many aspects as may normally be required. Each character or set of characters signify some important aspect about each item. These aspects are discussed with the help of an example of a nine characters codification system, whose features are discussed here.

A typical structure of a nine character code is as follows:

U V WWWW X Y Z

Each character or group of characters signify the following:

U	:	Type (Proprietary/General item)
V	:	Classification (Electrical, Mechanical, ... etc.)
WWWW	:	Part Description
X	:	Group (Earning/Non-Earning, Critical and Normal)
Y	:	Shelf-Life
Z	:	Value/Price Class

Details of each of these aspects are discussed in the following section.

(i) Type (U)

The first character indicates whether the item is one of general nature (code G), manufactured by several companies, or of proprietary nature (code P) available with the original equipment manufacturer only. This information is important for initiating the purchasing action and for deciding the subsequent storage location by the warehouse. Proprietary parts may not be stored in the warehouse but in an appropriate sub-store and vice versa.

Enquiries for quotations may be directed only to the original manufacturers in case of proprietary items, while in case of general items this first character will be only a first step in locating the appropriate sources of supply.

(ii) Classification (V)

The second character provides further information about the item as per various classes. For a process plant, the various classes can be codified as follows:

Classification	Code
i) Automotive	A
ii) Building Materials	B
iii) Castings	C
iv) Data Processing	D
v) Electrical	E

vi) Forgings	F
vii) Instrumentation	I
viii) Hydraulic	H
ix) Consumables	K
x) Mechanical	M
xi) Testing/QC	T
xii) Pneumatic	N
xiii) Recreation & Household Items	R
xiv) Safety & Security	S
xv) Packaging	P
xvi) Electronic	Q
xvii) Miscellaneous	Z

This is the second step towards locating a supplier, and it can also be used for finding out the total expenditure and pattern of expenses over a period of time for each class.

(iii) Part (WWWW)

This group of four characters specifies/ describes the part itself. Using this with the first and second characters of the code, the right sources of supply can be fully established.

This group of characters can also be used for other purposes such as:

i) Physical location of the item inside/outside the warehouse. For example, rubber parts and precision parts require protection from weather/dust etc., and must be located accordingly.

ii) Inventory status reports on any item or group of items.

iii) Pricing information on any one or group of items.

iv) Patterns and rates of consumption for modifying inventory levels.

The first two characters of this group can be alphabets (excluding 'o') and will indicate the general category of the part, while the remaining two characters can be numeric and can be specified further to make the code unique.

(iv) Group (X)

The seventh character in this unique code indicates whether an item is critical or normal and whether it is for an earning (production) equipment or non-earning equipment. Purchasing and expediting can use it for financial analysis.

Following is an exemplary list of the two groups:

Earning Group	Non-Earning Group
Quarrying Equipment	Cars/Pickups
Crushers	HVAC equipment

Feeders/Conveyors	Housing
Raw Mills	Road/Pavements
Kilns	Traffic Signals
Cement Mills	Buildings
Packing Plant	Safety/Security
CCR	Sewerage Treatment Plant
Workshops	-
Weighbridges	-
Laboratory	-
Bulk Loading Systems	-
Railway Yard	-
Fuel Station	-
Gas Turbine Station	-
-	
-	
-	

The following codes will be used:

Group	*Code*
Earning-Critical	1
Non-Earning-Critical	2
Earning-Normal	3
Non-Earning- Normal	4

(v) Shelf-Life (Y)

Many items require a limit on inventory levels and order quantities because of their limited shelf-life. For example, castable refractory and vulcanizing materials for jointing of conveyor belts have limited shelf-life. The eighth character specifies this important aspect. The following code may be followed for this character:

Shelf-Life	*Code*
Up to 3 months	0
Up to 4 months	1
Up to 5 months	2
Up to 6 months	3
Up to 9 months	4
Up to 1 year	5
Up to 2 years	6
Up to 3 years	7

Up to 4 years	8
Above 4 years	9

(vi) Value/Price Class (z)

The last (9th) character gives some idea about the unit value of the item in a broad range. This information will be helpful again in setting inventory levels, in preparing purchase requisitions, and their reviews and approvals.

Following is the suggested broad classification and codes:

Value (US$)	*Code*
Up to 500	0
Up to 1000	1
Up to 2500	2
Up to 5000	3
Up to 7500	4
Up to 10000	5
Up to 20000	6
Up to 35000	7
Up to 50000	8
Above 50000	9

These values are as per the standard unit of measurement in which the quantity of the particular item is specified, that is, No., Set, Meter, Kg, Tonne, etc.

(vii) Other Features

Any additional feature such as identification of different units of the organization, location of different units of the organization, different warehouses, items which are imported or are procured indigenously, equivalent items procured from different manufacturers/ suppliers can be given a suitable code by an additional character.

(viii) Overall Criteria

Whatever structure of the codification system is adapted, its suitability is judged by the information represented by it, features for management control included, and flexibility in the system, long life, and adaptability for computerization. The characters whether numerical or alphabets should be selected to meet these requirements.

CHAPTER 16

Standardization

INTRODUCTION

Standardization means uniformity and reduction in variety. Standardization can be attempted in many areas. Standardization of procedures, standardization of specifications say size, shape, color; standardization of design, standardization of machines, standardization of factory layout, if similar plants are to be repeated; standardization in building construction, standardization of test procedures etc. are some of the areas where standardization has been attempted successfully. Standardization in case of building construction means standard size of doors, windows, openings for window air conditioners, standard staircases, and standard norms of lighting.

Standardization helps in quality assurance. Today, Total Quality Management (TQM) or Total Quality Control (TQC) is aiming at improving the quality in every activity through standardization. Standardization of office procedures, stationery, furniture, uniforms are necessary for uniformity, orderliness and creating a common understanding in office functioning. Similarly standard sizes have revolutionized the manufacturing process where interchangeability of parts has a great importance. In this chapter, focus is on standardization of materials specifications, which has two aspects; first being variety reduction and second simplification.

VARIETY REDUCTION

Frequency of Use

Variety reduction is necessary to control inventory. Large number of sizes of nuts and bolts can be reduced to a select number of sizes. Similarly large number of oils and lubricants can be studied from the point of view of their characteristics or services required from them. Some grades of oils and lubricants can be eliminated and can be substituted by others, which can perform the same function or even better than it. The usage pattern is studied and the items that are similar to each other in certain characteristics are combined in one quality, which can serve the function of all, so that variety is reduced.

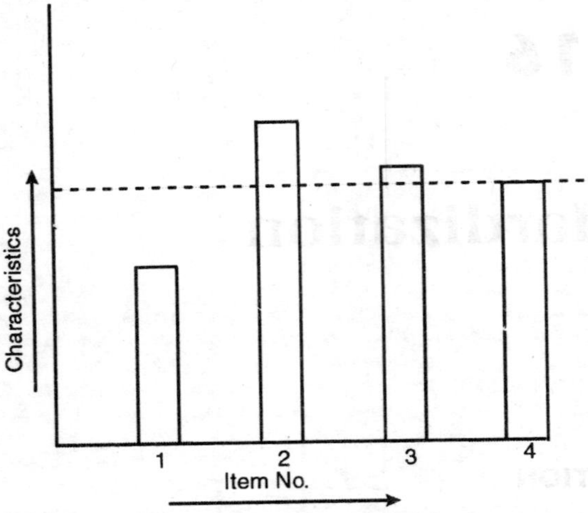

Fig. 16.1 Variety Reduction Through Selecting Average Characteristics

Out of the four items, which have very close characteristics as shown above, item 4 has an average characteristic and could be selected to achieve variety reduction (Fig 16.1). V belts of various sizes could be studied and a particular size, which could be used in place of two or three other sizes, could be selected by eliminating the use of others. A number of inventory items can be reduced to a great extent by this approach.

Preferred Number System

Some sizes, weights, and other characteristics are preferred over others to bring about reduction in variety. These sizes and weights are selected based on a preferred number system. For example, edible oil is sold in tins of 1 kg, 2 kg, and 5 kg capacities. Electrical bulbs are available in 0, 10, 15, 25, 40, 60, 100, 150, 200, 250, and 500 Watts ratings. Similarly, electrical cables are available in 1.5, 2.5, 4, 6, 10, 15, 25, 35,50, 70 and 95 mm^2 cross-sections.

It can be seen that the next size of these items by and large have a uniform increase or decrease. The sizes, in between the selected sizes, are left out and preferred numbers are selected based on the nearly uniform increase or decrease. This is explained in the following examples:

Items	Size	Increase in Wattage	Preferred number base
Bulbs	10 W		About 50 to 66.6 % increase from the lower size.
	15 W	+ 50 %	
	25 W	+ 66.6 %	
	40 W	+ 60 %	
	60 W	+ 50 %	
	100 W	+ 66.6 %	

Electrical Cables	$1.5\ mm^2$ $2.5\ mm^2$ $4.0\ mm^2$ $6.0\ mm^2$ $10\ mm^2$ $15\ mm^2$ $35\ mm^2$ $50\ mm^2$ $70\ mm^2$ $100\ mm^2$	+ 66.67 % + 60 % + 50 % + 66.67 % + 40.67 % + 42.85 % + 40 % + 42.85 %	Initial increase by 60–66.7 % and in later sizes, the increase is about 40–42.85 %.
Oil Tins	1 kg 2 kg 5 kg		Increasing value in an order.
Electrical Switches	5 Amperes 10 Amperes 15 Amperes 23 Amperes 33 Amperes 63 Amperes	+ 100 % + 50 % + 53.3 % + 43.48 % + 90.91 %	

The above examples show that certain preferred numbers are adopted in each case for reducing the variety of items.

ADVANTAGES OF STANDARDIZATION

1. Standardization helps in better understanding of the customer requirements. Every time, minor variations in quality requirements are not examined. Offers are received quickly with better prices from the vendors. Supplies are also received correctly as the items are standardized.
2. The process of standardization examines all aspects of the quality, both plus and minus points of the quality. Thus the final specifications meet the requirements most appropriately.
3. The cost of producing a nonstandard item is always higher than a standard item. Standardization helps in maintaining steady prices.
4. Large quantity orders are processed for the standard items as compared to small orders for nonstandard items. Better discounts are obtained while negotiating large orders.
5. Total processing time is reduced in purchases for standard items.
6. Less storage space is required for items of same specifications as compared to a variety of items that have to be kept separately.
7. Rate of obsolescence reduces by standardization.

8. Inventory turnover is increased and result in lower inventory for slow-moving items.
9. A standard item can be manufactured easily with an optimum operating time of machines. In fact, fewer machines are required to meet the requirements of standard items. The plant utilization factor can be improved, which indirectly helps in better utilization of the capital invested in plant, tools, materials, space, and men.
10. Standardization reduces demand on drawing office and design staff as fewer drawings and less number of designs are required.
11. Advance planning is possible for large-scale activities with standardization.
12. Standardization reduces the requirements of spare parts through variety reduction. The purchaser gets better after-sales-services. Fewer standardized spare parts can be made available easily.

SITUATIONS WHERE STANDARDIZATION IS NOT PREFERRED

Shape

Standardization is not preferred in cases where the item is defined by shape, which differs from case to case. For example glass tumblers of different shapes with different designs (Fig. 16.2).

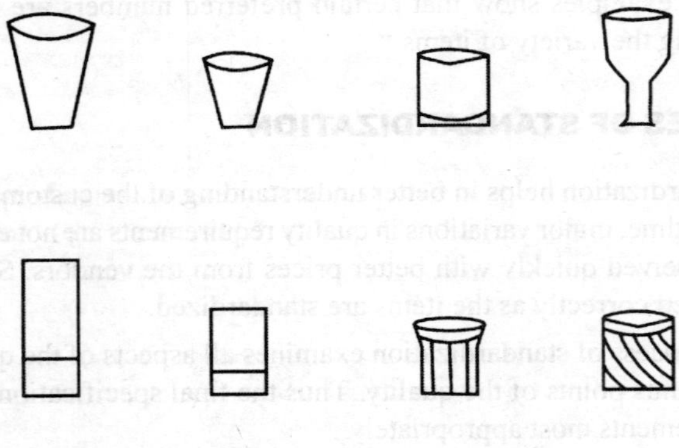

Fig. 16.2 Tumblers of Different Shapes

Novelty

In cases of decorative pieces or items of some specialty, standardization is not preferred. Each design should be unique. For example, jewellery is made with different designs to make it attractive thus sacrificing the concept of standardization.

Special Requirements

Some of the requirements are very typical and cannot be standardized. For example, new sizes or designs may be required in research applications.

Patented Items or Secret Designs

When a manufacturer wants to keep his product different from others for maintaining superiority, he may choose a nonstandard item. Similarly, when the intention is to keep the design secret, nonstandard items are preferred. This is true with industrial items, which are based on typical heat treatments where it is difficult to standardize the heat treatment.

STANDARDS

Standards can be classified as Engineering Standards, Government Standards, Industry Standards\ or even Company Standards.

Engineering Standards

Interchangeability of items in production processes, standardization of threads of pipes and fittings, and laying down standards for design of buildings is a part of Engineering Standards. For example, in a substation, a transformer room will have a requirement of minimum standard clearance all around the transformer and on top of the transformer. This is an example of standardization of engineering design. Standardization has been applied to composition of various materials such as carbon brushes for electrical motors and steel items. SAE steels are typical example of engineering material standardization.

Engineering standards are developed by involvement of all the interested parties and also those who can contribute to the subject of standardization. This may include manufacturers, users, purchasers, consultants, and even professors. Advantage is taken of the technical knowledge and experience of various experts in the area.

Industry Standards

Each industry has its specific requirements. Various industry organizations have been actively involved in studying the problems of the industry in specific, and in bringing out solutions through standardization, as may be applicable. For example, procedure for testing of cement has been standardized with the involvement of various research institutes for the industry. Various agencies such as USA Standards Institute, American Society for Testing Materials, Society of Automotive Engineers, National Electrical Manufacturer's Association, and National Council for Cement and Building Materials are some of the organizations, which have been sponsored for the development of industrial standards. Government agencies have also been active in such projects.

Government Standards

Various governments have established standards organizations such as Bureau of Standards in U.K. and India, SASO (Saudi Arabia Standards Organization) in Saudi Arabia etc. These organizations have been working for the development of standards for various industrial sectors. This service is reinforced by the promulgation of such standards and a certificate program to make it obligatory on the industry, to follow the standards developed. This facility lessens the burden of individual tests.

In addition to the efforts of standards organizations, various procurement agencies such as Armed Forces, Department of Supplies and Disposal have also laid down standards relevant to their activities. Attempts have been made to bring Government Standards and procurement practices closer to the industrial purchase requirements and prevailing manufacturing practices.

STANDARDIZATION PROGRAM

Various organizations have a standardization program, which is normally undertaken by a committee. The Standardization Committee comprises of representatives of various departments concerned with the specifications such as Production, Maintenance, Sales, Marketing, and Materials. Every departmental representative makes a contribution to the whole issue of standardization. The materials department, which represents storekeeping as well as purchasing, plays an important role in the standardization program.

The objectives of the standardization program are:

1. Standardize the materials used in the company.
2. To bring company standards as close to the Industry Standards as possible.
3. Variety reduction.
4. Establishing the specification of items to be purchased.

Normally the standardization committee meets once a month for discussing various issues that surface during production and maintenance, or complaints from the customers. These objectives are discussed with a view to improve materials specifications, variety reduction, and rationalization. In case the issue is urgent, a meeting could be called at any time. Records of the discussions are kept for each meeting and action points identified for further action in the matter. On the basis of various issues discussed at the standardization committee meetings, a program is prepared with time targets for completing the actions on each item. Regular review of the progress, problems faced in implementation, targets achieved are some of the functions of the Committee, and this is an important part of the standardization program.

REFERENCE

Menon, P.G., *Standardization and Simplification: Materials Management and O.R. in India*, MMJ Publications, D 409, Defence Colony, New Delhi - 3, 1968, pp. 155 – 175.

CHAPTER 17

Inventory Control Model

INTRODUCTION

Inventory is essential in an organization for production activities, maintenance of plant and machinery and for other operational requirements. The normal tendency is to have more inventory so that most of the items are available when needed. This results in blocking of money, which otherwise could have been used more productively. The management becomes very concerned if the inventory stocks are high. Inventory is a part of the assets in a company's balance sheet and therefore is under close management scrutiny. The management is very critical about any shortage of items required for production. Any increase in the downtime of the machines due to shortage of material leads to production loss. These two aspects call for continuous inventory control. Inventory control not only looks into the physical balance of various materials but also looks into aspects of minimizing the inventory cost. Another aspect of inventory control is control of the inventory-carrying cost.

Avoiding shortages, avoiding excessive stocking and increasing inventory turnover, are some of the main issues concerning inventory control. Further, methods of reducing the component of materials cost in the product cost is an important consideration in cost reduction. This means that the purchase of materials should be for the quantity needed and the purchase quantity should be neither more nor less. Purchases have to be made at the right time and at the most economic cost. Inventory control is therefore a strong management tool for cost reduction.

OBJECTIVES OF INVENTORY CONTROL

The objectives of inventory control are:

- Assurance of having the items needed:

  Assurance of having the needed items is not limited to projected requirements only, but also looks into the requirements that may arise from time to time. These requirements may be result of the delays in delivery, or items received but rejected on inspection.

- Economic buying:

  Economic buying, in addition to the economic order quantity, considers various other factors, which influence the overall cost. Economic buying not only determines the quantity to be procured but also considers the price fluctuation trend, quantity discounts, and other external factors having an impact on the price. One of important objectives of the economic buying is to reduce the procurement cost to the minimum.
- Avoiding any likely shortage of material.
- Avoiding overstocking of materials.
- Reducing inventory-carrying cost.
- Providing flexibility to the purchase department to apply appropriate purchasing policies such as:
  (i) taking quantity discounts for lower unit prices
  (ii) forward buying in case of cost likely to increase
  (iii) to adjust quantity to match with economic lots
  (iv) to order full truck load to reduce transportation cost
  (v) to adjust quantity conforming to standard packaging requirements

THEORETICAL INVENTORY CONTROL MODEL

The simplest form of inventory model is presented in Fig. 17.1. It shows that for normal inventory operation, the inventory level moves up and down between two set points, the 'Minimum Level' and the 'Maximum Level'. Inventory should not exceed the maximum level and should not go below the minimum level. Inventory crossing the maximum level means over-stocking and when it goes below the minimum level, it could result in a stock-out. In between these two set points, that is, the maximum and the minimum level of inventory, a reorder point is set. An order is placed for replenishment of inventory when the inventory reaches the reorder point. The order quantity is equal to the working quantity. By the time, the inventory reaches the minimum level, the quantity ordered is received. On receipt of the ordered quantity of the material, the inventory which had reached the minimum level increases to the maximum level and the consumption cycle restarts. The reorder point is set by keeping in view the leadtime for obtaining the items and making the same available for use. This means that if an order is placed for the working quantity, the material equal to the working quantity would be received at the end of the leadtime, and the inventory which had reached the minimum level once again jumps to the maximum level. This model is the theoretical inventory control model for the purpose of explaining the philosophy of inventory control. One of the most important point of consideration in the above model is the assumption that the consumption of inventory is at a uniform rate throughout the cycle, the order is placed when the inventory level reaches the reorder point, and the ordered quantity is received by the time inventory level reaches the minimum level. Further the leadtime does not change between the reorder point and the point when inventory reaches the minimum level when the fresh quantity is received.

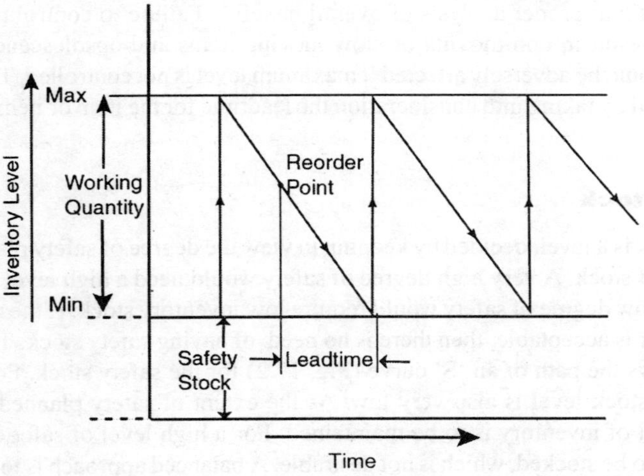

Fig. 17.1 Theoretical Inventory Control Model

ELEMENTS OF INVENTORY CONTROL MODEL

Various elements of an inventory control model are:

- Minimum stock
- Maximum stock
- Safety stock
- Leadtime
- Reorder level

Minimum Level

Minimum level is the level below which the inventory level is not allowed to fall. In case, for any reason, the stock goes below the minimum level, the matter is reported immediately and action is taken to ensure that the material is received at the earliest with extra efforts. For example, the items could be purchased from any other source even at a higher cost, or the items are received by a faster mode of transport say by air or by courier service. In fact, reaching minimum level is an indication of the danger of a likely stock-out situation. It is essential to keep an eye on all the items, which have reached the minimum level. Strict monitoring is necessary for these items.

Maximum Level

Maximum level is a control point to avoid any extra stock. An attempt is made to avoid excessive purchasing that may result in crossing the maximum level, and to ensure that the money is not blocked unnecessarily. However, in practice there are situations when maximum level is crossed intentionally to avail other benefits such as attractive discounts, saving on the transportation/freight charges, or strategic buying decisions. Crossing of maximum level reflects inadequate inventory control and should not be allowed without proper analysis of overall benefits. Failure to control the maximum level may result in non-moving or slow-moving items and obsolescence. Inventory turnover would be adversely affected if maximum level is not controlled. The maximum level is fixed by taking into consideration the leadtime for the item or items of the same group.

Safety Stock

Safety stock is a level, decided by keeping in view the degree of safety planned against being out of stock. A very high degree of safety would need a high level of inventory, whereas a low degree of safety would require low inventory stock. If the risk of being-out-of stock is acceptable, then there is no need of having safety stock. The inventory level follows the path of an 'S' curve (Fig. 17.2) for the safety stock. For a very low safety, the stock level is also very low. As the extent of safety planned increases, a higher level of inventory is to be maintained. For a high level of safety a very large quantity is to be stocked, which is not desirable. A balanced approach is to be followed, wherein, depending on the criticality of the stoppage of plant, the safety level is decided. According to the desired safety level, the inventory level, which is termed as 'Safety Stock' can be decided. Normally most of the organizations maintain a safety stock equal to the minimum stock level.

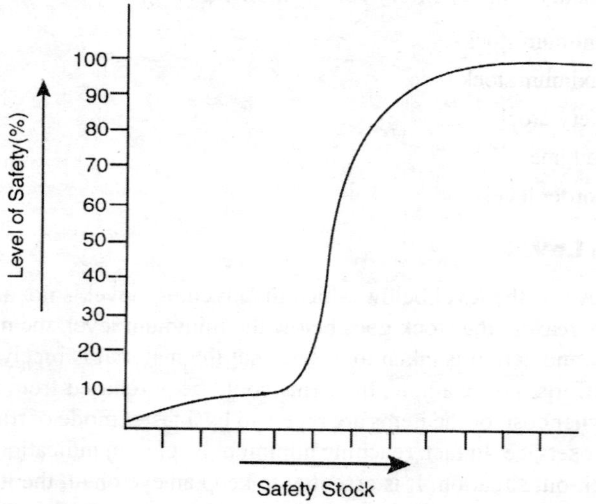

***Fig. 17.2** Safety Stock*

Leadtime

The time from the point a requisition for material is raised by the user or the inventory control section has raised a purchase requisition after review of stock level and future requirements, to the point when material is received, inspected, and is ready for use is known as the leadtime. Leadtime depends upon various factors both internal and external (Table 17.1). Internal factors are mostly under the control of the organization, but the external factors are not under its control. Correct planning, assessment, and monitoring of various elements of leadtime are necessary to get the item at the required time. Delay in delivery adversely affects the production and maintenance work, whereas early receipt of material increases inventory stock in excess of the maximum level and at times causes storage problems and spoilage of materials. Long delivery schedule puts pressure on the store staff to store materials for long. Storage of large quantity of material involves increased inventory-carrying cost, and also handing of materials which otherwise could have been avoided.

Table 17.1 Elements of Lead Time

Internal Lead Time	External Lead Time
Pre-order lead time	-
-	Ordering time
-	Production time
-	Dispatching time
-	Transportation time
Post-receipt lead time	-

Internal leadtime Internal leadtime has two components. The pre-order leadtime, that is, the time taken before placement of order and post-receipt leadtime is the time taken for inspection, making entry of the items in the store records, and the time in issuing the items to the users.

(i) Pre-order leadtime

The pre-order component of internal leadtime includes the following:

- time in raising requisition
- checking the specifications, average annual consumption, future requirements, current stock level, and review of outstanding items ordered but yet to be received
- approval of the purchase requisition and assigning it to the purchase division
- preparing inquiries
- issue of inquiries
- tabulation and evaluation of offers received from the suppliers
- Obtaining clarifications from the users about:
  a) additional technical specifications as may be required by the suppliers
  b) serial number of the machine
  c) item code of the manufacturer
  d) quantity review in case of large volumes or amount involved or to consider the alternatives offered by the suppliers.
- approval of the comparative statement/purchase proposals
- preparation of the purchase order

- signing of the purchase order
- issue of the purchase order

(ii) Post-receipt of material leadtime

The post-receipt of the material internal leadtime includes the following:

- unloading of the materials received from the supplier
- preparation of inspection note
- arranging inspection by the Materials Inspector and by the representative of the user department
- stock entries after acceptance of materials through inspection
- receiving issue notes for issue of the materials to the user
- collecting materials for issue from the bins in the store
- making the issue entries and handing over the materials to the staff of user department
- arranging replacement of any shortage and damaged material

External leadtime External leadtime has four components:

- ordering time
- production time
- dispatching time
- transportation time

(i) Ordering time

The ordering time is the time taken by the seller before receiving the order from the buyer and includes:

- Study of specifications including terms and conditions.
- Checking the availability of materials for production to meet the date of delivery as required by the purchaser.
- Seeking any clarifications on specifications, terms, and conditions say for terms of payment, mode of transportation, guarantee/warranty, and delivery schedules. Legal conditions of the contract also take time before an agreed offer could be made to the buyer.
- Preparation of offers.
- Negotiations regarding specifications, terms, and conditions.
- Placement of order by the buyer.
- Study of order placed by the buyer and providing acceptance.

(ii) Production time

It is the time taken by the supplier from the point of receiving the order till production of the items is completed. It includes the following:

- material and production planning
- material procurement

- production time/manufacturing time
- inspection time, before the items are ready for dispatch

(iii) Dispatch time

It is the time required in packaging, documentation, arranging transportation, and loading of the materials on to trucks, rail wagons, carriers or handing over the materials to the post office or courier. It also includes the activities relating to banking and export formalities.

(iv) Transportation time

It is the time taken by the transporter or carrier from the point of receiving it from the supplier until it reaches the destination. Each mode of transportation such as air, sea, road, or rails has its own requirements of time, documentation, and handling. It is not only the transporter who is responsible for this component of the leadtime, but also some government agencies like Customs Authorities, Toll Tax Authorities, Road Tax Authorities etc. Sometimes, a lot of time is lost in this kind of routine work.

Transportation time can vary due to various reasons such as traffic jams, temporary diversions of routes, strike by the transporters, accidents, political disturbances, or even non-availability of the appropriate transportation facilities. Large and heavy items need special facilities for loading and unloading and even permission from the local authorities for their transportation.

In case of imports, customs clearance and bank transactions are also time-consuming activities. There are occasions, when the documents are not received in time or are not complete or there are problems in the documents, which have to be resolved before the documents are accepted by the buyer and the bank.

Import requirements in case of chemicals and other classified items are to be fulfilled before such items could be cleared. Inspection of such items at Customs office takes time. In cases of shortages, damages, or loss, additional time is required for insurance survey and certification for processing the insurance claims.

Controllable elements of leadtime Certain elements of the leadtime can be controlled by the organization, while others can be controlled to some extent only by adopting appropriate terms and conditions in the order.

Proper planning, monitoring and controlling can, to a great extent, control the leadtime. However, obtaining clarifications regarding both technical and commercial aspects do take time, some times beyond the expectation of the buyer. Sometimes, the end user needs technical clarifications before making recommendations for the purchases. The suppliers, at times, take a long time to provide the required information. Thus, a lot of time is lost in the process. Similarly, some of the terms and conditions are agreed to only after protracted correspondence and negotiations. These include payment terms, warranty and guarantee clause, penalty clause and defect liability clause and so on.

The elements of external leadtime, that is, ordering time, production time and dispatch time can be worked out meticulously and agreed upon with the supplier.

These elements can be controlled to some extent with the imposition of the penalty clause. But there are some other elements, which are beyond the control of the buyer such as major shutdown of the plant and machinery in the seller's works, strike or shortage of power, and other external factors, which adversely affect the seller's production. Sometimes, pre-dispatch inspection by an external agency or the buyer's representative is required in cases of critical supplies. Inspectors take their own time to reach the site of the supplier for inspection.

Similarly, neither the buyer nor the supplier have complete control over the transportation period. Non-availability of transport facilities, traffic jams, accidents, or vehicle breakdowns on the way are some of the factors, which cannot be controlled by either of them. In case of urgency, a faster mode of transportation could be adopted to reduce the leadtime. However, the transportation cost and the nature of the items dictate the decision in such cases.

Insurance survey, customs clearances, and bank formalities in opening the letter of credit and transfer of documents take time which is not strictly under the control of the buyer. These activities should be monitored to keep the leadtime to a minimum.

Leadtime plays an important role in inventory control. It is necessary that every element of the leadtime be given due attention. The management should always keep an eye on the total leadtime, review it from time to time, and take timely corrective action.

Reorder Level

Reorder point is another important tool for controlling inventory mainly from the point of view that there should not be no stock-out. Reorder point is dependent on leadtime. It is set in such a manner that if the order is placed at the reorder point, the material for replenishment of the inventory item should be received by the time the inventory level reaches minimum level. The Reorder point shifts with the rate of consumption and is set based on average yearly consumption, if the leadtime is fixed. In practice, the leadtime is established quite correctly based on past experience. The reorder point is normally calculated by a computer automatically.

DYNAMIC NATURE OF THE INVENTORY CONTROL MODEL

Rate of consumption, order quantity, reorder point, and leadtime are not constant in practice and undergo changes for one reason or the other and disturb the theoretical inventory control model.

Changes in Rate of Consumption

The management decides the changes in the production on the basis of market demand. In case of a higher demand, the production is increased within the plant capabilities. Similarly, in case of market recession, the production is cut down. Changes in the production plans have a direct effect on the rate of consumption of inventory. The effect of higher rate of consumption on inventory is shown in Fig. 17.3 similarly the effect of lower rate of consumption on inventory is shown in Fig. 17.4.

Maintenance Requirements

Major shutdowns of plant and machinery due to emergency repairs results in high rate of consumption of the inventory items.

Delivery Schedule Changes

Lead time changes due to various reasons, both internal and external. In case the ordered material arrives earlier than the planned time, the inventory level increases and would cross the maximum level set (Fig. 17.5). In other cases, a delay in delivery of the material results in shortage of material (Fig. 17.6).

Reorder Point Fluctuations

Change in the reorder point influences the inventory control model. In practice it has been observed that human failures do take place, and there are delays in the review of inventory stocks by the staff. The inventory control staff fails to take timely action in raising the requirements on purchasing department. At other times the inventory group had taken timely action regarding review and raising requisitions for procurement, but the purchasing department did not take timely action in obtaining offers. Delay in ordering may result in shortage of materials (Fig. 17.7). On the other hand, an early ordering may result in excess of inventory (Fig.. 17.8).

Many a time, clarifications are needed on specifications by the suppliers as well as by the purchase executive from the supplier. The suppliers and their representatives at times are not able to identify the items due to their obsolescence or the item being out of production. Exchange of communication in clarification delays the ordering point, thus disturbing the inventory control model.

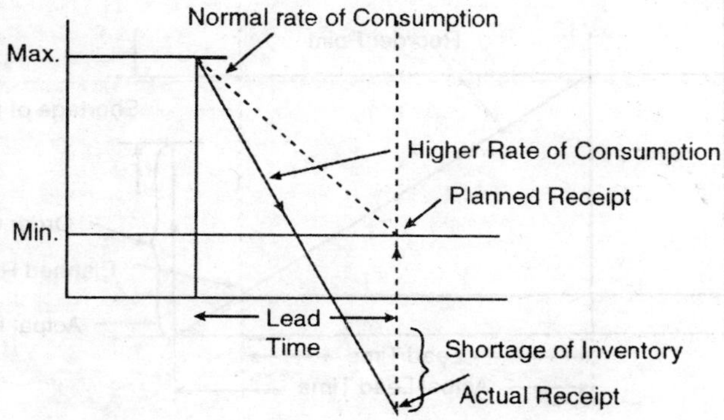

Fig. 17.3 *Effect of Higher Rate of Consumption on Inventory*

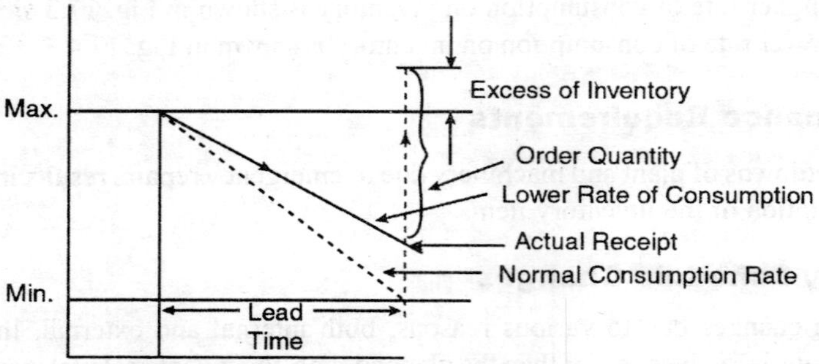

Fig. 17.4 Effect of Lower Rate of Consumption on Inventor

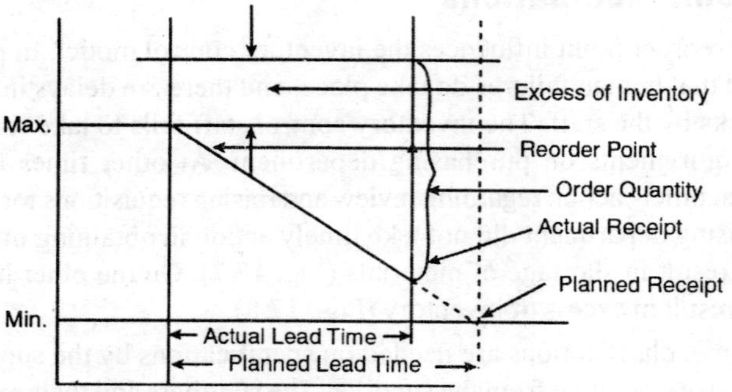

Fig. 17.5 Excess of Inventory due to Shorter Lead Time than the Planned Lead Time

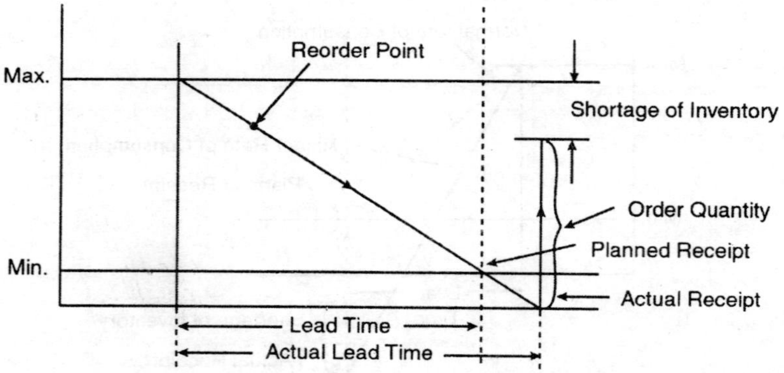

Fig. 17.6 Effect of Longer Lead Time than the Planned Lead Time on Inventory

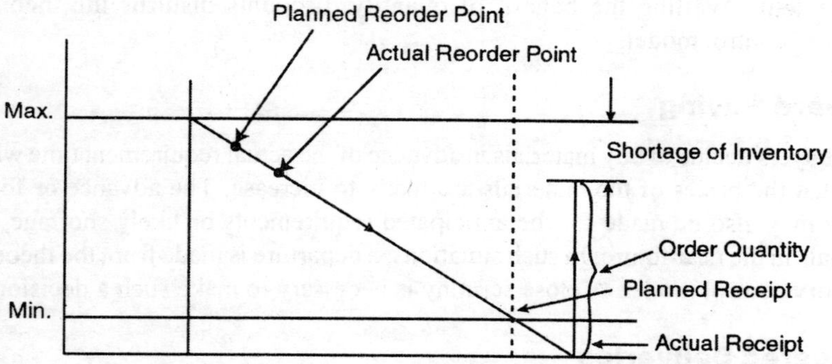

Fig. 17.7 Shortage of Inventory due to Delay in Reordering than the Set Reorder Point

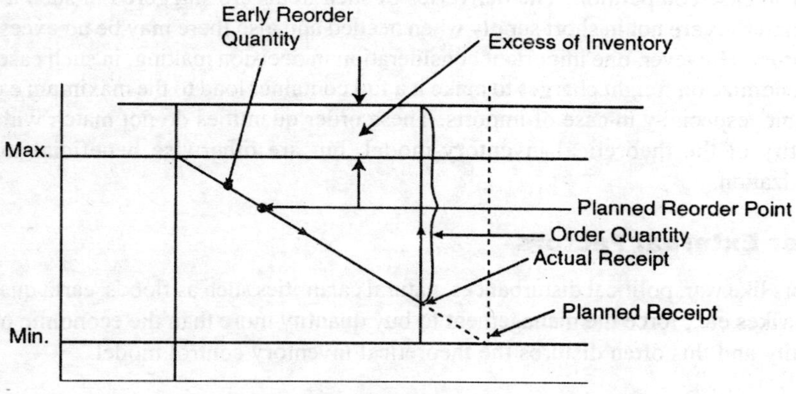

Fig. 17.8 Excess of Inventory due to Early Ordering than the Set Reorder Point

Bulk Purchasing

The concept of purchasing quantity equal to the Economic Order Quantity (EOQ) is often relaxed in favor of bulk purchasing to avail the benefit of attractive prices, for example, buying a complete shipload of raw material or a very large quantity required for a long period. In some other cases, government decisions may favor bulk purchases such as bilateral trade agreement with other countries or relaxation of some levies, taxes, or duties. These factors disturb the inventory control model and would call for continuous review and monitoring of the inventory.

Quantity Discounts

Quantity discounts are often offered by the suppliers to obtain big orders. The quantity offered under discount proposal may be more than the required quantity. In case of requirement of a continuous nature, the discounts may be so attractive that the buyer is tempted to buy the quantity offered even though it may be more than the normal requirement. Availing the benefit of quantity discounts disturbs the theoretical inventory control model.

Forward Buying

Some buyers decide to buy materials in advance of the actual requirement time with the hope that the prices of the materials are likely to increase. The advance or forward buying may also be made for the anticipated requirements or likely shortage of the materials in the near future. In such situations, a departure is made from the theoretical inventory control model. A close scrutiny is necessary to make such a decision.

Staggered Deliveries

For items of regular consumption involving high value, normal annual requirements are worked out and orders are placed at a very attractive prices after negotiations under intense competition. The deliveries of such items are staggered in such a way that materials are not in short supply when needed and also there may be no excessive inventory. However, one important consideration in decision making, in such cases, is to economize on freight charges to make it a full container load to the maximum extent possible, especially in case of imports. These order quantities do not match with the quantity of the theoretical inventory model, but are otherwise beneficial to the organization.

Other External Factors

Factors like war, political disturbances, natural calamities such as floods, earth quakes, and strikes etc., force the management to buy quantity more than the economic order quantity and this often disturbs the theoretical inventory control model.

REFERENCE

Patric J. Mountane and H. Charnov, *Management*, 3rd ed, 2000, Barron's Educational Series Inc., Hauppoouge, New York 11788, USA, pp. 398 – 403.

CHAPTER 18

Inventory Control Techniques

INTRODUCTION

There are a number of techniques which play an important role in the inventory control program. These techniques are very helpful in rationalization of inventory control approach and assist in formulation of inventory control policies. Some of these techniques forming part of the inventory control program are:

- Best order quantity
- ABC analysis
- VED
- HML
- FSN
- Codification
- Standardization
- Classification of items for strategic review

BEST ORDER QUANTITY

Quality and quantity of an item are the two most important aspects in its procurement. Once the quality is established, the question remains as to, how much to procure. A decision on the best quantity to purchase is quite a complicated one, if all the pertinent factors are considered and the number of items for procurement is very large. For a critical item, for example, raw material, which is critical for the production and is also to be purchased in large quantities, lots of time and effort is spent to decide on what quantity to procure. At the same time very little attention is given to a large number of other items. It is therefore essential to develop some sort of mathematical approach to determine the best quantity to purchase. With the help of computers, the calculation of best quantity to purchase has become very easy.

The total inventory cost has three elements:

- Cost of inventory purchased during the year.
- Acquisition cost or cost of ordering.
- Inventory-carrying cost.

The concept of 'best quantity to procure' gave way to 'Economic Order Quantity (EOQ)', which produces the lowest total cost. Acquisition Cost (AC) depends upon the number of orders placed during the year, whereas 'Inventory-Carrying Cost (ICC)' depends upon the volume of the inventory carried during the year. If the number of orders placed during the year is large, the acquisition cost will be much more. However, the case of inventory-carrying cost is otherwise. The inventory-carrying cost decreases with the increase in the volume of the inventory and is normally presented as percentage of inventory cost. As the acquisition cost/ordering cost increases, the inventory-carrying cost decreases.

Economic Order Quantity (EOQ)

The economic order quantity 'Q' is the quantity, which minimizes the sum of the acquisition cost and the inventory-carrying cost, that is the quantity related to the minimum 'variable costs'. The economic order quantity equation minimizes the total annual cost (Fig. 18.1).

Determining Economic Order Quantity (EOQ)

The following symbols are used in the EOQ formula:

Q Economic Order Quantity (EOQ)

q Order quantity

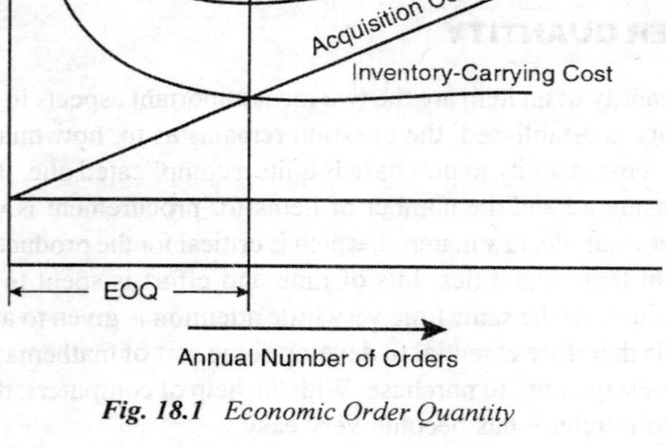

Fig. 18.1 Economic Order Quantity

U	Daily rate of usage, same as rate of receipt
n	number of working days in forecast period
A	ordering cost per order, in dollars per order
I	Inventory-carrying cost in dollars per order
C	Unit cost of items, dollars/unit of measurement

$$\text{Acquisition cost}\,(AC) = \frac{\text{Quantity used during the period}}{\text{Order quantity}} \times \text{Cost to order}$$

$$= \frac{nu}{q} \times A$$

$$\text{Inventory–carrying cost}\,(ICC) = \text{Average inventory} \times \text{unit cost} \times \text{carrying charges}$$

$$= \frac{q \times C}{2} \times 1$$

$$\text{Cost of inventory} = \text{Inventory used during the period} \times \text{unit cost}$$

$$= nUC$$

$$\text{Total annual cost }(T) = \text{Acquisition cost} + \text{Inventory - carrying Cost} + \text{Cost of Inventory}$$

$$= \frac{nUA}{q} + \frac{qCI}{2} + nUC \qquad (1)$$

The EOQ (Q) being the quantity at the minimum total annual cost can be determined by differentiating the above equation (1) with respect to q and then equating the equation to zero

$$\frac{dT}{dq} = -\frac{nUA}{q^2} + \frac{CI}{2} = 0$$

$$\frac{dT}{dq} = 0 \text{ or } -\frac{nUA}{q^2} + \frac{CI}{2} = 0$$

$$\text{or } q^2 = \frac{2nUA}{CI}$$

$$\text{or } q = \sqrt{\frac{2nUA}{CI}}$$

This equation could also be derived from the fact that the Acquisition cost and Inventory-carrying cost are equal at the minimum total annual cost (Fig. 18.1).

At EOQ,

Acquisition Cost (AC) = Inventory-Carrying Cost (ICC)

$$\frac{nU}{q}.A = \frac{qC}{2}.I$$

$$\text{or } q^2 = \frac{2nUA}{CI} \quad \text{or } q = \sqrt{\frac{2nUA}{CI}}$$

$$EOQ = \sqrt{\frac{2 \times \text{Annual usage} \times \text{Order Cost}}{\text{Unit Cost} \times \text{Inventory-Carrying Cost}}}$$

Once the order cost and inventory-carrying cost is determined for a company operation, the EOQ is related to only one variable, the total annual usage of the item under consideration.

$$EOQ = K \sqrt{\text{Annual Usage}}$$

where K is a constant.

Assumptions made in the use of formula The following assumptions are made in the above formula:

- Only one product is involved.
- Usage from the inventory is at a uniform rate during the whole period under consideration.
- The unit cost of the item includes direct labor, material, and that portion of overhead which varies with the size of the lot ordered.
- The calculated EOQ will be used every time of ordering during the period under consideration.

Limitations of the formula Some of the limitations in the formula are:

- Change in the unit price of the material or product is not considered.
- The formula does not reflect the price advantages of volume buying and quantity discounts.
- The order quantity calculated is likely to be adjusted arbitrarily to bring it into conformity with commercial practice to unit packages, full truck load quantities, economical manufacturing quantities, and quantity discounts.

Advantages of using the formula The mathematical approach to determine the best order quantity has many advantages, despite the limitations stated above. Some of the advantages are:

- The formula substitutes facts in place of judgement. Personal bias is reduced and the quantity decisions are consistent and in line with the policy.
- The formula can be used with the help of a computer with minimum effort.
- The mathematical method can be relied on more, relieving the buyer of all the responsibilities with assurance of the correct decisions
- The formula can be used without any moderation under stable conditions.
- The formula provides a useful starting point in cases where the final determination of the ordering quantity is influenced by price fluctuations, seasonal factors, advance coverage, and other elements not considered in the formula.

Variable Costs

Both acquisition cost and inventory-carrying cost vary according to quantity ordered. There a are number of factors which influence the acquisition cost and inventory-carrying cost. Both these costs are discussed in detail in the following sections.

Acquisition cost Inventory acquisition cost is the cost of procuring inventory items. The inventory acquisition cost largely depends upon the approach adopted in procurement and procurement policies. Issuing large number of orders involves a lots of effort and adds to cost. Consolidation of requirements results in less number of orders and therefore reduces acquisition cost.

A good vendor list helps greatly in reducing acquisition cost. Sending large number of inquiries takes up a lot of time before the offers are received. Their tabulation, analysis, and negotiations add to the acquisition cost. Similarly, if adequate inquiries are not sent, enough offers will not be received, and this makes it difficult to take a decision about purchasing the items. In many cases, inquiries are floated again, thus losing valuable time and effort and increasing acquisition cost.

The quality of manpower also affects the acquisition cost. Professional staff always finalize the terms and conditions of the purchase in minimum time, whereas untrained staff is unable to deal with some of the issues correctly and in fact create more problems in execution of the order. The professional staff is always in a better position to take advantage of the business environment and is able to negotiate the best prices for the organization.

Acquisition cost also largely depends upon the use of modern facilities like using fax, e-mail, computer networking etc. Fast communication is always beneficial in reducing the overall procurement cost. The cost of computerization in purchasing may appear to be high, but it always pays off very quickly. Computerization also helps in reducing the staff strength to handle the same amount of work. Lots of paperwork can be reduced with the help of computers. Lots of costly space could be saved, which otherwise would be occupied by old files. Modernization and automation helps in creating an efficient working environment and ultimately reduces acquisition cost.

Another factor in acquisition cost is the purchasing organization. Purchasing, if organized as a centralized activity or decentralized activity, affects the acquisition cost.

The various elements of the acquisition cost can be listed as follows:

- cost of building for the purchase department/its rental and its maintenance cost
- cost of paperwork
- cost of facilities such as computer terminals, PCs, typewriters, photocopying machines etc.
- cost of telephones, faxes, telex, e-mail
- cost of manpower employed
- cost of travel of purchasing engineers/executives to the market
- cost of testing and third party inspection, if any

Many companies have detailed information on the purchase order cost. A satisfactory value is determined by taking the total cost of operating the purchasing department, which includes all the salaries, expenses, and overhead charges on an annual basis and dividing this by the number of purchase orders issued during the year. Average acquisition cost per order will differ from organization to organization and may be in the range of US$ 5 – 15.

Inventory-carrying cost Carrying of inventory is an important element of production activity. Various elements of inventory-carrying cost are:

- interest on the inventory investment
- overhead charges for the storage space
- cost of handling facilities
- cost of manpower in stores division
- obsolescence cost
- insurance cost for the materials stored
- depreciation
- taxes

(i) Interest on the inventory investment

This cost is directly related to the size of the inventory, which depends upon various factors such as:

- excessive requirements of materials by the user departments
- storing large number of items as 'insurance spares'
- large number of slow-moving or obsolete items
- excessive quantity of material purchased to take advantage of bulk purchases and the discounts associated with them

A close control on the size of the inventory is very important as excess inventory increases interest on the inventory investment, and shortages in inventory may result in stoppage of plant thus losing production. A strict control in declaring an item as 'stock item', 'insurance item', or item 'when required' plays an important role in controlling the cost of interest on the inventory investment.

(ii) Overhead charges on storage space

Different types of spaces are required for storing of various items. For example, certain items are required to be stored in closed areas; some require air-conditioned space, while some others need a properly ventilated space. Costs of lighting, safety provisions, air-conditioning, ventilation, furniture, racks etc., are part of the overhead costs. These are important for safekeeping of the materials, but the design of the stores should be such that the expenditure on such facilities is with in limits.

(iii) Cost of handling facilities

Stores operations involve handling of heavy items, which include loading and unloading, internal transportation, and shifting. Normally, warehouses are equipped with EOT Cranes. In addition, forklift trucks, hydraulic trolleys, and wheelbarrows are used in the warehouse for handling materials. All these equipment require regular maintenance. EOT Crane need not be of a very high capacity as it is mostly required for normal operations. A very high-capacity EOT Crane will have a high maintenance cost as well as high electricity consumption. At the same time, the EOT Crane should not be below a capacity which may not be able to load /unload the materials handled. Normally EOT Cranes of five tonnes or ten tonnes capacity are installed in stores. The number of forklift trucks and hydraulic trolleys should be adequate, not more and not less. Excessive number of these items will add to the inventory-carrying cost.

(iv) Cost of manpower in stores division

The cost of manpower in the stores division depends upon the centralized or decentralized operations of the warehouse. More manpower is required to manage various activities of receiving materials, issue of materials and inventory check if there are number of warehouses or sub-stores. The warehouse location, layout, area/size, and number influence the inventory-carrying cost. If proper attention is not paid to these aspects, the inventory-carrying cost will be very high irrespective of the volume of production and will become a fixed cost.

(v) Obsolescence cost

Obsolescence of spares has been discussed in detail in Chapter 19 'Effective Management of Spares Parts'. Obsolete items should be disposed of regularly to keep the inventory low thereby controlling the inventory cost.

(vi) Other elements of inventory-carrying cost

Insurance, depreciation, and taxes are all related to the size of the inventory. Every effort should be made to keep the size of inventory low so as to control the inventory-carrying cost on these aspects.

(vii) Average inventory-carrying cost

The information on average inventory-carrying cost is available in most accounting systems. It is to be noted that the average cost in the quantity formula is for individual commodities; this would, therefore, require different actual carrying costs due to differences in bulk density of various items, the type of storage facilities, rate of depreciation etc. It is very difficult to work out carrying costs for each individual commodity. Normally one average cost figure is computed and adopted, which may be a percentage of the total inventory cost say 5 %.

ABC ANALYSIS

A big organization has a very large number of items, some times 50000 to 100000. All items cannot be given equal attention. It is therefore essential to determine the items or group of items that deserve the maximum control. One of the most important considerations for control is the value of annual consumption of inventory items. It has been observed that a small number of inventory items consume a very large share of inventory consumption during the year. Further, a little larger number of inventory items covers a moderate share of annual inventory consumption, and a very large number of items just cover a very small share of annual inventory consumption. This brought out the concept of ABC analysis. Various studies have shown that only 10% of items have 70% of the annual inventory consumption, 20% of items have 20% of the annual inventory consumption and 70% of items have only 10% of the annual inventory consumption (Fig. 18.2).

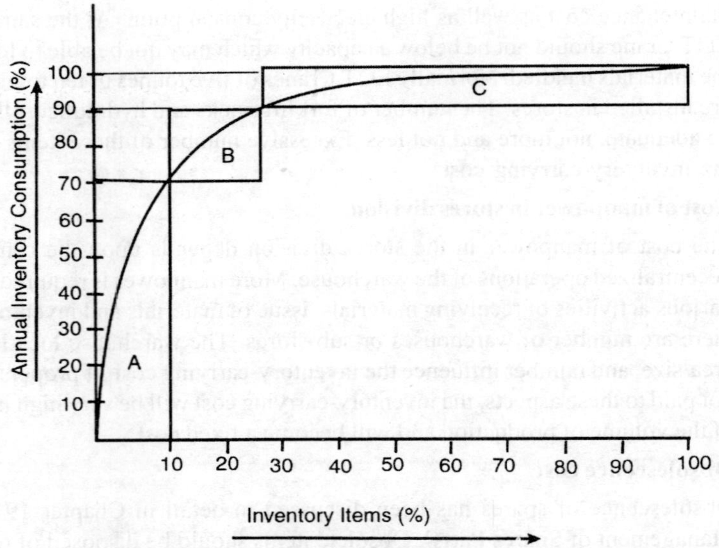

Fig. 18.2 ABC Analysis: Percentage of Inventory Items VS Annual Inventory Consumption %

The steps in computing ABC analysis are:

a) Calculate annual usage in units for each item for the past one year.

b) Calculate the annual usage in US$ for each item by multiplying the annual usage quantity with the average unit price of each item.

c) Rank the items from highest dollar usage annually to the lowest annual usage in dollars. Table 18.1 shows determination of ranks of the items according to the annual usage in US$ for 10 items.

Table 18.1 Determination of Ranks by Annual Usage in US$

Item No.	Average usage (units)	Unit cost (US$)	Annual usage (US$)	Rank
1	45	4	180	6
2	120	10	1200	3
3	16	30	480	4
4	180	8	1440	2
5	80	3	240	5
6	1632	5	8160	1
7	60	2	120	7
8	15	4	60	9
9	12	6	72	8
10	12	4	48	10

d) Arrange the items in the inventory by cumulative annual usage (dollars) and by cumulative percentage. Categorize the items in A, B, and C categories.

Table 18.2 shows arrangement of items in descending order according to their annual usage in US$. Table 18.2 also shows the cumulative annual usage in US$ of the items. The cumulative usage of inventory items is then divided by the total annual usage in the inventory to present the percentage cumulative annual usage. It is observed that item # 6, which constitutes 10% (1 item out of 10 items) of the total number of inventory items covers 68% of the annual inventory usage. Items 4 and 2, which constitutes 20% (2 items out of 10 items) of the inventory items covers 22% of the annual usage of the inventory. Items 3,5,1,7,9,8 and 10 constitute 70% (7 items out of 10 items) of the total inventory items and cover only 10% of the annual inventory usage. The items are divided in three categories A, B and C (Table 18.3). In general, only 10% of the inventory items cover about 70% of the annual inventory usage and are categorized as 'A' category items, 20% items cover about 20% of the annual inventory usage and are categorized as 'B' category items and the remaining 70% items cover only about 10% of the annual inventory usage and are categorized as 'C' category items.

Table 18.2 ABC Ranking

Item #	**Annual usage (US$)**	**Cumulative annual usage (US$)**	**Annaul Usage Percentage (%)**	**Category assigned**
6	8160	8160	68	A
4	1440	9600	80	B
2	1200	10800	90	B
3	480	11280	94	C
5	240	11520	96	C
1	180	11700	97.5	C
7	120	11820	98.5	C
9	72	11892	99.1	C
8	60	11952	99.6	C
10	48	12000	100	C
Total	12000			

Table 18.3 ABC Category-summary

Category	**Items #**	**% of items in inventory**	**Dollars in the category**	**% Dollars in the category**
A	6	10	8160	68
B	4, 2	20	2640	22
C	3, 5, 1, 7, 9, 8, 10	70	1200	10
Total	10	100	12000	

This calls for different attention to various categories of A, B, and C items. The most important point in ABC analysis is how to differentiate between a few important inventory items from the others, so that the management could focus its attention on them to get the best advantage.

The impact of the high cost of 'C' category items of inventory due to stock levels being more than the requirements is not much. However, any increase in inventory items of category 'A' when compared to their average annual consumption would have great impact on the inventory investment. Extra effort to keep the inventory of 'A' category items low without affecting the plant operations would give very good results. Therefore, category 'A' items require very tight inventory control. Items of category 'B' need moderate attention and category 'C' items need minimum attention.

In real life situations, there may not be a clear division of items in three categories of 'A', 'B' and 'C' and it may be required to divide the inventory into four or five categories, that is, 'A', 'B', 'C' and 'D' or 'A', 'B', 'C', 'D' and 'E'. The management may decide on such categorization for better control, based on the annual usage of the items.

Control through ABC Analysis

ABC analysis is an important tool to control the inventory investment in an organization. It provides good guidelines for adopting appropriate purchasing policy for different categories of items and also for the amount of attention, which is required from different levels of management, to be given to various items. According to the importance of 'A' category item, top level of management must devote a major part of its time in procurement of 'A' category items, both from the point of view of cost control as well as controlling the quantity to be procured. Creating a keen price competition for 'A' category items brings excellent results. Similarly, frequent purchases of 'A' category items in appropriate lots will ensure against any shortage. At the same time, no excessive stocks are built up for these items.

'B' category items also deserve attention from the top level of management, but not to the same extent as that of on 'A' category item. The middle level of management may be given the responsibility to monitor the procurement of this category of items. The top level of management should just oversee that actions for procurement of the 'B' category items are taken as per directions and guidelines laid down by it.

The lower level of management should manage the 'C' category items. The management should lay down systems for establishing rate contracts or blanket contracts with reputed suppliers to purchase materials without much effort and with minimum paper work. Even cash purchases may be permitted to procure immediate requirements of the 'C' category items. This approach of division in management attention will help in developing appropriate procurement policies and ensuring that the purchases are made in the most economical way and that at the same time there is no shortage of materials.

OTHER TECHNIQUES OF ANALYSIS

Each inventory item is different from another from the point of view of its importance. Each inventory item is examined from different considerations while deciding the importance attached to it. Some of these considerations could be criticality of the item for production, high cost of the item, or difficulty in procurement of the item. Some of the techniques adopted for control of inventory are:

- VED (Vital, Essential, and Desirable)
- HML (High, Medium, and Low cost)
- FSN (Fast, Slow, and Non-moving items)

These techniques have been discussed in detail in Chapter 19, 'Effective Management of Spares Parts'.

CODIFICATION

Codification is one of the important elements of inventory control activities. It helps in avoiding duplication of items in the inventory and enables correct entries in the bin cards, stock control cards, and account codes. Codification has been discussed in detail in Chapter 15, 'Codification'.

STANDARDIZATION

Standardization plays an important part in inventory control. Standardization helps in reducing variety and thus reducing the demand for storage space for less number of items.

Standardization also helps in higher inventory turnover and reduces the number of slow-moving items. It also assists in reducing the rate of obsolescence of spare parts. These aspects have been discussed in detail in Chapter 16, 'Standardization'.

CLASSIFICATION OF ITEMS FOR STRATEGIC REVIEW

There is always a demand from the Maintenance Department to cover more and more items in the category of stock items, Once an item is listed as a stock item, its replenishment is done automatically by the Inventory Control Section, even though the same may not be required for a very long period. This increases the inventory and adds to the slow-moving or non-moving items. The following points should be considered before declaring an item as a stock item:

- Continuity of usage of the item.
- Probability of failure.
- Criticality of item for the machine and criticality of the machine.
- Imported items and items of critical nature with long lead time should be stocked.
- Item with short lead time and not critical in nature need not be stocked.

Items in the stores are divided in different categories to distinguish one from the other for purpose of control. The items are given different codes and their replenishment policy is stated clearly (Table 18.4).

Table 18.4 Types of Items, Their Codes and Replenishment Policy

S.No.	Item Type	Code	Replenishment Policy
1	Standard/Stock	S	Items are in Part Master Record and are replenished by Inventory Control Section.
2	Non-stock	N	Items listed in Part Master Record. However their replenishment is done at the request of the user through Material Requisition.
3	Protected	P	These items should always be in stock. These are replenished by Inventory Control Section.
4	Record only	R	Record for purchase only. No quantity is kept on hand. Inventory Control Section does not replenish them. When received, these are issued against the Direct Issue Voucher (DISV).
5	General Item	G	There is no Part Master Record for these items. These are not in the inventory also; when received, they are issued against Direct Issue Voucher (DISV).
6	Obsolete	O	These items are in stock, but are not replenished.

REFERENCES

1. Patric J. Mountane and Bruce H. Charnov, *Management*, 3rd edition, 2000, Barronn's Educational Series Inc; Hauppoowage, New York 11788, USA, pp. 398 – 403.
2. Jack. K. Shiman Joel G. Siegel, *Operations Management*, 1999, Barron's Educational Series Inc; Hauppoowge, New York 11788, USA, pp. 268 – 297.

CHAPTER 19

Effective Management of Spare Parts

INTRODUCTION

A machine is made of a large number of parts. Every part is important in the smooth running of the machine. Even if one part fail or does not function properly, the machine will not function or will fail to function to its full capacity. Some parts never fail during the lifetime of the machine, whereas many fail repeatedly. Some other parts fail only once a while. There are also parts which wear out over period and create some problems, which if not attended to and corrected would result in jerks or vibrations in the machine; this may result in early failures of coupling bolts, or may even result in cracks in the body of the gear box, thus forcing replacement of the gear box itself.

The parts that are likely to fail and may need replacement are stocked to meet any eventuality and are therefore called 'Spare parts'. There are a large numbers of machines, big or small, in any plant and each requires spare parts to be stocked. Thus there are large numbers and variety of parts, which are to be kept in inventory. In some cases, suppliers of the main plant and machinery supply machines that are not of their own production but are bought by them from others. The Inventory Control Staff do not always know the details of such machines and their spare parts, including their source of suppliers. Often plant personnel need to look into the replacement of damaged components of these machines or another equivalent spare, which can exactly fit to the machinery. It is essential because changing the machine for a damaged component is not possible for various reasons, as it may be either very costly to replace the machine or a similar machine is not available. In such situations, all those who are involved with the management of spare parts of the machines, that is, the Store Keeper, Inventory Controller, and Purchaser join hands in attacking the problem so that the spares are available for replacement when needed.

FACTORS INFLUENCING THE STOCKING OF SPARE PARTS

Unpredictable Failures

It is often very difficult to predict when a part will fail or whether it would fail at all. This uncertainty always remains. The past experience of the maintenance staff plays an important role in maintaining the machine in operating condition by proper forecasting and planning of the spares in advance. The judgment of the maintenance staff has been the key factor till now, in deciding what and how much is to be stocked and at which stage? It is realized that the judgment of the maintenance staff to a great extent depends largely on the qualitative analysis about the quantity of the parts to be stored. It is often observed that in the early years of operation, the health of the machine is good and replacement of parts is not required very often. As the machine becomes old, its various parts undergo wear and tear and thus there is a greater need of the spare parts for replacement. This calls for scientific method of planning the quantity of spare parts, rather than depending on mere judgment. This brings out the concept of average life, which can be easily determined from the historical data of past failures or replacements. Maintaining history sheets for each machine or for their important components is of great importance.

The history sheet records the full details of maintenance activities carried out, parts replaced, condition of the parts for future guidance, and data of important parameters like vibration level, clearance between bearing and casing, temperature, oil condition etc., which gives an idea of the problems likely to be faced by the machine. The frequency of failure of the parts, life given by important components, and the details about the condition of the parts help in predicting the possibilities of failure and therefore in projecting the future requirements of spares. This gives rise to the concept of failure analysis.

Failure Analysis Helps in Working Out Projected Requirements of Spares

Failure analysis is based on a scientific approach. For example, knowing the vibration level and signature curve from the vibration analysis, it has become possible to predict the remaining expected life of the component or of the machine. In earlier days, the machine would stop whenever some part failed and man found himself helpless in controlling the machine time. Today, man has total control of the machine time by measuring certain parameters and deciding when the machine would stop functioning. This has been possible by the predictive maintenance techniques such as vibration analysis, oil analysis, measurement of belt tension, measurement of clearances, thermal analysis, measuring insulation level of electric motors and cables. This concept of maintenance has totally replaced the old concept of breakdown maintenance, which played havoc with the machines and also with the productivity of the organization. This scientific approach of maintenance has become essential from safety considerations in some cases to avoid any catastrophic situation like failure of an airplane.

Appropriate Maintenance Techniques

The predictive maintenance approach has greatly affected the management of spare parts. There is no need to stock an item until it is required and this can be known well in advance. Stoppage of a machine upon failure of a part results in loss of machine hours and necessitates emergency purchases of spares, which are procured at a very high price as compared to the price paid when procured in normal circumstances in a regular activity. In normal purchase, there is enough time to identify the right source for obtaining the best prices, negotiating best prices, consolidating shipments, and saving on transportation costs. It also helps to purchase items from the Original Equipment Manufacturer (OEM) of the item rather than to purchase it from the supplier of the main plant and machinery, who often charges very high rates.

Technical Evaluation of Machine Before Purchase

One of the very important factors in spare parts management, is the technical evaluation of the machine from the point of view of maintainability and reliability, before its selection for purchase. One examines the design aspects, operating parameters, and considers the operating condition of the machine. Some of the machines may be more prone to failures and therefore require more spares. There are machines, which have electronic controls in place of mechanical controls. These machines have less moving parts and therefore need fewer repairs. The initial cost of these machines may be higher, but their higher uptime and lower need for replacement of parts pay off more than the high initial cost. Machines having electronic controls require less number of spares.

Nearness of Service Centers and Dealer/Distributor

Availability of service centers of the machines influences the spare parts requirements. The spare parts, which may not be required for long but are critical for operations, and normally are to be stored may not be stored any more, as the same will be available with the service center. The risk of long downtime of the machine due to non-availability of spares is no longer there. Similarly, if the local dealers or distributors are close to the plant, the need for keeping the spares in store is reduced.

Nature of Items

In case of imported spare parts, the need for storing increases due to the long time required for various import formalities and customs clearance procedures. Opening of letter of credit in case payment terms are through letter of credit, takes time. Similarly, legalization of documents through Chamber of Commerce or Consulate Office takes time before the spares can be made available. In case of heavy items shipment is normally done through sea freight, which involves long delays and greatly depends upon the route of the ship and weather conditions affecting the sailing of the ship.

Nature of Plant and Machinery

A highly sophisticated and mechanized plant is vulnerable to breakdowns, which could be tackled by replacement of spares/components rather than repairs. The cost of downtime of these plants is normally so high that spare parts in machines with a possibility of failure are to be stored for immediate replacement of defective parts of plant and machinery.

Administrative Factors

Various administrative factors, for example, organization structure, procedures to be followed, storage facilities and records have a bearing on the spares to be stocked.

Organization structure Inventory control and purchasing activities are largely influenced by the fact, if the plant is a single unit or multi-unit. In a single unit organization, every item required has to be stocked. But in a multi-unit organization, pooling of the common spares reduces the inventory. The advantage of pooling of requirements has been greatly realized by many organizations. They prefer to cooperate with other organizations to share the inventory for certain high-value items, which are common and are used in their respective organizations. These items are stored centrally at one place. The inventory status is shared through computers so that every plant in the group knows the stock position of the items and meets its requirements without the risk of their becoming out of stock. Therefore the concept of centralization and decentralization of inventory control greatly influence spare parts management.

Procedures followed Very long clerical procedures involved in decision making, more documentation than required, long procedures in procurement, and wasting time on minor issues influence the stock level of spares. Inventory level can be reduced to a great extent if the system is efficient and response time is low. Computerization of inventory control and purchasing has greatly helped in this direction. Connecting the Purchasing Department with the suppliers through computers helps in obtaining quotes for items, information of availability of stock with the different suppliers instantaneously and helps in cutting down the procurement time.

Storage procedures Procedures of stocking items systematically with proper and reliable stock records greatly help in spares parts management. It is not unusual to see several parts unaccounted for in the cupboards of Maintenance Department. On most occasions, it is an informal storage. Quite often they are all stocked and the issue procedures are so complicated that a minimum one or two days are required to obtain a part from the store. Therefore the Maintenance Department prefers to keep critical spares under their direct control to meet emergency situations.

Storage space The availability of adequate storing space greatly influences the spare parts management. Proper racks with due marking, material handling equipment, proper lighting, ventilation, and air conditioned space helps in improving the efficiency and productivity of the store's operations. Quick reach to spares in the stores, efficient handling and protection from damage due to environmental conditions influences the availability of spare parts.

Inventory records Inventory records plays an important part in spare parts management. It is often seen that there is no consistency in physical quantities and the store records of the items. Items, which are physically available in the store, are not shown in the records. Similarly, items which are still on the record are not physically available. Items, which are received in the store, are not entered in the records for long. Reliability of records is very essential in inventory control. The whole exercise of inventory control goes out of gear, if records are not properly maintained.

Financial Factors

Various financial factors, which greatly influence the management of spare parts, are inventory-carrying cost, stock-out cost and cash availability.

Inventory-carrying costs For high-value items especially, inventory-carrying cost is a major consideration. Every case of over-stocking involves additional unnecessary costs.

Stock-out costs Careful study of stock-out costs guide the policy on stocking of spare parts. VED (Vital, Essential, Desirable) analysis helps in identifying the items that are critical to the functioning of a machine.

Cash availability There are times when an organization may face scarcity of funds. Shortage of funds has a great impact on spare parts and delays the purchase of spares. Over-stocking of inventory for fear of delay in procurement is a normal feature in plants, which are not managed well.

Obsolescence of Spare Parts

There are a large number of items in the inventory, which are in stock for long but no longer useful. Such obsolete items create numerous difficulties such as high inventory value, occupying useful space and requiring continuous attention for cleaning and accounting. Some of the reasons for obsolescence of spares are discussed here.

Improper provisioning at the time of procurement of main machinery At the time of purchase of the main machine, sometimes the user does not have a complete idea about which spares to buy and in how much quantity. The focus at this stage is normally about the features of the machine selected and its price. Spare parts planning and their initial procurement is not given due attention. Most of the time, it is left to the supplier of the main machinery to suggest a list of spares to be procured for a period of about two years. The suppliers of the main machinery at times recommend spares that are never required. It is done with a belief that the user might need these spares sometime or the other. The spares are sold as insurance spares, which may or may not be required but are to be maintained in the inventory. This is required to ensure running of the machine by avoiding uncontrolled shutdown. At times, the supplier is not concerned or serious and just dumps a lot of spares, which are never used. This situation is compounded by the fact that the user heavily depends on the supplier's recommendations and is ignorant about the real requirements. Further, the user also tries to over stock the spares with a fear that if there is any failure he should have spares for immediate replacement. These considerations are more prevalent in cases where machines are imported, and import of spares may take a long time at a later stage.

Procurement of spares without knowing that the machine is being phased out Inventory staff at times is unaware of plans for the machine being phased out or about its future plans. The user thinks that the inventory control staff should be informed, after a decision is taken, about the phasing out of the machine. In case the phasing-out is delayed for any reason, such as cash flow problem or lack of funds, the user does not want to take a risk of being out of stock and therefore, the inventory staff are not given any clue about the phasing-out of the machine. This results in replenishment of spare parts for the machine as a routine exercise.

Standardization Unplanned procurement of machines and equipment results in a variety of sizes and makes of machines and equipment for similar operations or activities. Expansion of plants is carried out at different stages. Different sizes of machines with technological differences are selected at each stage of expansion. Machines of different manufacturers are installed at different stages of expansions. This results in variety of spares. To avoid this phenomenon, organizations review the status and try to standardize the plant and machinery as much as possible. The process of standardization is very essential to reduce inventory size. However, there is a danger in attempting too much standardization resulting in obsolete spares.

Offshoot of bulk purchasing In case of bulk purchases, mainly for quantity discounts or for transportation economy, factors like annual consumption, shelf-life, and technological changes are overlooked. This, at times, results in items in the stock which are not used for long becoming obsolete.

Over-stocking Fear of being out of stock of spares, which may results in production loss, prompts the user to stock more than the real requirements. Over-stocking results in obsolescence of spare parts.

Incorrect forecasting The maintenance staff fail to assess the correct requirements and make wrong forecasting for spares.

Wrong inventory records Duplication in codification results in spare parts being kept in different locations. While one item of one code is consumed, the item with a different code is not consumed for long resulting in obsolescence.

Under-utilization of machines Under-utilization of machines results in low wear and tear of parts and therefore low requirements of spares.

STEPS FOR MANAGEMENT OF SPARE PARTS

Spare parts availability, efficient procurement, avoiding excessive stocking, and obsolescence can be achieved by following certain steps. These steps are discussed in the following section:

List of Spare Parts

A list of spare parts of each machine should be prepared and kept ready at all times. The list should contain a brief description, quantity required and working quantity, the suppliers or the manufacturers code number, and name of the original manufacturer.

Complete Specification

Complete specifications of each part should be developed. Specifications should very clearly describe the part. The serial number of the machine and model number, year of manufacturing, and manufacturer's name are part of specifications. Complete specifications enables one to procure spares in optimum time, otherwise a lot of time is lost in communication while obtaining the clarifications from the supplier, before an offer is received from him. Revised part numbers should be clearly indicated in the specifications. Updating the specifications is equally important as the development of specifications. There should be a group of people, who will be responsible for finalization of specifications. The Inventory group, user group, and purchasing group should mutually agree about the specifications.

Drawings

There are a number of machine parts, which can properly be described with the help of drawings only. Some of the drawings are received from the machinery manufacturers. In many cases, the machinery manufacturer does not give drawings. The user should develop drawings of spares. The spares can be purchased from sources other than the main machinery supplier with the help of drawings. By preparing drawings, the number of sources of suppliers can be increased and spares can be purchased at very economic prices and in shorter time. Development of drawings helps in removing the dependence of the buyer on the main machinery supplier. The inventory cost can also be reduced to a great extent.

Analysis of spare parts Some spares are more important than others. Therefore, the attention given to all the spare parts will not be the same. Spares of high value, high consumption, high weight, large volume, and for critical machines would deserve separate treatment. ABC analysis is used for focusing maximum attention to those 10% of the spares (A category items) which occupy 70% of the cost of the inventory used during the year, medium attention to 20% of the items (B category items) which accounts for the 20% of the cost, and least attention to those 70% of the items (C category items) which accounts to only 10 % of the cost. ABC analysis helps greatly in giving due attention to inventory items according to their value of importance, but still lacks certain other important aspects.

VED (Vital, Essential, Desirable) analysis examines the items from the importance of plant operations and is not related to the value of annual usage. Spares related to machinery on single line operations are very important. Their non-availability can result in stoppage of the plant. These spares may be of very low value but have great importance in plant operation. Spares, therefore, should also be examined from the point of view of vital, essential, or desirable nature. The ideal decision for the quantity to be purchased would be based on a balanced, combined approach of ABC and VED analyses. The attention to each item in the inventory to be purchased would be determined on consideration of the matrix of ABC and VED. For example, highest attention is to be given to 'A' category items in the category of 'Vital', next to be given to B category items in the 'Vital' category, and lowest attention is to be given to 'C' category items in the 'Desirable' category. For explaining this point, values of the inventory are given in the matrix as below:

	V	E	D
A	80	70	60
B	70	60	50
C	60	50	40

Such an analysis for inventory items would give optimum results with respect to availability of spares and also for the value of inventory investment.

Additional techniques of analysis of spares The items can be subjected to other classifications, such as FSN (fast, slow, and non-moving). Time limits are assigned for each category. For example, an item is termed as a fast-moving item if it is issued at least once in six months; slow-moving if issued once in two years; non-moving if the item is not issued in three years.

Other classifications can be SDE (scarce, difficult, and easy to obtain) and GOLF (government, ordinary, local, and foreign sources), SOS (Seasonal, off Seasonal), XYZ (the inventory value of items stored), HML (High, Medium, Low). The criteria for analysis in each classification are presented in Table 19.1.

Matrix of other techniques for analysis One of the matrixes can be examined between ABC and XYZ techniques.

Table 19.1 Criterion Considered in Different Classification of Spares in the Inventory

S. No.	Classification	Criteria
1	ABC	Annual value of consumption of the item.
2	VED (Vital, Essential, and Desirable)	Criticality of the spares for operation of the machine.
3	FSN (Fast-moving, Slow-moving and Non-moving)	Frequency of issue of the item from the stores.
4	SDE (Scarce, Difficult to obtain, and Easy to obtain)	Availability of the spares.
5	GOLF (Government, Ordinary, Local and Foreign)	Source of supply.
6	SOS (Seasonal, Off-Seasonal)	Seasonal availability.
7	HML (High, Medium, and Low)	Unit price of material.
8	XYZ	Inventory value of the items stored.

Control can be based on the guidelines as detailed in Table 19.2. Another matrix can be examined between XYZ and FSN items. Control can be based on the guidelines as detailed in Table 19.3

Table 19.2 Guideline from Matrix Between ABC and XYZ Analysis

	X	Y	Z
A	Reduce stock level with close control.	Attempt to reduce inventory value	Normal attention in review
B	Control consumption and stock by frequent reviews	Moderate control	Review twice a year
C	Identify the surplus items and dispose them off.	Strict control on stock	Review once a year

Table 19.3 Guideline from Matrix Between XYZ and FSN Analysis

	F	S	N
X	Very strict inventory control	Strict inventory control	Dispose item at the earliest at optimum price.
Y	Normal inventory control	Stock level to be low	Dispose item as early as possible
Z	Create enough stock to reduce clerical work	Stock level to be low	Dispose item even at lower prices

Similar combinations can be examined between ABC and HML and between ABC and GOLF.

Regular Review of Spares for Replenishment

The user should review all the spares at regular intervals so that there is no shortage or excess. The frequency of review will be different for different types of items. Spares can be classified in various categories to assign different review periods. These categories are as presented in Table 19.4 with nature of their movement.

All items introduced for the first time to inventory, either with or without bin location should be treated as 'W' (When required) until consumption pattern is established at least for three years.

Diagnostic Survey

A program of diagnostic survey should be prepared for measuring various parameters such as vibration measurements, measurement of shock pulse value of bearings, temperature measurement, oil analysis, crack detection of critical machine parts etc. The Maintenance Department should carry out such tests at regular frequency. On the basis of condition of the equipment, spare parts should be arranged. This would help reduce inventory of spare parts to a great extent.

Maintenance Approach

Maintenance approach plays an important role in spare parts management. Breakdown maintenance should be eliminated, and preventive and predictive maintenance should be adopted. Preventive maintenance needs regular checks of the machine and its parts, with the help of checklists, developed in advance. The objective of the preventive maintenance is to check in advance and take corrective action before the machine stops. This approach of maintenance has helped in reducing downtime of the machine to a great extent and has thereby reduced uncontrolled demand for the spare parts.

Table 19.4 Spares Classification for Replenishment Review

Notation	Description	Example(s)	Movement
R	Regular	Bearing, Seals etc.	Movement once in twelve months
I	Insurance	Thrust Roller	Indefinite
W	Indent when required	Chemical for temperature control of lubrication oil	On user's request, item is assigned location or under direct issue
S	Sporadic	Contactors	Infrequent consumption
C	Cyclical	Kiln Chains, Bricks	Consumption is cyclical
O	Obsolete	Any item declared obsolete	Non-moving items awaiting sanction for disposal. Items of scrapped equipment with no alternative use.
D	Written-off awaiting sale	Any item declared surplus/ obsolete	Written-off items after approval of management. Awaiting disposal.

Predictive maintenance is based on diagnostic study of various parameters, which help in predicting the condition of the machine or of its parts and to take corrective measure before the event of likely failure occurs. Predictive maintenance goes hand in hand with preventive maintenance. Today, the trend is for predictive maintenance, which automatically reduces the need for preventive maintenance, that is, the frequency of preventive maintenance checks could be reduced, if regular checks for monitoring the condition of the machine are carried out.

Storage Practices

Spare parts should be properly codified and kept in racks, which are properly identified with rack location, number, and location of the part. Any part, which is kept at two different locations, should be marked with both the locations. There should be regular physical checking of the spares to ensure that the spares are physically available and that the records are up-to-date at all times.

Procedure for Storing/Issuing

Correct procedures for storing of different items such as V belts, seals, bearings, electronic parts, and chemicals should be adopted.

Procedures for issue of items should be simple and the issue timing should be convenient to the operational staff. It should be understood that the main job of the operational staff is to properly maintain and operate machines and therefore they should not be overloaded with cumbersome procedures for issue of spares with inconvenient issue timing.

Initial Procurement of Spares

At the time of procurement of plant and machinery, the project team makes a final selection of the machines and do not bother about the adequate spare parts required. Spare parts as a package for two years time quoted by the supplier are taken/accepted. It is necessary to involve the Maintenance Department at the stage of initial procurement of spares as it would contribute in selecting the right spares, and would be able to decide on the correct quantity of spares to be procured. This would avoid dumping of unwanted spares by the machinery suppliers.

Cost Control

Control of cost of spare parts plays an important role in controlling the inventory. The Maintenance Department recommends a long list of spares for procurement without any cost consciousness. In case, an excess of spares is to be procured, a review is necessary by the user department. It has been observed that most of the time, the requirements of spares are reduced substantially after such reviews. This exercise of review of cost of spares keeps the inventory of spare parts at a low level.

Reconditioning and Overhauling of Parts

Reconditioning and overhauling of parts is usually resorted to, for maximizing the returns on the investment. There are parts, which wear out, develop cracks or are misaligned due to severe operating conditions. These are taken out for reconditioning and overhauling. Reconditioned items or overhauled items are as good as new parts. The cost of reconditioning, in most cases, is much less than the cost of new parts. Various considerations in the decision to recondition/overhaul the items are:

(a) Availability of the reconditioning facilities in the company's own plant or elsewhere. It should be examined if the existing facilities have the capacity to deal with the job of reconditioning/overhauling. Some of the parts, which are out of the production range of the main supplier/manufacturer, can be purchased from the reconditioned items with good expected life. An example of such an item is the electrical motor.

(b) Availability of repair facilities and their capacity.

(c) Availability of expertise:

If there are a large number of machines in operation, it is better to develop a team of experienced and trained personnel to repair or overhaul the part. It is especially applicable to transport vehicle repairs.

(d) Nature of parts:

If a part is standard and available off the shelf or it is a specialized or custom-made design, in case of a standard item, the important considerations in reconditioning are the cost of reconditioning, the quality of reconditioning facilities, and expertise.

(e) Economy of reconditioning:

This is an over-riding factor. The economy of reconditioning considers the cost of reconditioning as well as the expected life and reliability of operations after reconditioning. This should be compared with the cost of purchase of new spare parts and their expected life.

Management of Obsolete Parts

The management of obsolete parts deals mainly with two issues:

(i) How do you avoid obsolescence

(ii) What should you do with obsolete parts

How do you avoid obsolescence Avoiding obsolescence of parts involves a careful planning at the stage of conceiving the project. It is necessary to avoid a variety of machines, as much as possible, while selecting the machines. It is better to have the same capacity of production line from the same source of supply, so that spare parts can be used interchangeably for all the production lines.

Overstocking and hoarding should be avoided by closely monitoring the requirements. Standardization, which may result in obsolescence, should be examined for the overall objective to take advantage of variety reduction. Inventory staff should be informed well in time of any future plans of phasing out of machines, expansions, and new projects. Whenever a new machine is to be purchased as a replacement for an old one, the replacement decision should also consider the spares in stock. It should be ensured that all the spares of the old machines, which are not likely to be used and are therefore surplus, should be disposed of.

- to plan and control price of product
- to fix the product price in a competitive market environment. Strategic decisions are required to be taken in a competitive situation
- to evaluate purchase performance
- to find alternative materials with the objective of cost reduction. For example, some of the waste materials from other industrial sectors could be used as raw material for the product. Some examples of this are
  (i) Gas generated during oil exploration is a very useful fuel.
  (ii) Fly ash from powerhouse can be used for producing clinker/cement.
  (iii) Slag from steel industry is used for making slag cement.

VALUATION OF MATERIAL ISSUES

Various methods can be used for valuation of materials issue, which are:

- First in first out (FIFO)
- Last in first out (LIFO)
- Highest in first out (HIFO)
- Next in first out (NIFO)
- Average
- Weighted average

First In First Out (FIFO)

In this method, the value of materials issued is worked out on the basis of the cost of materials received earliest in the warehouse. If an inventory item is procured at two different times at unit price of US$ 10/PC and US$ 15/PC, the material issued is valued by taking the unit price of US$ 10/PC, till the quantity in stock is available from the lot procured at US$ 10/PC. If the quantity issued is higher than the stock quantity of the earliest procurement lot, the value of issues will be at the rate of price of the earliest lot for the quantity issued from that lot plus the value of the issues for the quantity from the next lot at the price of second lot. This is explained in Table 20.1.

Table 20.1 Valuation of Material Issues Under First in First Out Method

Date	Purchases			Issues		
	Quantity (PCS)	Price (US$/PC)	Value (US$)	Quantity (PCS)	Price (US$/PC)	Value (US$)
5.1.2001	200	10	2000			
20.1.2001	400	15	6000			
22.1.2001				100	10	1000
30.1.2001				100	10	1000
15.2.2001				100	15	1500
25.2.2001				300	15	4500

The value of issue is the same as the value of purchase or as the material received in the stores. The issues are in the same chronological order of purchase/receipts and are valued at the same purchase value.

This method ensures that the materials are issued at the actual cost and thereby no profit or loss is incurred in the valuation. If the cost of materials purchased is low, the value of issues worked out with this method represents a lower value than the present value of the materials issued. In other words, this is a case of undervaluation of issues. The cost of production, therefore, is lower than the actual prevailing cost of materials if procured just prior to production. This method is easy to work with, provided the price fluctuations are reasonable during a specific period.. Under inflationary conditions, the profits are inflated thereby advancing the payment of taxes. This method is therefore not preferred by the Finance Managers.

Last In First Out (LIFO)

The value of the material issued under this method is based on the price of last purchase. If the price of an item procured, at two different times are US$ 10/PC and US$ 15/PC; the issue value will be based on the last price of US$ 15/PC, till the stock contains items procured at this price. This method ensures that materials are issued at actual cost, but it is opposite of the FIFO method. Table 20.2 explains the method of valuation of issues under this method.

Table 20.2 Valuation of Material Issues Under Last in First Out Method

Date	Purchases			Issues		
	Quantity (PCS)	Price (US$/PC)	Value (US$)	Quantity (PCS)	Price (US$/PC)	Value (US$)
5.1.2001	200	10	2000			
20.1.2001	400	15	6000			
22.1.2001				100	15	1500
30.1.2001				100	15	1500
15.2.2001				200	15	3000
25.2.2001				200	10	2000

Though the stocks are at cost they do not represent the current price level. During falling prices, the value of stock is lower and therefore losses are to be written off. Under this method, the profits are not shown immediately and consequently, tax liability is deferred.

In a rising price trend, this is the present value of the materials issued. The main advantage of this method of valuation is that the cost of material charged to production is closely related to the current price level, provided that the material is purchased recently. This method is not preferred in cases of materials whose prices réduce over a period.

Highest In First Out (HIFO)

In this method the highest value is taken for the issues. For example, if there are different prices for the materials in the warehouse, for example, US$ 15/PC, US$ 10/PC and US$ 12/PC, the issues will be valued at US$ 15/PC.

Next In First Out (NIFO)

In this method, the market prices of the items are considered for valuation of issues. In other words it is the replacement cost of the items issued. For example, if the value of purchase is US$ 10/PC but the present market price is US$ 15/PC, the issues will be valued at US$ 15/PC.

Simple Average Method

The simple average method takes into consideration the price of the new consignment along with the prices of earlier consignments, whose material is still in stock. Each time a new consignment is received at a new price, the average of the price paid per unit of the stock still in stores and the price of the new consignment is worked out. For example, if the present stock of an item in the warehouse is 100 units at a price of US$ 10/PC and on additional 200 units are received at a price of US$ 15/PC, the simple average price of this item will be (10+15) ÷ 2 == US$ 12.5/PC. This price will be used till the next change in the price occurs. This process involves a lot of calculation and therefore needs computer support.

This method of costing is favored in a situation where the price fluctuates rapidly over a narrow range. It gives stability to the product costing and is considered as a useful method. However, very high or very low change in the prices will have to be closely monitored. In a situation where the prices of the items with short leadtime are charged, the value of issue will not represent the true value of the issues.

Weighted Average Cost Method

First in first out (FIFO), Last in first out (LIFO) and simple average methods of valuation of issues have problems due to price fluctuations of the various items procured. The inventory is either valued at a lower level or at a higher level than its real worth. These methods therefore have favorable or adverse effects on the price of the products and also affect competition in the market. The basic purpose of the management is to recover the cost of materials procured from the sales of the product. The weighted average method removes these difficulties. The method of calculating the issue price is shown in Table 20.3.

This method involves more calculations as it considers the total cost by considering the total quantities unlike the simple average method where only the average price is considered. The method is favored in case of price fluctuations and variation in order quantities.

Table 20.3 Weighted Average Method for Calculation of Issue Price

Date	Purchases			Issues		
	Quantity (PCS)	Price (US$/PC)	Value (US$)	Quantity (PCS)	Price (US$/PC)	Value (US$)
5.1.2001	200	10	2000			
20.1.2001	400	15	6000			
22.1.2001				100	13.33(1)	1333
25.2.2001				300	13.33	3999
30.3.2001	100	12	1200	50	12.89(2)	644.5

1: $(200 \times 10 + 400 \times 15) \div (200 + 400) = 13.33$

2: $[(600 - 400) \times 13.33 + 100 \times 12] \div [(600 - 400) + 100] = 12.89$

FACTORS CONSIDERED IN SELECTION OF METHOD OF VALUATION OF INVENTORY

As discussed in the earlier sections, the method of valuation of issues is independent of the method of valuation of inventories, which is a part of balance sheet of the company. The various factors considered in the selection of the method of valuation of inventories are:

- Nature of inventories (consumables, spare parts, and raw materials)
- Trend of price fluctuations (decreasing or increasing trend and frequency of fluctuation)
- Turnover
- Value of inventory
- Tax laws

Normally, spare parts and consumable inventories are valued following the Weighted Average Method of valuation. The Weighted average is adjusted after each addition of the inventory items.

Raw materials are normally purchased through contracts. The price of raw materials is normally fixed for the duration of the contract, except for the variable costs associated with the purchase of raw materials. For example, insurance charges, transportation cost, cost of third party inspection, customs clearance and port charges (in case of imports), and government levies, if any, vary from consignment to consignment. Contract price and other charges as applicable are considered for valuation of raw materials.

Valuation of semi-finished and finished goods take into account the accumulated expenses of each Cost Center. Any loss of materials such as material lost during storage and handling such as loss due to material flying away with the wind or being washed away with the rains, spilled over or spoiled due to environmental conditions

Table 20.4 Profits as Worked Out on the Basis of FIFO and LIFO Method of Valuation of Inventories

Method of valuation	Year	Inventory Jan 1		Purchases		Inventories Dec. 31		Cost of sales	Sales	Gross profit
		Quantity	Price	Quantity	Price	Quantity	Price			
		PCS	US$/PC	PCS	US$/PC	PCS	US$/PC	US$	US$	US$
FIFO	1998	100	1	100	1	100	1	100	150	50
	1999	100	1	100	1.5	100	1.5	100	250	150
	2000	100	1.5	100	0.8	100	0.8	150	100	–50
LIFO	1998	100	1	100	1	100	1	100	150	50
	1999	100	1	100	1.5	100	1	150	250	100
	2000	100	1	100	0.8	100	1	80	100	20

1. Under FIFO method, profits is higher in the year of high price.
2. Under LIFO method, sales are high when prices are high and low when prices are low.
3. Under LIFO, inventory may show a value (US$100) higher than the market value (US$ 80) as in 2000

are considered and adjusted while working out the cost of semi-finished or finished goods. Service costs are allocated to the production cost center on a fixed percentage established on the basis of past data.

The method of inventory valuation has a considerable effect on the profit and loss of a company. Table 20.4 shows the effect of valuation of inventory on the profit by FIFO and LIFO methods.

High inventory valuation results in

- Estimation of earnings at a higher level
- Working capital looks better
- There is a possibility of higher dividends/bonus
- More tax payments

A low inventory valuation results in

- Reduced financial strength of the company
- Heavy taxation

Index

S/UBS/80-5951/07/03